W9-BRC-794

WHO'S SORRY NOW

WHO'S SORRY NOW

The True Story of a Stand-Up Guy

Joe Pantoliano

With David Evanier

DUTTON

DUTTON
Published by the Penguin Group
Penguin Putnam Inc., 375 Hudson Street, New York, New York 10014, U.S.A.
Penguin Books Ltd, 80 Strand, London WC2R 0RL, England
Penguin Books Australia Ltd, 250 Camberwell Road,
Camberwell, Victoria 3124, Australia
Penguin Books Canada Ltd, 10 Alcorn Avenue, Toronto, Ontario, Canada M4V 3B2
Penguin Books (N.Z.) Ltd, 182–190 Wairau Road, Auckland 10, New Zealand

Penguin Books Ltd, Registered Offices: Harmondsworth, Middlesex, England

Published by Dutton, a member of Penguin Putnam Inc.

First printing, October 2002
1 3 5 7 9 10 8 6 4 2

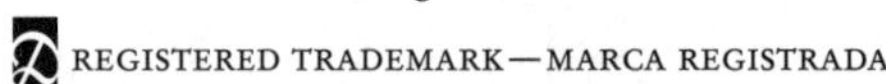

LIBRARY OF CONGRESS CATALOGING-IN-PUBLICATION DATA
Pantoliano, Joe.
Who's sorry now : the true story of a stand-up guy / Joe Pantoliano with David Evanier.
p. cm.
ISBN 0-525-94677-2 (alk. paper)
1. Pantoliano, Joe. 2. Actors—United States—Biography. 3. Sopranos (Television program) I. Evanier, David. II. Title.
PN2287.P227 A3 2002
791.43'028'092—dc21
[B] 2002027110

Printed in the United States of America
Set in Stempel Garamond

This book is printed on acid-free paper. ∞

To Mommy and Nancy,
the two great women of my life.

ACKNOWLEDGMENTS

Special thanks to Danny Roth and Bonnie Solow, who both saw a book in the story of my humble beginnings; to Bonnie, for introducing me to Maureen O'Brien, who began this journey with me and proved to be a true stand-up guy along the way; to David Evanier, who swore on a stack of bibles that he could do it, and did it in spades—I will be forever grateful, David; to Brian Tart, whom I picked over all the rest because I knew in my gut that he was the guy; to Amy Hughes, who grew on me like a new pair of legs and proved to be our team's MVP; to Lisa Johnson and the PR folks at Dutton, thanks in advance and only if you do a good job and sell this friggin' thing; to Gibson Patterson, Sue Patricola and everybody at PLPR; to Nick Stevens, my agent of fifteen years, who's still wondering how a guy who can't read or spell can manage to write a book; to Lisa Hallerman, Howard Cohen, Alex Schaffel and everybody at United Talent Agency; to my sister, Maryann Pantoliano-Higginson, and family, for putting up with all my inquiries and being such an integral part in this process; to Patty DeRiso and the DeRiso family, for a lifetime of friendship and for reminding me of all the little details I'd chosen to forget; to Antoinette May and Tony Centrella, for their crucial insight on their dear friends Mary, Monk and Florie; to Judy, Roseann, Janoots and the entire Guidese family, and Patty Cocucci, Louise Cocucci and the Cocucci family, who were instrumental in helping me uncover the good, bad and ugly of our family history and family legends, and who've shown their support and love for me throughout this book and throughout my life; to Travis Malloy, for pioneering the storied road to the Hoboken of my youth; and finally to Gleb Klioner, for introducing me to the great Eddie Mordujovich, without whom my voice would have been rendered but a faint whisper in the gutters of that great mile-square.

All of the following people helped make this book possible and my love and gratitude goes out to all of them:

Marie Gallo and Chicky Centrella, for all those wonderful family pictures; Anthony and Louis Pantoliano; Florie Branda and family; Pete and Louise Centrella and the Centrella family; Mary and Sal Tropea and the Tropea Family; Mario Abbattista; Lucille Tobin; Vinny and John Fiore of Fiore's House of Quality in Hoboken, for providing me with memories of my family's voracious appetite for Hoboken's finest mozzarella; Bill Bergen, for keeping a tight ship at the Hoboken Fire Museum and giving that precious piece of history its due recognition; Anthony Russo, Steve Capiello, Jimmy Ferina, John Marotta, Al Labook, Jude Fitzgibbons and Frank Monte Magno at Hoboken City Hall, for sharing their enlightening and entertaining stories with me and providing me with helpful information about Hoboken's multihued past; Donna Damiano, John Fredericks, Bobby Lewis and John Lehne, my teachers whom I learned from the most; Marcia Gay Harden and Thadius Shields, for their unwavering support on this project; Tommy Lee Jones;

Joe Belella; Robert Downey, Jr.; Patricia Hearst-Shaw and Bernard Shaw; Diane Lane; Andy Garcia; Mary McCusker; Chazz Palminteri; Elizabeth Peña; Camryn Manheim; Jason Schwartzman; Bobby Costanzo; Ron Berkle; Steve Railsback; Tony Spiradakus; Darius Anderson; Robin Bronk; Lynn Colomello, for her amazing transcription skills and her uncanny insights into the bonds that exist between Italian-American mothers and their sons; Jessica Samples; Juan Carlos Rodriguez, who's always taking me places; Chris Milnes and the Axis 360.com guys, for their creative dedication to joeypants.com; Francine Spiegel of Tenderoni.com, for her inspired artwork; David Chase, Ilene Landress, Dominic Chianese and cast, crew and writers of *The Sopranos*; Tony Goldwyn and Jane Muskey; Malachy McCourt; Andy and Larry Wachowski; Alisa Blasingame and Thea Bloom; Robert Kennedy, Jr.; Nick Mele; Robert Picardo; Carrie-Anne Moss; R.J. Wagner and Natalie Wood, my first mentors and angels in the land of LA—I will forever be indebted to you; Aunt Rita Pantoliano and Uncle Walter Pantoliano; Uncle Frankie "The Mayor" Lia, who made it past one hundred and never missed a beat; Morgan Kester, for being a great mother to my son, and Patti Arpaia, for smoothing out the rough edges—thank you both for being there for me; Christina Landaverde for loving my children as much as I do; to my children, Marco, Melody, Daniella and Isabella, who, if all goes well, will be wiping my ass in the end; and to Nancy, my wife, thank you for absolutely everything. Finally, to Joe A., K.C. and Matti O., who died in those tall towers that Tuesday morning, and who will forever be in my heart.

Introduction

Kiss My Ass and Make It a Love Story

There I was, sitting in the back of a New York City detective car in Hoboken, handcuffed and wondering how the hell I had gotten myself there. "We have an outstanding warrant for your arrest, Mr. Pantoliano," the detective had said, very politely.

"You can call me Joey. What the hell did I do?"

"Multiple E-ZPass violations, Mr.— Joey. I hate to do this to you, but the city's doing a major sweep on all E-ZPass violators. We have to bring you in." With all the stuff I pulled off as a little runt in these very streets, I can't believe it's a measly toll-paying white box hiding behind my rearview mirror partially out of sight and entirely out of mind that gets me in the end. My teenage counterpart would be laughing in my face (or perhaps pelting the car with jumbo grade A nonorganic eggs) if he knew what this old cigar-puffing geezer was getting turned in for. And not like you asked, but no need to wonder about what my mother would think. I'd never have mentioned it to her. Not my mother.

But I digress. Back in the Crown Vic, my NYPD hosts were explaining that they wanted to spare me the embarrassment because I was a celebrity. So they arranged to bring me in the station through the back to prevent the press from getting their hands on me. They were worried I'd be a Page Six byline by morning, and appeared to feel very strongly about preventing that from happening. They were nice guys, I gotta hand it to them, but don't they know that's just the kind of publicity I could use for my upcoming memoir? Not to mention it's definitely my favorite kind of publicity—the free kind. As I'm getting a courtesy drive to the bar on Tenth and Willow in Hoboken, where my twenty-one-year-old son Marco works and where I had planned to have dinner with my wife and kids, my mind started drifting. It was the same bar where we'd had our dinner the night of my father Monk's wake fifteen years ago. It never had a name as far as I can remember. It was just the bar on Tenth and Willow. What else would you call it? We had walked the four short blocks from Failla's Memorial to the bar that night, four short blocks from where I now keep an apartment that I share with Marco. Failla's Memorial Home was the funeral parlor where I laid all my immediate family to rest—my mother, my father, my aunts and uncles, my mother's father, his father before him—the list goes on. And here I was, almost fifty-one years old, driving through the streets of Hoboken with a shiny new pair of handcuffs around my wrists and wondering if I ever really left the projects thirty-three years ago. I just knew it would end up like this, that somehow, I wouldn't escape the fate my childhood seemed sure to deliver, and I'd end up with a pair of cuffs not very different from those my "cousin" Florie wore time and again while shackled for more years of his life than he ever cared to acknowledge.

They had to keep the cuffs on me. "Procedure," they said. At least these guys were thoughtful enough to put the cuffs in the front and place my jacket over them so as not to alarm my two little kids upon seeing their old man in dire straits. Then again, how much harm could that scene have done? I turned out kinda okay, didn't I? My mind flashed to the time when I was eight years old and Aunt Lizzie, Florie's mother, had died. They had given Florie his own courtesy delivery, flying him back to New York from his new home at the Atlanta Federal Penitentiary, where he was serving a fifteen-year sentence, and had escorted him into the funeral parlor in New York City. I remember watching him, the solemn figure in handcuffs standing over his mother's coffin, as that still moment of bittersweet courtesy forever etched itself into my brain. My situation, of course, was a little different. After all, I was dealing with an E-ZPass violation. All right, *multiple* E-ZPass violations, but the point is, I hadn't hijacked the Hoboken ferry along with 375 of its passengers and their cars and trucks and sent them on a short detour up the Hudson to Poughkeepsie or nothin'. Nah, that was Florie's big scam that literally sent him up the river. Me, I'd go in, get processed, pay my fine and leave. Maybe I'd be a bit inconvenienced, missing a family dinner and all. But the next day was Easter, and we'd have plenty of time to spend together. And, after all, I was on a hit HBO show, and I still had a movie career. Yeah, I guess I had done OK for a kid from Hoboken, New Jersey. So what if I got a pair of handcuffs on, I mean, some people wear them for fun.

We made a left on Willow and pulled up to the Tenth Street bar. I could see the front room of the bar was already filling up with people and it wasn't even eight o'clock yet. I thought, that's great for Marco, after all these years the place is still attracting Hoboken's finest, the liquid dinner crowd. Admittedly, I was feeling a bit light-headed from all the peculiar events that night in March, but the thing that really had me wondering if perhaps I had indeed taken the red pill was the fact that we'd actually found a parking spot right there in front of the entrance on a Saturday night. Had Frank Sinatra himself greeted us on the street equipped with a forty-piece band gutting out a passionate rendition of "Billie Jean Is Not My Lover," I wouldn't have been more stunned. Hoboken is notorious for never having available parking spots, let alone on a Saturday night. As long as I can remember, people double-parked along the streets at night and woke up every morning to the sounds of car horns, the early birds alerting their neighbors to come on down and let them out so they could drive to work or just bathe in the satisfaction of having dragged that son of a bitch from apartment 3A out of bed. It was the established routine. That should have tipped me off right then and there. But I had a lot on my mind. The ghosts of Hoboken surrounded me that night in my thoughts, not to mention that swiftly approaching publisher's deadline.

We got out of the car and the well-mannered detectives took me in through the back of the place so the people at the front of the bar wouldn't notice. I was accompanied by Anthony Falco, captain of the Hoboken Police Department, who had tried unsuccessfully to get me off the hook. They just couldn't do that, the fellows from the NYPD had insisted. We walked into the secluded back room, past the pool table and toward the curtain separating off the adjacent room where I had sat with my sister and contemplated my father's life once upon a time. One of the detectives made a motion for me to lead the way, so I pulled back the curtain and walked smack into a room full of shouting, hooting and whooping close personal friends and family. There were about a hundred and fifty of them.

Admittedly, my first thought was how the hell did they fit them all in there? I remember the place being just roomy enough for two dozen of us, a couple of tables and a fat loaf of sausage bread. But here they were, and they seemed to be comfortable enough. I turned back and sent a brief but kind glance toward my detective hosts, motioning to my still-cuffed wrists. "You fucking bastards." As usual, I meant it in the warmest way possible. In my world, that translates to "job well done—the both of you are decent, good-natured chaps regardless of what they may say about you." Incidentally, I think I still owe E-ZPass some toll money. If any E-ZPass representatives are reading this, please bill HBO, ATTN: Joey Pants's I CAN'T BELIEVE I GOTTA DRIVE ALL THE WAY OUT TO NEWARK FOR ONE FRIGGIN' SCENE Fund. Thanks.

It was a belated surprise birthday party, my fiftieth. My wife, Nancy, had planned a surprise party on my actual birthday, September 12. It seemed like good timing, with the Emmy Awards being in town that week, because all my friends, East

Coasters and West Coasters alike, would have the opportunity to surprise me and be merry, and of course to roast me to their hearts' content. But September 12 wasn't what Nancy or anyone else for that matter ever imagined it would be. On the day prior, my son had stood at the river's edge, watching the second plane crash into the South Tower, witnessing the hopes and dreams of thousands of innocent lives come crumbling down, carrying our own hopes and dreams with them. I used to stand at the same point on the river's edge as my son had, only I'd watched in amazement as the towers gracefully inched their way up to the sky. Walking into that crowded room in the Tenth Street bar, surrounded by family and friends and angels that had molded my life—the elders, the cousins, the movie stars and the celebrities—I remembered a more innocent time. I remembered that the source of my lifelong dream of becoming an actor wasn't rooted in fame or money, but in a frightening insecurity that when I died, there wouldn't be any evidence that I had ever existed. If at least I could leave a film behind, there I would be, Joey Pants, long after my last breath. As a kid, I'd watch *Million Dollar Movie*, and see all of these old flicks and think about how incredible it was that some of those people were dead, but there they were, right in front of me, living on in Technicolor. I wanted to have that kind of a legacy. I wanted to be a Technicolor ghost.

With a cigar in my hand and good company to every side of me in the old Tenth Street Bar, I revised that old dream. The proof stood right there, one hundred and fifty independent verifications from wall to gritty wall. The *true* legacy I leave behind is the love and the memories that will last in the hearts of the people who know me, in the hearts of my children, in the hearts of my friends. My own heart, after all, is a shelter to all the memories, the lessons learned, the time shared—good and bad and worse—with all those lives that came before and have since gone, and to the pain of losing them. And I've lost a lot of people. I guess that's part of growing old. The heart is stubborn. Rumor has it God borrowed the first heart from an old woman in Naples and never returned it (she was definitely related to my mother; that's why she had no qualms about taking God's name in vain). Since then hearts everywhere hold tight to their possessions. Once it lets something in, it ain't ever gonna let it leave. Somehow, I think, through all of it, through the Storm of the Century that was my upbringing in this quaint little town that stands in the shadows of the vanished towers, here I am, I survived, with a dream intact.

— BRIEF INTERLUDE —

Right about now, there's a guy sitting in his plaid worn living room reclining chair somewhere in Jersey City reading this and saying, "Fuck this, I buy Joey Pants's book and he gets soft on me. What the hell? Where's the friggin' return policy on this thing?"

I know you're out there. Just calm down, relax and read this like the good boy that you are, unless, of course, you'd rather I come over there and show you a little disciplinary trick or two I picked up from a couple of the outstanding specimens of humanity I've portrayed over the years. You might be upset to know how natural those roles actually are for a guy like me.

NOTE TO EVERYONE ELSE EXCEPT THIS GUY: Over my thirty-year career, I've had the distinguishable honor of playing the guy you love to hate every now and again. Every time someone comes up to me on the street and says, "I *hated* you in that movie!" well, then I know I did my job. As an actor, I am responsible for defending these despicable characters on set as wholeheartedly as Johnnie Cochran would in a court of law. Needless to say, I hereby detach myself from any of the sick and twisted personality traits and psychopathic tendencies I've occasionally taken up on screen, with two noted exceptions: their typically incessant charm (my dear brothers and sisters, some things are beyond my control) and, of course, the occasional heavy cursing. It's a hard habit to break when the words that rhyme with "trucking" and "runt" were used far more often in my house growing up than "dinner's" and "ready." I mean well, and anybody who knows me knows that. Got it? Good. Now, shut up and read.

— END BRIEF INTERLUDE —

This is a story of unconditional and unconventional love. The strongest love imaginable, the harshest love imaginable. And no one embodied that double-edged love as well as my mother, Mary "Mariacella" Centrella—or as I still refer to her to this day, Mommy. When I was a kid, if I ever asked one too many questions of her, she would turn around and ask me, in her plain, true Hobokenese, "What're you writin' a book?"

"Yeah," I'd tell her every time.

And she'd reply like clockwork, "Well, kiss my ass and make it a love story." These were Mommy's tender words to me, every one of which rang true.

Twenty years now, dead and gone, and the sweet sound of Mommy's voice calling me home to eat still rings in my ears like it was only yesterday.

"Joey!"

Okay, so it wasn't so sweet.

"Hey, Joey!"

At this point, I'm probably the only one on the block who's not looking up at her as she's leaning out of our fifth-floor apartment window.

I'm down on the concrete courtyard below, playing with a few of my fellow ten-year-old pals and cousins from the projects. She spots one of us. "Hey, Beaver! Where's my Joey? JOSEPH!!"

I'm definitely in trouble now, but I play it cool in front of the other kids. "Whatcha want, Mommy?" I shout over my shoulder. "Can't you see I'm in the middle of somethin'?"

"It's time to eat, you little sumanabitch! Get your fat ass upstairs!"

"Ahll-right, I'm comin'." I surrender. I may have been smug, but I wasn't dumb. Before she has a chance to clear her throat for the next sound-off, I've already double-stepped my way up the five flights of stairs and charged through the unlocked steel front door of our pocket-sized three-bedroom apartment. She greeted me with a smothering hug, a wide smile and a smack on the face.

Mommy taught me what tough love was all about. She taught me that saying "I love you" was not necessarily the strongest way to communicate that sentiment. Mommy could masterfully wrap up her love in any number of disparaging phrases and pet names, but you knew what she really meant when the biting words came out. At least I'd like to think we knew what she meant.

She showed me life for what it was, never shielding my curious eyes with a G-rated screen. She showed me death for what it was too, and not only did she withhold censorship of the event, she quite literally put my face in it.

"Joey, come along with Mommy," she said to me after straightening my tie and spitting on her hand to try and take the cowlick from my hair. Grabbing my hand, she walked me up the dark burgundy carpet of Failla's Memorial Home and up to the gold velvet kneeler in front of the imitation mahogany casket. "Say a prayer now, Joey, because our friend Danny has gone to heaven."

Danny Magliano was the guy who used to come over our house during Christmas and take Mommy down to his car so she could pick from a wide selection of brand-new chemistry sets and basketballs and toy fire engines and all sorts of children's toys all packed conveniently in the trunk. Everything in that exciting trunk had been stolen without a gun, "swag" as we called it. Danny was the closest thing to Santa Claus I ever had.

He'd been shot dead in the swamps along the Hudson River up near Edgewater Road.

Mommy and I bowed our heads for a moment of reverence to the recently deceased, and before I could say "amen," she gave me a tug on my sleeve and spoke into my ear. "Joey, look at his head." I craned my neck to look into the casket, and there he was, swag Danny, lifeless and pale. "You see that? He was shot in the head three times, and you can't even see the holes!"

"Wow!" She was right. One second of reverence for the deceased, followed by a minute of awe for the deceased's corpse. I stepped up on the kneeler and leaned over for a closer look. "Tell me more, Mommy, tell me more!"

"Jesus Christ, Joey!" she snapped. "What do you think this is, a party? Lower your voice and have some respect for the dead."

Amen. Mommy insisted on taking me and my little sister Maryann to every wake held at Failla's. We were usually the only kids there and we never missed a one. She'd dress us up and show us off. They were my favorite family get-togethers. It's no wonder that I still love a good funeral. They brought out the best and the worst in everyone. I was fascinated by death, and fascinated by the ritual surrounding it. The food, the dramatic scenes, the monumental fights, the men hanging out in the back room of the parlor smoking cigarettes and cigars and telling stories while the women stayed up front with the casket and gossiped and whispered and checked out the flowers—death stood still in the center of the room while the spirit of our family was alive and kicking all around it. But Mommy never let me forget why we were there. She always made me have a peek.

My Mommy, my dear endlessly loving Mommy, the part-time bookie, the full-time seamstress and the interminable gambler. She'd bet on anything. She bet on my father's life and on her children's future, and it was probably the only bet she ever won fair and square. My dear Mommy, she'd bet on a raindrop if she could, and for all I know she had. "Twenty that the raindrop to the right's gonna hit the windowsill first." And if she could have somehow found a way to cheat God himself . . . I'll be damned if He hadn't lost an Andrew Jackson every now and then to Mary Centrella.

Which is why I'm sure the All Powerful and All Knowing had a soft spot in His Neapolitan heart, or come to think of it, more like a chip on His divine shoulder, for my dad, Dominique "Monk" Pantoliano, since He had chosen poor Monk for the thankless and altogether sacrificial task of being Mary Centrella's personal and portable punching bag. Daddy can best be described by the items thoughtfully placed in his casket when he gracefully punched out of this world: a racing form, a pack of cards, a box of cheap cigars and his trusty black hat and raincoat. He never underestimated the value of that hat and raincoat, not when the wrath of Mommy was a sure bet no matter the weather. It was always sunny skies and clear with a 100 percent chance of rain for the Monk.

Not that they didn't have anything in common. Daddy was every bit the gambler that Mommy was, and she never let him forget it when money was tight around the house. And money was always tight around the house. My father wasn't what you'd call a man of means. Aside from gambling, he shared his professional life between the local factory where he worked as a foreman and the local funeral parlor where he was the hearse chauffeur. But with the horse track just across town, he could have been a brain surgeon with a law degree and managed the Backstreet Boys on the side, he'd still have been broke his whole life for all I'm concerned. And yet he was the nicest guy you'd ever want to meet, and you would have quickly forgiven his plaid polyester leisure suit wardrobe. He may have been a loud dresser, but one thing's for sure, he knew to keep his mouth shut.

For all of my family's ritual gatherings and habitual gambling, it was apparent that one key habit was left out: paying the rent. Instead, they had opted for the ritual of packing and moving. We had moved ten times by the time I reached high school. Any new place we settled in was rarely more than several blocks, or floors, from the last place. The notion of "home" to me was as stable and comforting as riding in a train car. You walked in and had a seat, but you never got too comfortable, because you knew your stop was always coming up next. As these moves divided up the chapters of my childhood and adolescence, so they will divide the chapters in my book. In *Poor Richard's Almanack*, Ben Franklin pointed out that "what maintains one vice would bring up two children." Between Mommy and Daddy, they could have raised an entire Pantoliano litter in one, and only one, charming single-family home had they played their cards right. Or in their case, had they not played their cards at all.

Mommy and Daddy. Quite the pair.

Oh? Did I say pair? Parental units tend to come in twos for most Joes I know, but I was fortunate enough to be blessed with a bona fide threesome. Three may have been company, but two was certainly a bitch. Had not Florio Isabella, my other father, my honorary stepfather and third cousin to my mother, stepped on to the scene in time, I'd be sending this manuscript to my cell mate Bud's sister's husband's cousin's good friend's ex-coworker's lover who knows a guy in Scranton who knows a literary agent in Pittsburgh, and the return address would be Attica, New York, New York. And that's assuming I'd have gotten the knack of distinguishing my *b*s from my *d*s from the tattoo on my thigh proclaiming Bud's property rights. Everybody knew him as Florie, and if it wasn't for him, Tommy Lee Jones would still be looking for the perfect guy to play his sidekick in *The Fugitive*. The man saved my life. I mean Florie, not Tommy Lee, although for all I know the latter may beg to differ. Though his final days were spent making an honest but meager living delivering freshly pressed clothes in the dry cleaning business, Florie spent twenty-one out of his seventy-seven years locked up in federal penitentiaries, and spent much of the rest doing the Cajun two-step with the wrong side of the law. But the only dance he ever cared to see me in involved "tights and a fucking tutu" so that I could make a true "fairy-ass" out of myself. At least that's how my mother referred to the acting career that Florie relentlessly encouraged, straight through the day I said goodbye and headed for the Big City to find my fairy-ass destiny.

Mary, Monk and Florie. They were my angels. She tortured the both of them mercilessly, but they loved her through it all, and they all loved their Joey unquestionably.

Multiply that love by an extended family of Pantolianos and Centrellas numbering in the hundreds, and all living within walking distance, make that shouting distance, from any one of the ten addresses we called home in and around Hoboken, and you begin to understand why I consider myself blessed. Blessed that I was part of a time and a place and an immigrant culture that has long since disappeared. That would be classic Italian-American postwar pre-Yuppie urban New Jersey. Blessed that I was able to thrive on the collective strength of a supremely loving, huge and unruly, huggin' and kissin', screamin' and cryin' tribe. We were dirt-poor but proud, and had plenty of heart to go around.

And I was blessed that I got the fuck out of there before they ate me up alive.

This is my love story.

—1—

201 Park Avenue

Lucky Me

My father had been staying at a friend's apartment in South Jersey the night he passed away. He'd been suffering from cancer for the last four months and, earlier that evening, developed a severe pain in his left leg. His pal immediately drove him to a nearby hospital. Upon their arrival at the emergency room, a young attending physician began to treat Daddy and, in an apparent attempt to take his mind off the pain, engaged him in some small talk, just as I'm sure he'd been instructed to do back at med school. "So, where you from?"

"Hoboken," Daddy replied.

The doctor's face lit up. "Oh! Frank Sinatra country!" He was obviously a fan and didn't hold back his excitement.

Upon hearing this, with his arms still attached to tubes and IVs, Daddy lifted himself up from the bed and grabbed his buddy's arm. "Fuck this hospital, I don't wanna die here." Then he turned his head around and locked eyes with the doctor and said, "Fuck you and fuck Frank Sinatra."

They hastily released Daddy, and his friend drove him to the next nearest hospital, twenty minutes away. He died less than an hour later.

Hoboken, New Jersey. Frank Sinatra country. Frank was always a hero of mine. We were both made from the same stuff, homegrown Hoboken Italian-America. He was born and raised a couple of houses down from where my mother was born and raised, which was just down the road from where my father was born and raised. He beat the odds and became Hoboken's first big success story, and I've always admired him for that. He put my hometown on the map, gave it a story of its own apart from the shadows cast by the big skyscrapers and looming egos across the river. I knew there had been some bad blood toward the Sinatras on my family's part, dating back to an incident with my grandfather in 1943, but as I listened to the story about my father's final moments, my childhood suddenly came to life in a flash, and for the first time, it all made sense. My father was old Hoboken, and old Hoboken, my Hoboken, was a world unto itself. It was a microcosm of old-school values and customs, indifferent to the ever-changing social mores that existed beyond the Hudson waterfront—and in that little world, nothing was sacred.

Looking back now, I realize I'm a lucky son of a bitch. In fact, I admit it, I'm pretty much the luckiest guy I know. The fact that I beat the odds and survived my childhood alone is reason plenty. The fact that I can look back on it not with anger but with gratitude, a sentimental wink and a smile, gives me the gall to even refer to myself as lucky. The fact that I get to share this with all of you, well, I guess that could just make me a prick with a good agent. Regardless, I'm every bit a product of that little wacky old world that is just a seven-minute ferry ride from Manhattan, and it amazes me every day.

Perhaps it was the stark contrast with the metropolis so nearby that accentuated Hoboken's quirky nature and that of its inhabitants. Maybe it was in the water. Either way, growing up penniless in the company of degenerate gamblers and professional bullshit artists was just the motivation this kid needed to go out and actively seek his own calling in the world. Some folks say you learn best by negative example. If those folks are right, I am a genius. If, however, that statement is ever proven less than accurate, and I have a fleeting suspicion that's the case, then at the very least God knows my first nineteen spins on this Earth gave me the goods to work with. And God also knows I've spent the next thirty regaling my fellow cast members and friends on the set with small tales and tall tales and tales of every size about my wild and wonderful childhood, so I figured it's about time they got the true story.

My mother spent ten years praying to St. Joseph every night asking the good saint to bring her a baby boy. He granted her the favor and she granted me his name in return on the morning of September 12, 1951. I was born on Park Avenue. This was not the Eva Gabor lapdog-toting, high-society version, but the other one, about two miles and many more worlds away across the Hudson River in the spaghetti-and-meatball section of Hoboken. *My* Park Avenue was my first playground, and the first of many home addresses I had while growing up in the heart of my hero's hometown.

Nobody lived better or worse than *mi famiglia.* Had the good stork dropped me off anywhere else in the world, I would have missed out on the best goddamn childhood that a kid could have asked for. And I mean that sincerely. It wasn't a glamorous lifestyle by any recognized standards, borderline respectable at most, but I had a ball. What else did I know? It was like growing up in a Frank-Capra-meets-Martin-Scorsese matinee movie, circa 1951. *It's a Wonderful Life* meets *Mean Streets*, only instead of New York City's Little Italy, it was Hoboken USA. The set was picture-perfect, equipped with tightly spaced brown tenement apartment buildings, time-worn cement-stepped doorways, packs of potbellied men socializing in front of bars and unadorned social clubs, stray dogs catching shade under frayed storefront awnings, kids making the street their ultimate playground, a steady parade of festivals with their accompanying onslaught of first-rate Italian food.

The parades were something else. They'd easily stretch two city blocks, and the procession would march down the streets shooting off fireworks as the band shot off tune after wonderful old Italian tune to cheering and dancing crowds. The long march would invariably lead to the big feast, where the singing would continue, muffled only by the sofrittos and calzones being put away by the dozens. Heimlich maneuver posters on street lamps might have been useful. Then again, if anyone could break the shackles of human evolution and handle the feat of eating, singing and/or screaming at the same time, it was us Italians. Darwin would have had a field day in 1950s Hoboken, a virtual Galapagos of groundbreaking humanity.

Hoboken was built on the banks of the Hudson River and on the backs of generations of Dutch, German, Irish, Italian and Puerto Rican immigrants who found their promised land among its shipping ports and industrial factories. Because it was a seaport town, its residents developed their own combination accent that rivaled the better known Brooklyn and New Orleans flavors of English. The Hoboken accent is unique, combining mainly its Dutch, German and Irish influences. My father, for instance, would eat a ham "sangwich" and drop by your "haich" to say hello after he was done. Just leave the door unlocked, he'll help himself in. Back in the 1920s and 1930s Hoboken was a vibrant, raw and swinging town. There were at least 15 theaters throughout the city and more than 240 saloons on the River Street waterfront, more per square foot than anywhere in the world. I'm sure that didn't stop every man in my family from personally getting to know every bartender and his mother's maiden name at every single one of them. In the 1950s, the waterfront bars used to close for one hour every night so they could clean them up and ready them for the migration of thirsty Manhattanites as they arrived off the ferryboat in the wee hours of the morning, fleeing the cries of "Last call!" back in New York City. Manufacturers deserted Hoboken after World War II for sprawling industrial parks, and by the early 1950s, factory buildings stood crumbling and empty. Hoboken became a city of grimy smokestacks and decaying storefronts. It was heaven on earth, and it set the stage for a truly sensory-packed upbringing.

When I trip down memory lane nowadays, the sound I remember most, besides Mommy's screeching voice sounding off my name, is the hum of the crowds gathered outside to hear the Christmas carols in December and the popular ballads of the day infiltrating the very chemistry of the neighborhood air all night and day in Hoboken. These sounds didn't come from the windows of our ragtag apartments, but from the city's public address system, which piped down music from tinny amplifiers that were rigged to the top of street lamps on the corner of every block of our gritty little one-square-mile paradise. Up and down Adams Street, over to Monroe Street, all along Jackson Street, oxygen played second fiddle to the voices of Frank Sinatra, Nat King Cole and Bing Crosby.

"Fly me to the moon . . ."

It was the backdrop to my childhood: circa 1950s and 1960s *On the Waterfront* Hoboken, the seaport town of boats and docks and Manhattan-bound ferries, the melting pot for the huge Pantoliano and Centrella tribe, a rowdy bunch of tough-talking first- and second-generation Italians living in what became with hindsight one of the last genuine Italian-American urban ghettos. *The Sopranos* is certainly what we weren't. No high-line suburban lifestyle for us, no marble floors, no poolside lunches. I guess we were old-fashioned. Poor in our pockets but rich in ways you couldn't imagine. I often think it's the kind of upbringing that some of my "tough guy" characters would have had, if they'd had the good fortune to have been surrounded by true rough-around-the-edges angels like I had watching over me from day one. I thank my lucky stars every day for that.

Hoboken was basically all blue-collar working class, most of whom worked the nearby docks. Monroe Street, five blocks over from Park, was all Italian, and that's where my parents both grew up. My mother was born at 512 Monroe, down the street from 410 Monroe, where Sinatra lived. Everybody knew everybody on that street. There were the Alfanos, the Pantolianos and Centrellas, the Sinatras, the Citros, the Cocuccis, the Brandas and the Guideses. It was lower-class housing for those who lived beyond class distinctions. Everyone was pretty much at the same socioeconomic level—that is, dirt-poor. As a result, it was character that mattered; character alone could distinguish you from the rest. Luckily for us, there was plenty of character to spare. We could have exported the stuff had someone found a way to extract it and package it up nice and pretty. I can see the label clearly:

CHARACTEROL

Character Enhancing Supplements extracted from the richest character deposits of Hoboken, New Jersey. Take twice daily to infuse your spirit with a rich, zealous appetite for life and a "bah fungo" attitude.
Pending FDA approval.

And however tight money was, there was always food to spare, and always time to spare after eating. We'd all congregate after dinner, a cacophony of jabbering Italians, crazy and funny and well-fed Italians, warm and passionate human specimens, superb storytellers. I can still smell the aroma of steaming coffee mixed with a splash of anisette and a gush of cigar smoke coming from Aunt Dannah's kitchen on a Sunday afternoon, as Sambuca shots were poured one by one into coffee-filled mugs by the family men and women. It was their Sunday routine—different house, same alcohol ratio.

And while our daddies were drinking and our mommies were playing canasta, the kids of Hoboken owned the streets. We'd be drinking Coca-Colas and playing Kick the Can, Johnny on a Pony and Moon's Up beneath an endless canopy of clotheslines that hung from building to building across the streets. Damp shirts and pants, blouses and overalls, bedsheets and tablecloths forever swaying above us in the summer breeze—they were our American flags. The sight was outright impressive. We had a constant support system around us, which was made especially noticeable during the summer months, when people would spend countless hours looking down from their windows, occasionally yelling down to someone below. There was no air conditioning, so the windows were always open and people had pillows stationed permanently on the sills. Folks would just lean out and get any little breeze they could grab coming off the Hudson River and New York Bay. And they watched everything. It gave the average mother an underlying sense of security when the kids were doing their thing outside the house. Of course, ask any scrawny kid back then and he'd tell you that sense of security was as unfounded as the chew-your-meat-forty-times rule. Somehow the bad apples always managed to earn their title, and Lord knows I dealt with my share of bad apples. They were a dime a dozen in Hoboken, and they came in all shapes, sizes and varieties.

My parents and I lived at 201 Park Avenue in a low-rent

ground-floor apartment until I was about three years old. It had three tiny rooms: a bedroom, a kitchen and a bathroom down the hall that you shared with the other apartments on the floor. Each apartment had a separate light switch in the bathroom so they didn't pay for each other's electricity. It had a toilet, but there was no sink or bathtub, and you had to bring your own toilet paper. In those days, we took what we called "whore baths"—sponge baths in our kitchen. Soaking up the soapsuds in the kitchen sink, I didn't have a yellow rubber ducky but I had slippery clean dishes galore and I was the happiest kid on the planet. Clueless, perhaps, but you know what they say, ignorance *is* bliss. And thank you, Lord, for my ignorance at 201 Park Avenue.

My Mommy and Daddy were first-generation Italian-American hometown sweethearts turned sparring gladiators fighting to the death. Actually, it was Mommy who did most of the "gladiating." Daddy was more of a hapless lion who found himself half-sedated in a stadium full of sneering Romans who all looked like Mommy and were ready to come charging down at any given moment with knife blades in hand and get a piece of the action. Daddy was a soft-spoken genuine nice guy, a World War II veteran who had helped fight the Nazis in Germany by driving trucks filled with bombs in between battle positions. That was a piece of cake compared to his life with Mommy, a mouthy, popular and pretty young woman with a major chip on her shoulder and a mean streak a mile wide, especially when it came to men.

They were married ten years before I came on to the scene, but I got there just in time for World War III. Not for me, mind you. It was "little Joey, my Joey" and "Monk, you no-good dirty rat bastard" all in the same breath, which more often than not occupied the brief space in between deep long drags from a Chesterfield cigarette. I was her ally, while Daddy was strolling around like Mr. Magoo with a bull's-eye taped to his back. The war that began raging in earnest once I joined the family was strictly between Mommy and Daddy. "You good for nothing sumanabitch!" was her battle cry. Nothing was ever good enough for Mommy, not if Daddy was involved. Needless to say, they were in major hate with each other by the time I showed up. But I never doubted their love for me. I lucked out and became the instant object of their mutual affections.

Getting hitched to Mommy in the first place wasn't an easy task for the Monk. It was pretty much a lousy sequence of rather regrettable events that finally brought them together in front of Father John Pasquariello at St. Anne's Church in Hoboken on August 16, 1941. When Mommy met Daddy at a community youth dance, she was an innocent fifteen and he was a cool eighteen, and they fell very much in love. Both Mommy and Daddy had left school by that point, Daddy never getting past the fourth grade and Mommy leaving after the seventh grade to work. I'm convinced that Daddy's moves on the dance floor must have reeled her in. The Pantolianos were known to be good dancers, and the Monk was no exception. He loved to do the Peabody, and I imagine him swiftly picking young Mariacella up from the punch table, her long full dress swinging out as he twirls her to attention and pulls her to his right side, and Daddy, not missing a beat, leading her into an alternating cross-step, lock-step as the ragtime bounces off the band's instruments and rattles the punch bowl that she abandoned. Just take Tony Manero, throw out the disco ball and throw on a bowler derby and there's Daddy. Yeah, those two were in love once, Mommy and Daddy. They were pretty much inseparable from the beginning. Cousin Antoinette May, who was best friends with Mommy back then, remembers her crying like a baby all the time because she was so in love.

But things weren't looking so good for Daddy's chances, Peabody and all. Mommy's father, Cosimo "Dopey Gus" Centrella, wasn't a big fan of her new beau. It seemed to come down to the fact that, well, the Monk just couldn't hold down a job for the life of him. Grandpa Gus made his opinion on the issue clear enough. "If he can't hold a job, he's not made for this family, and if you ain't marrying him, you ain't gonna be seeing him either." Enda story. I guess Daddy was just too busy reinventing the fox-trot to busy himself with the whole breadwinning game. So my mother and Monk had to do a fair share of sneaking around town to get any time together. Antoinette and a couple of the neighborhood girls would come by Mommy's house and pick her up on their way to work at her family's dressmaking factory. She'd walk two blocks with them to the corner of Fifth and Adams and then they'd leave her there with Monk, who'd be waiting for her on that same corner every morning. Monk would never be allowed inside the house, so Mommy would go down her list of excuses and made-up dates with girlfriends and sneak out of the house just about every night to be with him. Antoinette recalls the frustration her cousin felt, especially because all of her female cousins, Antoinette included, had their boyfriends pretty much "accepted" into the family. Only Mariacella's Monk was denied the official Centrella seal of approval. As Antoinette put it, "Monk and Mary wouldn't dare sit in the living room, like I could with my boyfriend. She couldn't. They'd be on the corner. We'd go to school, Monk and Mary'd be on the corner." It was a dire situation and, eventually, too much for Mary to handle. In desperation, she broke up with Monk and soon after started dating another guy, named Red.

Now, I assume Red was gainfully employed, since the guy was immediately okayed by the powers that be and given full privileges (well, almost—they were Catholic, after all). So it seemed to be all over for the Monk and Mary. If this had been a scene from the Italian-American version of *Back to the Future*, a Polaroid snapshot of my sister and me with her "Fuck Mickey Mouse" sweatshirt and my A&P cap-and-apron outfit would be disappearing right about now.

Several months went by. It was June and cousin Antoinette had announced her plans to marry. My mother threw her a shower the Saturday night before the wedding and had all the family and friends over her house. Grandpa Gus got wasted and hit the town, but everybody else stayed and celebrated with Antoinette. That is, until Mary decided that the party was over and kicked everybody out of the house. "You gotta leave. Now!" and that was that. Everybody had to go—Antoinette, her new in-laws, all the guests, even her mother, Mamie. The party moved over to Antoinette's new in-laws' house and the coast was clear for Mary's date with Red. She had set the whole thing up to work that way. She knew her father would get drunk if she threw the shower at the house. She knew her mother would be loyal to the bride-to-be and move on to wherever the party continued. She also knew no one would think twice if she suddenly freaked out; I guess she already had somewhat of a reputation for that sort of thing.

Red came over as planned and they quickly got down to business on the living room sofa. Just as quickly, Grandpa Gus stumbled in drunk and found the two of them going at it. Red flipped out. Grandpa Gus was a physically intimidating character and had a reputation for being a hair shy of insane besides. In a desperate moment of self-preservation, Red spilled the spoiled beans to my grandfather: "For fuck's sake, I wasn't her first!" And then Red ran like the wind.

Sunday morning Antoinette got woken up by a phone call. It was Mary on the other line. She sounded resigned and almost content. "I'm marrying Monk. This August."

Daddy was the default choice. Grandpa never really gave his blessings; it was more a necessary enforcement of the Centrella rule of law. Pull out the Polaroid snapshot again and boom there we are. Joey and Maryann. And we owe it all to a guy named Red.

My parents' wedding in August was what you call a football wedding: beer, Italian cookies and wrapped sandwiches that they'd throw at you from behind the serving table. It was catered by the great character actor Vincent Gardenia's father, who had an Italian traveling theater company, Comedia del Arte, that played the town pretty regularly and, yes, he also sold sandwiches on the side. Hoboken was always a breeding ground of subliminal influences for aspiring actors and performers; it was impossible to escape the aroma of theater, even at our football weddings.

Daddy eventually found work as a foreman at Standard Brands in the old Lipton Tea building on Washington and Fifteenth Street, right on the Hudson River. Of course, he still managed to spend most of his weekdays and weekly paychecks at the Aqueduct racetrack. Everybody really liked the Monk, everybody but Mommy that is. He was a straight shooter. A working man. Well, sorta, but he sure kept his ducks in a row. Wherever he walked, he always stopped every fifteen steps or so and checked the back of his shoes to see if he'd stepped in shit. He was careful, cautious and clean, and you could be damn sure that the soles of his shoes were 100 percent dogshit-free.

The Pantoliano side of the family was huge. Daddy had nine brothers and sisters, and every single one of them was an entertainer. They hung out at the Rex Bar run by Cousin Kelly Cocucci and would make the windows shake singing everything from "Sweet Georgia Brown" to "Sweet Sue." Uncle Popeye would belt out a drunken rendition of "The Roses of Picardy" and for an encore he'd frighten the little kids like me with "You're Nobody Till Somebody Loves You." Daddy's sister, Aunt Dannah, and his eldest brother, Uncle Joe, were great tap dancers. If I knew the people then that I know today, there would never have been room on the pop charts for the Jackson Five, and I'll tell you now, that Partridge bunch and those Brady kids would have had a thing or two to learn from the Pantoliano clan.

My uncles and aunts on my father's side were testimony to

the characteristic Neapolitan sense of humor and comedy and unending sense of play. Their father, Grandpa Pete, played quite the role model. Like his children, Grandpa Pete was good-natured and fun-loving, and his life was a textbook success story for Italian immigrants in America. Arriving to New York as a teenager with an eight-word English vocabulary ("hello," "how much costs a beer?" and "thank you"), he learned the glass-working trade until he gained his U.S. citizenship, then moved across the river in 1908 and joined the Hoboken Fire Department, where he eventually worked his way up to the top job, serving as fire captain of Engine #5 until his retirement in 1943. He was a legend in town. Becoming captain wasn't an easy feat by any measure, considering that the Hoboken Fire Department at the time was 99 percent Irish. Reading down his company list from 1927, my grandfather sticks out like a sore thumb: O'Reilly, Ryan, Delaney, Kearnen, O'Donald, McKinsey, MacMahon, Fitzpatrick, O'Brien. They were all listed under Captain Pantoliano. But he must have made the right impression with the right people, and fire department politics were on his side. Leave it to a Pantoliano to bridge the cultural divide. He was a true stand-up guy, and there's no question that he lay seed to my family. The sections of the Hoboken Fire Department code cited for a violation he received on Sept. 19, 1940, during his tenure as captain, read like a genuine family biography:

> **Sec. 121:** Officers of the department will be expected to set an example for subordinates in the matter of due regard of respect for rules of discipline.

> **Sec. 129:** Members shall be held responsible at all times whether on or off duty for conduct unbecoming a member of the department, or tending to lower their service in the estimation of the public.
>
> **Sec. 131:** No member shall sign his warrant in whole or part or refuse or unreasonably neglect to pay his just debts.
>
> **Sec. 132(F):** The following offense is forbidden: conduct prejudicial to good order and discipline.
>
> **Sec. 153:** Officers and members shall not commit any assault or breach of peace, due to any act for which they can or may be arrested, confined or imprisoned, and shall not sell or resign their salaries, borrow any money from or procure one another to endorse any note, check or assignment of salary, or evidence of debt refused within thirty days to liquidate any debtness incurred from necessaries, or loan, sell or give away any public property.

Looks like Grandpa Pete was no stranger to the gambling, debt procuring, creditor avoiding and unabashedly unbecoming social conduct that went a long way toward defining my family in those days. Of course, to his benefit, he did get nineteen days paid vacation out of the deal.

As his retirement was nearing in 1943, Grandpa Pete was approached by a friend of his, the first mother of crooners everywhere, Dolly Sinatra, with a proposal. She wanted Grandpa Pete to appoint her husband, Marty O'Brien, also a fireman, as his successor once he retired. "Pick Marty," she said, "and my Frankie will give you a thousand bucks." Grandpa Pete remembered her son from the days he would sing for the dancers over at Jefferson Street Hall. He figured a little cash boost to kick off his golden years didn't sound so bad, so if your little troubadour wants to pay up, well, your Marty might as well start picking out a new rug for the office.

Once the new fire captain assignment had officially been made, my father Monk drove Grandpa Pete to pick up his payment at the Paramount Theater in Times Square in Manhattan, where Sinatra was performing three shows a night. Grandpa Pete went backstage and gave the attendant his name. Five minutes later the kid comes back and relays a message from Mr. Sinatra: "I don't know no Pete Pantoliano. Tell him to get lost." And with that, he slammed the door on Grandpa, and Grandpa Pete never got the money. Anyway, that's the official Pantoliano version. Recently I learned of a not-so-far-fetched rumor flying around that Sinatra gave the money directly to Grandpa's bookie, Gyp de Carlo, instead, so Sinatra may have actually made good on his promise after all. Either way, after driving his father back empty-handed that evening, there would be a thousand-dollar chip on Daddy's shoulder for Frank Sinatra. It stayed there all Monk's life, and was there an hour before he died.

Personally, I think Daddy just needed an outlet to dispense the wrath he absorbed on a daily basis with Mommy. And why not Frank Sinatra? He was an easy, intangible target, removed from everyday life. One thing's for sure, Daddy never let out any aggression on his kids, or his wife for that matter. That was all Mommy's job. But Mommy could always count on a dependable, unfailing excuse for her seething temper. It was a very serious condition that actually affected the entire family, and there appeared to be no cure at the time. We're not sure if it was hereditary, as I haven't shown any symptoms for the last thirty years, but we think instead it may have been airborne, perhaps even a by-product of the toxic smoke from Mommy's Chesterfields. After numerous examinations and false diagnoses, and tremendous advances in the fields of theoretical physics, applied mathematics and chaos theory, the condition was eventually identified and diagnosed correctly. "Chronic Insolvency," the accountant said. Together and on their own, my parents gambled away every cent they made. Mommy did this at church bingo, where she spent five nights a week and played sixteen cards at a time while chain-smoking cigarettes and gossiping with the girls, and Daddy at the track, usually the Big A. Both padded the pockets of the local bookie to the tune of four to eight bucks a week, which was plenty of dough in those days. Daddy inevitably took most of the blame, but believe me, they were equal partners in crime on this account.

I was an only child at 201 Park Avenue; it wasn't for another six years after me that my sister, Maryann, was born. And being the only child after ten childless years with my father, my mother was always deathly afraid that something would happen to me. Describing her as protective, overbearing and overreactive would be an understatement, kind of like describing Patty Hearst as that actress with the exposed cleavage in *Pecker*. One of my clearest memories from Park Avenue was sitting in the living room with Mommy and Daddy eating dinner and watching *The Martha Raye Show* as the snow fell outside. There were some kids playing outside and throwing snowballs. A snowball came crashing through the living room window, landing perfectly intact on the floor. To Mommy, it was a grenade in disguise. She jumped up and grabbed me, screaming, "Get away from the window! Somebody's trying to kill Joey!" I had cut my hand on a bottle of milk that fell and cracked in the chaos. Mommy was hysterical. I started screaming. Daddy was wrapping my hand with a dishrag. Blood was everywhere. Mommy screamed straight through the eighteenth stitch at the hospital. "Somebody tried to kill my Joey!"

I learned a lot about Mommy during those early years. She took me to the annual parade on Washington Street, about two blocks from our apartment, and pushed our way into the front line of the procession just as a clown entertaining the crowd was approaching. It was my turn and I could see him going right for me and I freaked. "Why are you crying, honey? Say hello to the nice clown." That didn't help. "Look, he's not really a clown. It's your Uncle Popeye." Even though I was still young enough to be in a stroller, I had sense enough to know that my mother was lying. "That's not Uncle Popeye!" I wailed. I could tell that straightaway. I didn't smell dead dog, cheap whiskey and stale cigars, only the spooky sweet cotton-candy scent of clown. She'd never have guessed I knew the difference. From that point on, I knew Mommy would lie to try to make everything okay, or at least a little better.

Mommy was a full-time housewife and a part-time seamstress. She worked at home from the kitchen table. She did "piecework" and got paid for each piece she sewed finishing touches on. She would cut uniform patches, the kind that sergeants and corporals wear in the Army, off a big roll she'd receive every week. I would help her out by counting them up in blocks of ten and tying them off for her. The smell of glue would engulf the kitchen, together with cigarette smoke, just enough to get a spankin' good buzz going for a four-year-old kid.

The fact of the matter is I would have done anything she asked if I thought it would make her happy. She knew it, and boy did she make use of it.

"Joey, get Mommy her cigarettes."

"Baby Doll, give Mommy a bite of your sangwich."

"Sweet Jesus, Joseph and Mary . . . give your Mommy that fifty bucks you got for your first communion. You owe me for the party."

Yes, she was a natural-born con. Didn't matter who, didn't matter when, but the only problem was she wasn't very good at it. Even as a kid, I could spot her tricks like they were wrapped in cellophane.

Some of the closest times I had with her were when she taught me how to play cards—I mean when she taught me how to cheat at cards.

During one of our ritual evening poker games at the kitchen table, Mommy got up to get coffee and I saw a card, a king of spades, stuck to her ass. She came back, sat down and gave me a quick slap on the hand.

"Did you look at my hand?" she asked.

"No, Mommy."

She picked up her hand of cards and eyed me suspiciously. "Then quit playing with yourself and make a bet."

I studied the hand and pushed a small stack of nickels toward the pile of coins in the middle of the table.

She sat there with her cigarette dangling out of the side of her mouth, still eyeing me suspiciously. "What the fuck is that supposed to mean?"

"I'm raising you thirty-five cents," I replied.

"You little snake bastard, you . . ." She paused. "You trying to bluff your own mother?"

"Maybe," I said with a grin. "Maybe not."

She folded her cards with a frightening glare, and slowly a smile spread across her face. She was positively glowing. "Thadda boy," she said. "And you did it without looking like an asshole. That's good."

I felt like I had just brought home an *A* on my report card. I reached forward to collect my winnings. Mommy stopped me. "But not good enough, sweetheart," she said as she showed four kings, including the one that had been stuck to her rear end. I'd been had again.

Truth is, though, aside from cleaning me out of my piggy bank change, she wasn't gettin' very much of Lady Luck's charity either. She never won big at bingo. Her daily number very rarely came in. Still, she never stopped trying. The hustle was in her blood. She loved the action, and she had muscle in her every bone.

Looking back at my parents' life together, I guess the unceasing combat was inevitable. Both of their ancestors were from the legendary tough-blooded region of Avellino in Naples, Italy. Legend has it that one of my mother's relatives, Pellerino Morano, was one of the "founding fathers" of the Cosa Nostra in New York City at the turn of the century. La Cosa Nostra means "This thing of ours," and was often used to label the establishment of an Italian community and family away from the old country. Pellerino met and married Diletta Centrella. Pellerino decided Hoboken was a good place to open a bar, but he wasn't a United States citizen so he needed a front man. He chose his second wife's brother, Cosimo "Dopey Gus" Centrella, who happened to be my grandfather on my mother's side. The bar was placed in Gus's name, but Pellerino owned it and young Achille "Kelly" Cocucci, his stepson and Diletta's son, operated it.

The Rex Bar eventually became a staple landmark of my childhood. Years later, as a toddler, I became a regular there, thanks to my father's fondness for the place, and got some of my earliest lessons of life hanging out watching all the action. Cousin Kelly had taken over control of the bar by then, and his tough-guy-with-a-heart-of-gold attitude and unwavering moral sensibility made me proud to be related to him, even as a kid. He ran one hell of a bar back in the day, not to mention one tight ship of a household. He was a strict disciplinarian with his kids, but managed to earn their respect and love and maintain it even during their teenage years, and if he needed any vindication at all, every one of his kids turned out to be rock-solid salt-of-the-earth adults. It's a tight rope to walk sometimes, and as a parent of teenagers now, I'm realizing more and more how much I learned from Cousin Kelly. That's right, kids, you can blame him. He was without doubt my first role model and proved to be a significant positive influence in my life.

But there's a bad seed in every bunch. Convicted murdering turn-of-the-century gangsters aside, that prize went to my maternal grandfather, Dopey Gus. I never knew him—he died before I was born—but from scraps of anecdotes picked up over the years, I have every reason to believe the man was a total prick. It didn't help his case that Mommy never had a kind word to say about him when his name was brought up in conversation. In her later years, she'd always remind me that she refused to be buried on top of her father on the family plot, to make sure she was buried on top of her mother. It was pretty clear that she hated her father.

Grandpa Gus ran a small factory that assembled women's clothing, mainly dresses. It was a big union shop, and he was the head guy, or the chairman, as they called it. Mommy and cousin Antoinette and Antoinette's brother Tony Centrella and numerous other Centrellas all at one time or another worked together at Gus's factory. That's why everybody in the family could sew. He was a dressmaker. He did the machine work, the gals did the handwork, and Tony swept the floors for two dollars a week. You wouldn't call Gus a tailor, though. He just made dresses. There's a difference. They'd receive the dresses in partially preassembled pieces of fabric and they'd put it all together there, while Grandpa Gus operated the machines and the gals operated with their hands. As Antoinette recalls, he was a top-notch crackerjack operator, the boss of the dressmaking operation and the boss of the family. Grandpa Gus was a strong man physically and a tough-guy gambling man. But when he'd get drunk, and he got drunk a lot, he'd do weird stuff, or so the story goes. It was enough to earn him the title "Dopey Gus," which is what everybody in town knew him by. "Dopey" has funny connotations, but make no mistake, there was nothing funny about my Grandfather Gus. Wild, drunken and absolutely mad, perhaps, but not funny, or cute, or anything resembling the dwarf by the same name.

Grandpa Gus used to run the Italian lottery in Hoboken for Vito Genovese during Don Vito's rise to the top. As kids, my mother and her brother Pete would drive into Manhattan's Lower East Side with the numbers, complete with receipts and cash, and give them to Vito's brother, who'd check them against the winning numbers from the Naples horse track. Involving his children in the dirty business was one thing, but it was his penchant for trigger pulling that really soured my grandfather's reputation. Grandpa Gus's temper was legendary. My mother used to sit me on her lap and frighten me with the story of the sorry spitter. My mother, no older than seven or eight, went up to her father one day after school and told him that there was a guy that sat at the same spot and spit at her every day when she walked home from school. "Which way you walk home?" he asked her in his heavily accented English.

"By John the Florist," she answered.

"Okay, tomorrow you walk same way and show me."

The next day, Grandpa Gus watched as his daughter and cousin Antoinette walked by a middle-aged man seated in front of a doorway, and lo and behold, they pass him and "what-too!" he spit on the street just behind them.

Mommy and Antoinette weren't ten feet from the man when Grandpa Gus crossed the street, pulled out his pistol and shot the guy in the leg. Blood splattered everywhere on the sidewalk. The man screamed in pain and hit the pavement with a thud. Grandpa Gus, his temper even, walked over matter-offactly, stopped and leaned down so his face was only inches from the wounded man's face. In Italian, Grandpa Gus said to him, calmly, "You spit on my kid again, and I kill you. *Capische?*"

The man was terrified beyond belief. He was gasping and wheezing, fighting for air and unable to speak a full sentence. "I didn't . . . didn't . . . spit . . . on kid . . . I gotta . . . spit . . . I gotta . . . condition . . . I gotta . . . condition!" It turned out the poor guy spit all the time because he had a severe sinus problem. It had nothing to do with my mother.

She was not very happy about the turn of events. She cried as she stood on the sidewalk, her white blouse peppered with blood.

Not that there aren't fond memories of him anywhere in my family. Tony Centrella, my third cousin, Antoinette's brother, remembers when he was a kid and Gus would give him a dime to go around collecting numbers. "Boy, it was like giving me a treasure. That's how I knew he liked me," remembers Tony. If you give a kid a dime every time you see him and pat him on the back and say, "Go get 'em, Tony, go get 'em!" and "Here you go, go treat yourself, kid," the kid's gonna see a nice man. Tony hadn't known the details of what Gus was up to, except for overhearing the occasional rumor exchanged by his sister and mother. "As far as I knew, he was a mellow, nice person." But as he grew older, Tony, like everyone else, came to know the Crazy in the Dopey.

But his daughter, Mommy, had the unfortunate privilege of getting the early scoop. The privilege really didn't please her much. Grandpa Gus and Mommy clashed all the time. He was strict with her to the point of exaggeration, and she was belligerent in return. She often went against him, and you couldn't go against Grandpa Gus, at least not without consequence.

Grandpa Gus was odd and frightening all in one. In a fit of rage after picking a fight with his wife once while cousin Antoinette was at the house visiting Mary, he asked his niece who should go first: "Me or your Aunt Mamie? One of us has gotta go, Antoinette. One's gonna die. Who do you want to die?" Antoinette always thought a man's gotta die first, and besides, she liked Aunt Mamie. But I'm sure she got the hell out of there quick after answering him.

While Gus didn't have many fans in the family, he had fans all over Hoboken, and he screwed every last one of those gals. I'm not sure if his infidelity was a matter of conscience for him, but it doesn't seem likely. He wasn't a devout Catholic and didn't recall that whole fuss about the Ten Commandments. Surprising for a guy who was a genuine stickler for keeping Catholic holiday tradition. Palm Sunday in particular must have been a real favorite of his. I can still hear Mommy reminiscing about that Norman Rockwell Palm Sunday family dinner when she was twelve. The aroma of the feast Grandma Mamie had prepared all day had slipped into every nook and cranny in the house, and by now had probably worked itself well outside the walls, kick-starting salivary glands and stomach pangs all the way to Weehawken. Grandma Mamie was busy getting everything ready in the kitchen and Grandpa Gus, Mommy and her younger brother and sister, Pete and Tilly, were all sitting and waiting at the junior-sized dining table when Grandpa Gus called out to his wife, "Mamie, make sure everything's done before you sit down 'cause I don't want you to have to get up. Make sure you take care of everything." So she finished up doing a couple of things in the kitchen and went to join her family. As she was settling into her chair, Grandpa Gus asked her, "You got any idea of what you're supposed to do?"

"Yeah, Gus, I got everything," she answered.

"You didn't forget nothin'?"

"No, Gus, I didn't forget nothin'."

And with that last innocuous reply, he smacked her. He smacked her right across the face. The kids were shocked into paralysis, Grandma Mamie was holding her head and reeling from the pain and Grandpa Gus got out of his chair, walked over to the window and opened it, then walked back and around the table, picked up the four corners of the tablecloth, with the macaroni and the turkey and the gravy, the water glasses and silverware, the flower-print cloth napkins folded into perfect rectangles, and in one single motion threw the whole thing out the window. The picturesque warm family Sunday holiday fare fell five stories onto the street below. Mommy remembered hearing glass shatter and metal silverware clang first, then the crash and boom of forty-five pounds of lasagna, turkey, macaroni, struffoli and their containers smashing against sidewalk, fence and street.

Grandpa Gus kicked Mommy, Aunt Tilly, Uncle Pete and Grandma Mamie out of the apartment and made them sleep in the hallway that night. They never quite got to Hosanna. But Grandpa Gus did get to finish off Grandma Mamie's special

Palm Sunday pastiera, which, luckily, hadn't made it to the table before the table made it to the curb.

Days passed before anyone found out what had ticked him off. Mommy figured her mother had forgotten his ice, but it turned out that she'd neglected to place the little palm next to his plate, while all the kids had gotten one. Mommy's house had a tradition of cutting pieces of palm tree frond into little crosses and using them as lapels on Palm Sunday.

Grandpa Gus smacked my Grandma Mamie around on a regular basis. She was his punching bag. Mommy was deeply afraid of him. Quite regrettably, the echo of her father's abuse rang loudly in every chord she sang and every strike she delivered to her very own punching bag, the Monk. She told me that she blamed my grandfather for her mother's death. They had gotten into a fight one day and he choked her, and shortly after that she developed throat cancer. My mother nursed her until she died several months later. Those several months for her were the most profoundly sad and tragic of her life, tragic in epic proportions. Mommy believed Grandpa Gus caused the cancer that killed her mother. She had been traumatized beyond the point of no return, and I later found out that the origin of that pain went even deeper than her mother's death, a few ruined dinners and a disastrous family life. "I'll tell you when we're alone," says cousin Antoinette when I ask her about it. "I'll tell you when we're alone, not now."

Mommy never let go of her rage, only harnessed it and amplified it further, and subsequently channeled it toward every man in her life thereafter. She became a focused and driven and highly capable expert in the art of man-hating. And yet men fell for her. Had they been deceived, or was she masterfully capable of harboring a genuine unrestrained love and vicious stinging hate for the same object, simultaneously? For whatever she let the world see of her, it seemed clear that she was engaged in a lifelong subversion aimed at the male species. And if I knew my mother well at all, I knew that she didn't give a rat's ass about what anyone else thought of her, and if that's what they thought of her, so be it and go sing it to the papers till the little fairy muse falls out of your ass for all she cares. She had the ability to control her on-and-off rage with the flip of a switch or a flick of a cigarette.

But everything aside, no one expressed her love as well as Mommy could when she wanted to. And when she didn't want to, you knew, and so did the whole neighborhood. She was admired, feared and ridiculed all at once. She was larger than life. A goddess, in a really bad fucking mood. A Neapolitan masterpiece.

I was a three-year-old with a family life about as calm as a Muhammad Ali–Joe Frazier news conference. It's no wonder that I found an escape path from the get-go, in the form of a small black-and-white TV in the living room. I used to watch *The Martha Raye Show* and I vividly remember loving her. She was loud and she was funny and she reminded me of all my big-mouthed relatives. And I spent countless hours watching *The Merry Mailman* with Ray Heatherton. But what really fueled the fire in my belly like nothing else was watching Elia Kazan's *On the Waterfront* some years after the movie's 1954 release. I knew it had been filmed right there in my neighborhood, and I was mesmerized. The story was uncovered and written by Budd Schulberg and was based on the life of Tony Mike Gustoso, who ran a bakery with that name on Fifth Street between Adams and Jefferson, where my mother bought her fresh bread. Daddy had taken me to the docks at the age of two to watch them shoot the scenes there.

On the Waterfront brought film history, acting history and directing history right to my doorstep. The giants were here—Brando, Kazan, Karl Malden, Lee J. Cobb, Eva Marie Saint. Daddy and I went to see the film every time it played in Hoboken, and it burned its way right into my six-year-old consciousness, leaving an indelible imprint. Genius can be a little contagious, and once you get a whiff of it, it's downright inspiring. All of my uncles and cousins were extras in the film—even Uncle Popeye and his best friend John Wayne (a.k.a. Matty Russo, who got the name not from his involvement in the film business per se, but because back in the day his father had a horse-drawn fruit cart and he'd let young Matty ride it around town on Sundays; he was the only kid in Hoboken with a horse). They bragged about being in it till the Grim Reaper himself decided he'd heard enough and came knocking. People talked about it all the time. They were so proud it was made here and they still are.

The older I got the more the film meant to me. It continues to resonate in my life. Brando uncovered a deeper reality of acting, but with all the beauty and purity and grit and balls and reality and heart captured in that film. When I see it now, I see old Hoboken, I see my childhood and I envision myself as an infant staring at the sets and the actors and the directors and the gaffers and all the activity and all the excitement and all the possibility or bullshitting, that is. I stood by the houseboat next to Daddy after watching the film one afternoon in 1957 and looked across the river to the most fabulous view of Manhattan, glittering from the sunset over New Jersey. The waterfront docks on the New York side were like arms stretching out from the city, inviting me to give it a shot. Though I know I didn't understand it at the time, the seed had been planted for sure, standing there on the waterfront. I had discovered a loophole in the system—you could make a living out of lying. It was just about taking the art of bullshitting to a whole new level. Daddy always pointed out the irony of Brando, the longshoreman, having the bruises cleaned off of his face as his limo would pull up to take him back the big city. I could hear Daddy call out to me as I ran ahead of him, up the ramp that led back to the dock, the same ramp and dock where they had shot the famous final scene several years earlier.

"Where you goin', Joey?" Daddy yelled playfully. Joey who? I wasn't Joey, I was Terry Malloy, staggering across the dock toward the loading pier, leading a cheering crowd of longshoremen behind me.

—2—

202 Monroe Street

Sweet Summer

"No way! I ain't fucking riding in Uncle Popeye's car!" Not without a gas mask. At six years old, I had the mouth of a kid at least twice my age.

"Monk! Look what you done to him! You made a goddamn sissy outta this fucking kid! Joey, get the hell in the fucking car before I break you in half!"

"Could you really blame me? I'm gonna die in there, Mommy!"

"You ain't gonna have the chance 'cause I'm gonna get to you first if you're not in your uncle's car at the count of three. One . . . two . . ."

She's gonna be sorry when we get to the shore and I'm deader than the dead dog that was lying in Uncle Popeye's trunk less than an hour ago.

"Three!"

From as young as I can remember, dozens of Pantolianos and Centrellas would drive out in caravan style to Long Branch down on the Jersey shore for the summer. All the families would pitch in to rent a weather-beaten boardinghouse on Chelsea Avenue for ten dollars a week. The house was owned by Mrs. Brodsky and her Orthodox Jewish family, who lived there together with their summer houseguests, a feisty bunch of Italians escaping the heat, the stench and the boredom of July and August in Hoboken.

I looked forward to those trips all year round. Getting there was the only hard part. All the male cousins always got stuck riding in my uncle Popeye's car. They called him Popeye because he bore a striking resemblance to the crusty cartoon character, down to the anchor tattoo on his arm and the cigar that was glued to his mouth day and night and could easily have passed for the trademark cartoon pipe. I had nothing against him—in fact, he was one of my favorite uncles. He was a kind-hearted, caring man and a natural clown. You never left his company without a couple of good laughs as a parting gift. It was Uncle Popeye's profession that was the problem. Popeye was the unwitting gestapo for Hoboken's stray animal population. As Hoboken's full-time dogcatcher, he was called in to transport stray dogs and cats and the occasional roadkill to the makeshift dog pound on Fourteenth Street. It was just a garage along the river's edge and our very own Bronx Zoo.

We used to beg Popeye to take us there. At the garage, he would put the live dogs in a cage and keep them there, sometimes for days, until he had collected enough to proceed to the next step, which was the gas chamber. The gas chamber was a large metal tank that could hold about half a dozen large mutts. The tank's chamber was connected to a pipe that passed through the adjacent wall and was accessible from outside the garage. The carbon monoxide supply came from the only available source—Popeye's rusting late-model Rambler. He'd hook one end of a hose to the Rambler's exhaust pipe, the other end to the tank pipe sticking out of the wall and let the engine run for fifteen to twenty minutes. That usually did the trick. I think a guy came by with a city truck once a week to pick up the dead animals. Popeye's garage was a veritable house of horrors for the canine and feline community. The recently formed Humane Society clearly hadn't had the time yet to set its sights on northern Jersey.

He had taken the job after returning home a World War II hero, and he held the post for thirty years. He was good at what he did. Unfortunately for us, the City of Hoboken hadn't provided him with any special vehicle for the job, so Uncle Popeye used his Rambler, since it was equipped with a sizeable trunk that was just roomy enough for a couple of tragedy-stricken house pets. Popeye took his job seriously; no question about it. He was almost as dedicated a dogcatcher as he was a loyal Rex Bar patron. No matter where in Hoboken a call would take him, the old Rex Bar was always a convenient pit stop along the route back to the garage. He'd usually stop in for a couple of drinks with buddies, and by the third round he had no cares in the world. If it happened to be a Friday, Popeye might forget about the animal cargo he was carrying in the car. If he happened to have picked up a dead one, he'd easily forget about it the entire weekend. By Monday, he'd notice the stink rising above the underlying stench of stale cigar smoke, and by then it was too late. Enough occurrences of this sort led Popeye to be the proud owner of the foulest-smelling car in the entire state of New Jersey.

With the oppressive heat already bearing down in late June or early July, me and Popeye's two older sons, Anthony, who we called Beaver because of his buck teeth, and his younger brother, Eddie, as well as my cousin Patty DeRiso from my mother's side, were all forced to ride in the car for the two or three suffocating hours it took to get out to shore. The four of us kids were the Popeye transport regulars. There were always two or three more male cousins packed in with us, but they were lucky enough to make the rounds with the other vehicles every year. Me, Patty-boy and Popeye's kids were the default regulars. We had no choice.

Life out at the shore with the saltwater breezes mixing together with the aroma of my family's Italian cooking all day was the ultimate recipe for freedom for a cooped-up, hyper little city kid like me. In their heyday back in the 1920s, those boardinghouses we rented were probably elegant bed-and-breakfast joints. By the time we took them over in the fifties, they were classic oceanside dives. We'd squeeze six families into each house. Each house had seven rooms and seven refrigerators in the common kitchen. God knows there was always plenty for us to eat.

Our moms, along with about half of the female population of Long Branch, would spend the entire day together poolside smoking cigarettes, playing cards and gossiping under the glaring Jersey sun. The huge town pool ran almost a full block along Chelsea Avenue just two blocks away from our summer shacks. The kids were allowed to come and go as we pleased, so we spent half the time at the pool and half the time converting the streets of Long Branch into our extended Hoboken playground. The first time I found out that Mommy worked as a bookie was during one of those carefree early summers.

She didn't sew patches in the summer; she ran numbers instead, to help with the household finances. Naturally, I would assist her. It was a part-time deal for the two of us. Me being not more than six at the time actually worked in our favor. Nobody would ever suspect that a little kid like me was in on a numbers game.

She worked for the local bookies in Long Branch and was assigned to Chelsea Avenue, picking up the numbers for the horse races at Aqueduct and Monmouth Park and collecting the money from other avid vacationing bettors. The bookies paid her a piece of the action. In the mornings, Mommy would go from boardinghouse to boardinghouse collecting bets from the old men who'd been hanging out on their big front porches since sunrise. Once she'd gathered a hefty amount of their social security and pension earnings, she'd move on to the women who placed their bets poolside. That's when I'd come into the picture. Every day around noon, I'd show up in my junior swim trunks, flip-flops and Coppertone tan and pick up the money Mommy had collected that morning. She would wrap up the cash and receipts in a sheet of yellow legal-pad paper that had all the information for the bookie written on it in pencil and stuff the whole thing down the fishnet inside pocket of my swim trunks.

After two or three practice runs accompanied by Mommy, I knew exactly what to do next. With my flip-flops flapping away on the steaming pavement, I'd run down Chelsea Avenue to the Italian bakery around the corner.

"Hey, look who's here. Mary's little Joey," Mikey the baker would greet me every time from behind the counter. He was a large, round man with a thick gray mustache straight from the old country. "Come back around here, kid," he'd say, and our routine kicked in.

I'd pull the wrapped stack of bills out of my bathing suit shorts and hand the dampened delivery over to Mikey. The aroma of extra-strength cappuccino danced loops around the scent of almond paste as Mikey would riffle through Mommy's easily earned stash. He'd lick his thumb every four or five seconds as he counted out loud. While I waited, I'd stand on my tiptoes and peer into the glass display case filled with syrupy "baba rum" custard cakes and crispy cannoli overflowing with freshly made vanilla cream and every other bite-sized Italian miracle imaginable. The same two old Italian men wearing plaid wool caps, despite the ninety-degree temperature, were always seated in the back of the shop at a small café table, reading the racing forms and sipping espresso from tiny, porcelain cups that required their pinkies to be out in full salute when handled.

When Mikey was done counting, he'd fold up the wad of cash, give me a stern look in the eye and say, "Good job, Joey! Good job. Now go home and be a good boy." With that, he'd swat me on my ass and I'd run like the wind back to the pool, but not before he gave me my favorite pay, a steaming hot cruller fresh out of the oven. No wage I've ever earned since has been nearly as sweet.

In July of '58 Mommy and some of her cousins decided to

take advantage of the brief delay that occurred between the end of a race at Monmouth and the time the news reached Long Branch to make a little extra money off her part-time bookie gig. The simple scam they came up with involved two of her cousins. Georgie and his sister Rosie Fat would go down to the Monmouth Racetrack to get the daily double winners from the first two races, and then run to a telephone booth off the property to call Mommy back in Long Branch with the winning numbers. To prevent exactly this kind of thing from happening, they didn't have public phones at the racetrack grounds, but that didn't stop Mommy and her cousins. If there was a will, there was always a way for a Centrella. Whether or not you pulled it off was another story.

Mommy held a list of local clients who played the daily double. To win you had to pick the winning horses in the first two races. If you picked horse number 8 in the first race and horse number 9 in the second race, your daily double number was 89. Mommy listed the bets on her yellow legal pad, putting the name of the bettor next to the amount of the bet for each race. She'd leave one empty space for the winning numbers phoned in by her cousins. The call from Monmouth would come in several minutes after two o'clock. Mommy would fill in the blank space next to the winning numbers with one of her cousin's names in time to deliver the sheets of yellow pad to her bosses, who'd come to the Brodsky boardinghouse to pick them up at 2:15 sharp every day. She shared the earnings with her two accomplices, never more than fifteen or twenty bucks total a week so as not to arouse any suspicion. For several weeks she actually pulled it off and made out well by bringing in about an extra buck and a half a day. It wasn't much, but a dollar could stretch a long way back then—from her pocketbook all the way to the canasta table eight hours later.

I was home the day her bosses confronted her. It had only been a matter of time, and I think Mommy was surprised herself it had lasted as long as it did. From her performance that afternoon, it was apparent that she'd prepared herself for the eventuality. It was around four o'clock when Mommy answered the door and two slick-haired gentlemen in their thirties let themselves in. They both wore linen pants, brown leather sandals and Cuban-style guayabera shirts with side vents to let the ocean breeze in, one of them plain white and one with a blue swirl pattern over the pleated stripes that ran down the front. It was hard to tell the two apart save for the unlit cigar hanging listlessly from one guy's lips. As imposing as they appeared to me, Mommy was as cool as if the local Mormon missionary boys had just invited themselves in for milk and cookies. "What can I do for you boys? Didn't you get enough a me already today?"

They explained with polite jest that they never could get enough of her and then got straight to business. They had begun to notice an odd series of wins over the last several weeks "and we just wanna make sure you got nothin' to do with it."

It was Mommy's cue.

First came shock. "What?! This is a joke, right?" She looked at them with wide, intense eyes.

Then, indignation. "You walk into my house and call me

a thief in front of my son? You sumanabitch bastards! You sumanabitches! I won't take this!"

Finally, there was pain. "How could you fucking accuse me of something like this? I can't believe you would do that. How could you think I would ever do that to you? Really, how could you?" The tears were welling up in her eyes.

She had her bosses begging for forgiveness by the third act. "Mary, look, we're sorry . . . We didn't mean to offend . . . It's hot outside, the heat gets to your head sometimes . . . It was all a big mistake." What started out as a scene straight out of *Scarface* became something more akin to a video lecture on the three steps for exercising the powers of persuasion through tapping your emotional range, with Professor Mary Centrella. By the time they left the house, Mommy had gotten a two-dollar raise. Next to Brando, it was the greatest acting lesson I had received to date. She continued the scam for a week, figuring the immediate break in winnings would be obvious, and then called it off for good.

Once our fathers used up their two weeks of summer vacation time, they would commute on the weekends to meet up with the family and then head back to town and their jobs before dawn every Monday morning. It was just the women and the kids for the better part of the summer, and as much freedom as having half the parental units gone for most of the week may have meant for some of my cousins, for me it was just four-and-a-half days of Mommy unchecked. Daddy wasn't around for the crucial "Leave the kid alone, Mary" and "Let the kid have some fun, Mary" and "You're gonna make him crazy, Mary" interjections that would occasionally put a damper on the situation or, at the very least, divert Mommy's attention over to him.

Mommy came by her temperament honestly, from her father, Dopey Gus. Her obscenely overprotective nature made it apparent to everyone that she had inherited more from him than she cared to admit. She was as paranoid that strangers were out to get her little Joey as she was convinced of the malicious intent of Mother Nature. Snowballs turned into grenades thrown by plotting children in the winter, and thunderstorms conspired against me in the summer.

One year, when I was six, the first week after our fathers had gone back to Hoboken, we'd been lounging around the pool when a summer storm snuck up on us. All the moms and kids picked up and ran back toward the house. Halfway there, a lightning bolt hit a tree right in front of us, causing a limb to fall down to the sidewalk. We all froze in our tracks for a moment, and after gathering their wits, the rest of the family jolted ahead to the house. But Mommy grabbed me and forced me to stay behind with her. She wouldn't let me move forward.

"Mommy, let's go!" I screamed. We were getting soaked, and I was afraid the lightning was going to strike again and get us. But she was frozen still.

"No! Stay away from there! It's quicksand! You're gonna drown in the quicksand!" Aunt Minnie had run back to see what was going on. Her quizzical expression told me she had heard Mommy screaming about the quicksand.

"C'mon, Mary, get Joey to the house!" Aunt Minnie yelled.

But Mommy insisted that the ground around the fallen limb had become quicksand. Aunt Minnie ran toward us and, grabbing my arm and Mommy's, pulled us across the treacherous terrain.

At six years old, I wasn't quite convinced that Mommy was being irrational. At the same time, I was also old enough to be embarrassed by her reaction, especially when nobody else seemed to fear the sidewalk was anything more than met the eye. It was an incredibly awkward moment for me when Aunt Minnie, Mommy and I returned to the house drenched and frazzled. The whole family was shaking off the frightening moment with hearty laughs, but I was convinced they were laughing at me and Mommy. The quicksand on Chelsea Avenue made me very jittery about getting myself into any precarious situation that might make Mommy embarrass us both. But precariousness is not something a kid on summer vacation is very good at avoiding.

Summers were full of temptations and opportunities to test your limits, like swimming out beyond the shallow area off the beach, where only the big kids were allowed to go. There was a rope lined with round white buoys set up every morning to mark the area off. I was strictly forbidden to pass it. That was all the motivation I needed to convince myself I was a strong enough swimmer to handle the deep area. I waded in slowly, looking behind me to make sure there weren't any adults watching, and off I went, swimming as fast as I could. I reached the rope and ducked under, and it was just me and Mother Atlantic. I hadn't even realized how exhausted I was. The thrill of swimming past the rope had consumed me. Not ten feet on the other side, I lost my energy. Having reached my goal, my adrenaline engine shut down, and it became an effort just to keep my head above water. I started to panic and tried to scream, but I couldn't get a sound out of my mouth; I was too scared and the waves kept rushing over my head. Just before I lost consciousness, I felt a tug at my hair and an arm come from behind and grab hold of my upper torso and I was pulled out of the water. Patty-boy's older sister, Mary Ann, swam me back to shore as I coughed and cried. She had been keeping an eye on me the whole time.

"It's okay, Joey. It's okay. I got you. I got you," she said to comfort me. But I kept crying as she put me down on the sand. "You're okay, Joey. Take it easy."

"No! Please don't tell my Mommy!"

Once the fear for my life passed, the fear of Mommy's reaction set in. I don't know which was worse. I could just picture Mommy screaming at the top of her lungs that Captain Nemo had tried to kidnap her Joey.

"I won't," she promised. She didn't.

No matter what grave danger I had encountered or how close I may have come to death, it was the humiliation that I feared most.

It was my fear of humiliation that sent me running up a tree later that summer after getting hit by a car. A big truck used to come by every day at dusk and spray pesticide to kill the mosquitoes, and all the kids would run behind the truck and play in the cloud of poison that trailed it. We'd spent ten minutes merrily filling up our lungs with DDT one evening when the sound of car brakes interrupted our fun. I was facing away from the car when it hit me and knocked me to the ground, though it was probably going no more than five miles an hour at the time. The loud thump triggered complete chaos behind the mosquito truck. My cousins were panicking, and I could hear some of them run into my house screaming, "Joey got hit by a car! . . . Oh my god! He's under the car! . . . He's dead! He's dead!" while the driver got out of his car to see if I was okay.

Seconds later, the sound of Mommy's scream pierced the background hum of commotion. I hadn't been hurt that bad, just scraped from the impact on the pavement, and I immediately picked myself up and ran away from the direction of my house, toward Aunt Dannah's bungalow several doors down. While everyone was looking for me under the car, I had climbed up a tree in Aunt Dannah's backyard to hide away from the world. I'm not sure how I was able even to reach the first branch on my climb up—I was running on my primal instincts. As I settled on a branch and folded my arms around my knees, I could hear the car that hit me peel away. I didn't witness Mommy's confrontation with the driver, but I can imagine some fifth-column enemy agent accusations had been thrown around. There was probably no question in her mind that the driver had been following a top-priority Communist mission to destroy her son.

Aunt Dannah had seen me run past the side gate into the backyard and found me up in the tree. "Joey! Get down from there."

"No!"

"Get down, Joey! Are you hurt?

"No!"

"Did you get hit by that car?

"No!"

"Are you lying to me?"

"No!"

This exchange went on for several minutes, until the rest of the family cued in and came over to Aunt Dannah's backyard to surround me under the tree. Mommy led the procession. "Get down from that fucking tree right this instant, you little sumanabitch!"

"No!"

"Why not?"

"Because I like it up here."

Everyone laughed except Mommy. She began to climb up herself. The sight of her attempt was too much for me to bear. She wasn't considered an athletic woman by any measure, but she had strong legs and had wrapped them around the trunk of the tree to support the rest of her body, splitting her blouse in the process. I was afraid she was going to fall down on her face, so I climbed down before she could get any farther. With her arms and face covered in dirt and her blouse ripped and stained with tree bark, she grabbed me near the bottom and pulled me in close to her, giving me a smack on my face that silenced the crowd of cousins and aunts. "Don't you ever do that again!"

I didn't know if she meant don't ever get hit by a car again or don't ever hide from her in a tree again. But I didn't have much time to contemplate as she nearly squeezed the life out of me with a hug and didn't let me go until I was begging for air. Her eyes were watery.

"I think he's bleeding internally!" she started saying to the others. If I hadn't been before, I may have been now, after that hug. "Look at his face, it's all red!"

Aunt Dannah said she was going to call a doctor and told her to bring me back to the house. She grabbed my hand and we all walked slowly back out to the sidewalk, everyone but Aunt Dannah following us into our house. Mommy's sister Tilly was trying to convince Mommy that I was okay. I was trying to do the same. "I bet I feel better than the car does," I told her.

"I bet you do. That piece of trash thinks he's gonna ride through here like he's back on his fucking ranch? There are children out here for Christ's sake." To my surprise, Mommy began smiling and joking with everybody else about the people who lived out in the boondocks and drove around these parts like they owned it. But they were mistaken—we owned it now, the summer refugees from Hoboken. These were our streets.

I helped Mommy and Aunt Tilly chop onions and celery in the kitchen after the doctor confirmed that I wasn't going to die in my sleep that night. Funny, no one ever gave a second thought to us dancing around in the pesticide cloud. In this world, the only dangers were the visible ones, or the occasional supernatural phenomenon that got Mommy riled up. Mommy was calm and in good humor as she threw a handful of chopped garlic into a steaming pan of olive oil. The hint of a great meal to come overtook the kitchen. She leaned against the wall for a moment, taking a drag from her cigarette as a new Connie Francis tune played from a small transistor radio. It was amazing how quickly she could recover from the most agitated states. It was truly a gift. She got better and better at it too, even as the sources for her agitation would grow with every new year. For now, like any mother, she was just happy that I was alive. There was still some time before she'd have taken that one back.

When you're a kid, summer vacation *is* life. Everything else is punctuation. Coming back to Hoboken at the end of August was something like the feeling you get waking up from a serene and utterly satisfying dream, when the reality you were convinced was yours suddenly dissolves around you and you're left with the reality you're not too sure you want to be yours. Even for an innocent little half-pint, reality could be a real pisser.

I dreaded starting school in the fall, still haunted by my first, exceptionally disastrous year at Public School 9. My feelings about kindergarten were summed up best by a particular experience one fateful afternoon in the beginning of the year when I was chosen to clean the chalkboard erasers in my classroom. Every day the teacher would pick a different boy to clean all the erasers in the boys' room sink. It was perceived by the kindergarten male population to be an honorable privilege and a big treat besides to be able to do that. I was overjoyed that I'd finally been picked after having been overlooked for weeks. With an eager grin, I walked into the boys' room cradling all the erasers in my arms and dropped them into the sink just as two delinquent kids jumped out from behind the stalls and assaulted me. They were big kids, probably fourth graders. One of them pinned me down on the cold tile floor while the other unzipped his trousers and urinated all over me. He just emptied himself out like a faucet. Somehow I managed to break free, leaving the kindergarten room erasers in the sink and running home as fast as I could. I was hysterical and sobbing all the way there. But I never squealed on them. Even at that age, I knew that to do that was unforgivable.

Kindergarten hadn't left an especially positive impression on me, and the first grade wasn't looking to be any more alluring. It was becoming clear that I had a problem with reading. I would be diagnosed as being severely dyslexic years later in high school, and in the meantime, I would become used to the fact that my place was at the bottom of the class. School was a struggle from day one. Why couldn't I just stay home with Mommy and watch television? I was so damn good at that.

Home had been an old dive tenement building at 202 Monroe Street for a little over a year now. First in apartment 3A, then in 2B. Mommy wasn't happy with the paint job in the original place. It was peeling, and she had never liked the dull off-white tone and she hated to move the furniture around just to paint. She felt it was easier to paint an empty apartment and then move the furniture down a flight of steps. If you've attempted to find the logic to this and failed, don't be too hard on yourself. In fact, number 2B was a little bigger than number 3A, and there was another reason for the move, as the family was about to get a little bigger with the approach of summer 1958.

For whatever reason, Mommy's pregnancy had been kept secret from me. She had always felt that what I didn't know wouldn't hurt me. I was a very clingy Momma's boy. I still slept in between my mother and father every night in their bed, and perhaps she feared I wouldn't be happy with a new challenge for her affection. I had no concept of what pregnancy was and had completely overlooked Mommy's growing belly over the last nine months, until the night I woke up wanting a glass of milk and turned to wake Mommy up, only to find Aunt Rose Lia, one of my father's sisters, lying there beside me. I was convinced Mommy had morphed into Aunt Rosie and I was mortified. I had always been afraid of Aunt Rosie, and all her attempts at calming me down were fruitless. "Yes, I know I'm not your Mommy, Joey. Your Mommy's not here. She went to the hospital. She's having a little baby."

Yeah, great, whatever you say, lady. Just give me my Mommy back, and while we're at it, what the heck did you do with Daddy? Aunt Rosie decided the best thing to do was to take me to the hospital, even though Mommy's wishes were that I stay home. I don't blame her, I could be really nasty when I wasn't happy. I had learned that skill young. When I got to the hospital, Mommy was holding my new baby sister, Maryann. I was thrilled to have this cute little thing to play with. It was one of the happiest moments in my life when early the following morning we returned triumphantly to Monroe Street with Maryann. Mommy and Daddy were clearly invigorated. I even saw them kiss on the mouth once or twice that first week. How weird, I thought. At the time, I didn't equate childbirth with any loving or sexual act, so it had never occurred to me that they were anything more than platonic bedfellows.

Over the next several weeks, all the relatives came by to celebrate and meet the newest cast member in the Pantoliano family. The star of the show was unquestionably the newborn, but my hunger for attention was more than satisfied with the increase in traffic in and out of our apartment. The way I saw it, I had a new playful companion at home now, *and* countless more opportunities to charm the aunts and uncles and neighborhood adults. The shared spotlight was a small price to pay.

Despite the fact that I had to be dragged kicking and screaming to Public School 9 every day that following fall, things generally seemed to be running smoothly in the Pantoliano household, thanks in large part to the novelty of my sister's arrival. It was not until the afternoon I came home from school at the start of the four-day Thanksgiving weekend, to an apartment that had neither heat nor electricity flowing through it, that the halcyon days officially ended for me. Four school-free days at home minus a working television set equaled serious boredom. Add to that the approaching winter and the four layers of clothes you're wearing under your coat just to keep warm inside the house, and your total sum becomes absolutely miserable. Apparently, things had been so hunky-dory lately that my parents must not have wanted to spoil the party by paying heed to the bills. Even our telephone service had been disconnected for nonpayment. My mother resorted to conning the phone company into restoring our service time and again by giving them fake "new" names that she pulled from the obituaries. They grew wise to her after they noticed the same pattern in apartment 2B as they had seen in 3A, where three or four "new" customers had neglected to pay their bills and where service had eventually been shut down "until further notice." They did the same thing at 2B after the second dead name had ignored the phone company's bill collectors.

After two weeks of crashing with Uncle Popeye and Aunt Minnie and the kids, the electric and gas utility made a deal with us to get around the fact that they could extend us not one cent of credit. They would install two meters in our apartment that had slots for quarters. Any time you wanted to use any appliance that required electric power, or if you wanted to heat up the house or shower with warm water or cook on the gas stove, you would just insert two quarters in the appropriate meter and get around four hours of usage time. For the next two years at Monroe Street, life revolved around the frantic search for quarters. God help us if we didn't have enough lying around to run the heater all night. You bet we still kept our coats within arm's reach of our beds.

I think of my folks as farmers living off their slice of land the only way they knew how, using the resources available to them. Like farmers, their livelihood was subject to the whims of a wholly uncontrollable force. Had they been growing red beans in Minnesota, the weather would have worked closely with the soil we tilled to dictate how much Hoboken-packed Maxwell House coffee they could have kept in the kitchen. In Hoboken, the fickle Lady Luck worked closely with the mathematical principles of probability, permutations and combinations (or, with the bets they placed) to determine how many Minnesota beans we could have on the table. Leaving a weekly Standard Brands paycheck unadulterated by a stampede of numbered thoroughbreds was unheard of in my household. The idea was as ridiculous as Mommy placing the fourteen dollars in cash she earned a week from her sewing "homework" into a bank for safekeeping and not on top of a pile in the center of a fold-up card table at St. Anne's Church. She spent a lot of time there. Until I was fifteen, I thought "writing out a check" was what Daddy did when he placed a check mark next to his favorite horses listed in the sports page.

When the fog of good cheer had cleared and left us shivering in bed, Mommy began to focus her energies on blaming Daddy for our misfortunes. She could be as rough as a prizefighter, as ruthless as a headsman and as precise as a surgeon, knowing exactly where to strike.

"Joey, run down to Fannie's and get me a pack of Chesterfields." We had just finished dinner in the kitchen, and Mommy was talking to me from the other end of the table as she crushed out her cigarette while glaring at the back of Daddy's head. Monk was busy washing dishes in the sink. Upon hearing Mommy, he looked up from the dishes and turned to her. "There were two new packs on the—" He eyed the table warily as he realized it was now empty of cigarettes boxes.

Mommy grabbed the last smoke, lit it and slowly crushed the empty pack. I waited for the money as she went through her purse, flipping past several dollar bills and cigarettes before she snapped it shut. "I'm out," she said. "Get money from your father."

I went up to Daddy as he dried his hands and slowly dug into his pockets. He pulled out a small handful of change and began counting pennies and nickels. Mommy hadn't stopped staring at him.

Daddy was counting the change in his hand. "Thirty-eight, forty-five . . . Hmm. Check my coat over there."

I went to the chair, checked the pockets and found nothing. Mommy exhaled a stream of smoke in Daddy's direction. "Where's the money I gave you this morning?"

"What money, Mary?"

"Don't play dumb with me! You know what money. Where is it?"

"You didn't give me any money this morning."

"Goddamn you! What do you wanna feed the kids this week? Huh? The hell with 'em. Joey, you hungry? Too bad. Where'd it go, Monk? Which horse?"

Daddy looked helpless and vulnerable, standing with his back against the sink as he shook his head to Mary's accusations.

"I give you five bucks and you take it to the fucking track!"

"Two dollars," Monk uttered.

"You lying rat bastard. We needed that money to feed the kids, and you pissed it away! We got a baby to feed, Monk!"

Maryann fidgeted in her stroller next to Mommy's chair, aroused from her nap by the yelling. Her wool white cap had fallen off her head, and Mommy was replacing it as Daddy yelled back across the kitchen. "Two dollars! I bought those cigarettes. They were right there on the table!"

"Fuck us, Monk! Is that it? Well, fuck you, your mother's twat!"

"Don't you talk about my mother like that, goddamnit!" Daddy said as he pointed his index finger toward Mommy.

Mommy stopped in her tracks, and then retreated. "I'm sorry,

Monk, I'm sorry." There was a brief second of hopeful silence. "Your sister's twat."

My father's fist hit the dish rack, sending suds splashing against the wall. Baby Maryann started to cry.

"Go ahead!" Mommy screamed. "Break the fucking dishes. Break 'em all! See if I care."

Tears were welling up in Daddy's eyes. He'd reached his breaking point with Mommy's taunting. "How many times do I gotta tell you? Don't talk about my family like that!"

Mommy didn't wait for Monk to finish before she broke into an off-key rendition of the Connie Francis hit being played on the radio nonstop since the summer. "Who's sorry now? Who's sorry now? Whose heart is aching from breaking each vow?"

"What do I gotta do?" Monk continued. "I didn't touch that money. I got no clue what you're talking about, Mary. No clue! What do I gotta do?"

". . . Just like I cried over you."

She accused him constantly of fouling up their financial situation without taking any of the blame for herself. She believed it was a man's job, regardless of her own behavior, to make sure both vital and trivial expenses were taken care of. If Monk could neither support her nightly ante nor keep the Chesterfields stocked and the electric company collection department at bay, what good was he?

It wasn't only finances and inappropriate insults that had my parents up in arms. There were accusations of all sorts being thrown around by Mommy. The birth of their daughter had been the last piece of good news she'd let Daddy revel in at home.

He happened to be an excellent bowler, good enough to have gone pro if he'd been a man of ambitions. He belonged to several teams and leagues, and he spent countless evenings at the bowling alleys. He was actually too good for the Standard Brands factory team and was required to keep his average down just so he wouldn't overly intimidate his fellow teammates. I never quite got the hang of Daddy's favorite sport. He had gotten me my own bowling ball for Christmas that year, but the best I'd done with it was toss it at the Christmas tree, knocking the fake evergreen down, breaking a bulb and starting a small fire in the living room.

Mommy never gave him any credit for his bowling talent, even when it occasionally brought some extra cash into the house. He bowled a perfect game once—300, earning him the tournament title, twenty-five bucks, a free suit at Guisemeyer's, the local department store, and a picture in the paper to boot. He stumbled home drunk with a huge trophy in hand to find my mother and me in the kitchen playing cards. I'd just dealt her a hand that she must not have been very happy with, because on seeing Daddy she threw her hand on the table, causing the cards to slide off and flutter to the ground. Had her hand been a good one, she'd have set them down lightly.

"You cocksucker. You're fucking that twat again."

In his drunken stupor, Daddy's childish grin grew wider. "You're wrong, Mary. I was bowlin'. In fact, I got the proof right here," he said as he cocked his head to the side and pointed to the trophy in his hand.

"Stick it up your ass," she yelled as she jumped out of her chair and went right for the trophy, easily wresting it from Daddy's grip and, in one brisk movement, slamming it hard over his left shoulder. Pieces of the trophy flew off of Daddy as he collapsed to the ground. He lay there on his side holding his upper torso and screaming bloody Mary as she stormed out of the room. I stood up but was speechless as I stared at Daddy crying from the pain.

"Joey," he said in between sobs, "call your Uncle Popeye and tell him to come here with his car."

I did as he said. Ten minutes later, Uncle Popeye helped Daddy to the car and drove him to the hospital. We found out later that Mommy had actually broken his collarbone.

When Popeye and Daddy left, Mommy came out from the bedroom, where she'd locked herself in, sat back down at the kitchen table and lit up a cigarette. I looked at her and asked, "Why did you do that to Daddy?"

"Because he deserved it."

With every cigarette that Mommy lit, there was half a pack of cigarette butts still smoldering in her ashtray, each one a reminder that the cross Daddy bore at home was not for his sins alone. Each tirade was a distorted avowal that mixed the baggage from her past and the sore points of the present with her insecurities for the future. The ashtray on that kitchen table was a landfill for all that she considered regrettable.

— 3 —

701 Adams Street

King of the Feast

Daddy was still recovering from his broken collarbone when the final guest arrived on the Baby Maryann shower tour. His name was Florio Isabella, a third cousin of Mommy's with connections on both sides of her family, not to mention connections with an entirely different kind of family, but I wasn't aware of the latter at the time. All I knew was that as soon as he dropped by to visit late in August, it was Christmastime in our house. There were toys for me, perfumes for Mommy, cigars for Daddy, and all of it looked expensive.

The last time he'd visited had been on the Baby Joey tour, so it was a tremendous thrill when he had arrived unannounced at our house. Cousin Florie was back in New York after having been locked up for the last six years for some work he had allegedly done for the Genovese crime family in lower Manhattan. He started to visit us on Monroe Street a couple of times a week, usually during the day when Daddy was at the factory. Daddy would occasionally come home during a break from work with some coffee cake in one arm and his other arm strapped to his chest. Together with Mommy and Florie, they'd sit around the kitchen table and chatter about adult stuff and laugh and smoke cigarettes.

Florie was a playful and energetic guy. He would always pick me up and throw me in the air. He seemed ten feet tall as he'd sit me on top of the refrigerator. I felt like I was sitting on top of the world, and when he'd say, "Jump, Joey! Jump!" I'd stand up on top of the fridge and fly straight for his arms. He caught me every time.

From the moment he came back into our lives, it was as if he'd always been there. In a way, he always had. Mommy referred to her Cousin Florie often in conversation, making him out to be something of a superhero, straight out of a comic book, so he became a legend in my eyes. Mommy had talked about him as if he truly existed, but I never had any proof. Now the proof was here and I was hooked. He was the most exciting relative to ever walk through our door. His attention was a valuable commodity, and when I managed to get it, I felt like the luckiest kid in town.

Most people referred to him either as Florie or, as Mommy typically addressed him, simply Flo. Florie was a tall and dashing man with a full head of wavy hair that was white in front and faded toward black in back. He was three years shy of fifty just like Daddy and wore fancy monogrammed shirts with his initials on the cuffs and five-hundred-dollar suits, very unlike Daddy. He was movie-star handsome, with a perfect chiseled chin and nose, and he had blue eyes, just like me (my perfect nose came later in life).

My parents always needed that certain something to kick them out of their shared misery and allow them to actually enjoy each other's company for a change. Next to Maryann's birth, it was Florie's frequent visits that consistently lifted both their spirits. Mommy was always cooking something up for him when he was there, and Daddy was always serving him something to drink. When they'd all sit and talk, Mommy and Daddy would talk to each other as if they actually liked each other. That's how I know that deep down inside, they did in fact like each other. They just needed a little more help than most couples do to see that. Unfortunately, the outside world usually provided more insult than help to their cause. Regardless, Florie's "I'm here for good" ended up being too good to be true. Within six months of showing up in our lives, he managed to get himself into a wee bit of trouble on the Hoboken ferry.

The Hoboken ferry was one of the last steam ferryboats on the Hudson River, a survivor of the new era of tunnels and bridges. While passenger traffic had dwindled to a sprinkling by the late 1950s with all the alternative methods for river crossing available, the double-decked and double-ended ferryboat was shuttling large amounts of freight between downtown Manhattan and Hoboken. All the better for Florie, since it was the freight he was interested in.

After some weeks of research and due diligence, Florie discovered the schedule for the Seagram's trucks carrying loads of beer and liquor on the ferry, and decided it would be easy to overtake these trucks during their brief seven-minute passage across the river. His plan was simple: He would take control of the driver and drive the loaded truck onto land when the ferry docked. The trucks would park on the ferry on the way into Manhattan, and Florie would just have to tap on the window and discreetly show his gun. Since so many drivers were used to getting robbed, he figured they would just slide over and say something like, "All right, just don't shoot" and let him drive off with the truck as long as he spared them their lives.

He recruited five guys for the job: one guy to help him take over the first truck, two guys to take over a second truck, and two guys to stand lookout. Once the driver succumbed, each lookout guy would jump in one and each truck would drive off with four passengers, including the hostage driver, and enough alcohol to make the entire Hudson waterfront giddy.

It was a Friday morning when Florie boarded the ferry on the Hoboken side with his five partners and found to his dismay that more passenger cars than usual were on board. He briefly wondered if that would be a problem, but decided that it shouldn't make any difference at all. As soon as the ferry departed, Florie and his partner walked over to the first truck and Florie tapped on the window. The driver, as if he'd been expecting Florie, automatically and quite nonchalantly slid over to the passenger side, just as planned. When the man began to speak, Florie half expected him to say, "What happened to you? You're late!" But instead, he calmly informed Florie that the clutch on his truck "sticks and it's a real pain in the ass." He wanted no trouble, but said, "Listen, pal, let me drive this thing for you."

Florie was apprehensive and downright humored by the offer. "Get the hell out of here," he told the guy.

But the driver insisted. "Nah, look, I swear to Christ I'm

not bullshittin' you. Trust me, it'll jump on you. You're gonna want me to drive this truck."

Florie stood firm with this plan. Turning to his partner as he went to start the truck, he said with a smirk, "This guy's full of shit," and before he could dot his *i* and cross his *t*, the truck lurched forward two feet and hit the car in front of it, which lurched forward itself and hit the next car in line, until the last car at the front of the boat dove into the fence and nearly tipped over the side into the river.

The three of them instinctively jumped out of the truck. With his nerves on sudden overdrive, Florie turned to his partner, telling him to stay put, and dashed over to the captain, who was standing at the wheel eyeing the final car intently. Florie realized this operation had gotten a tad bigger than he'd originally planned and serious improvisation was now required. The captain barely noticed Florie initially, but took heed when Florie, with gun cocked and aimed, uttered the classic line, "Captain, we've got a mutiny." It was the first thing that had come to mind.

The captain flinched upon hearing his armed passenger's voice, and then, with a quizzical expression, he asked him to repeat what he had said. After he realized that he'd heard him correctly, the captain asked him where he wanted him to go.

"Just keep going like nothing's the matter," Florie replied.

When the ferry arrived at its dock in lower Manhattan, Florie and his guys, along with the two hostage drivers, rode the trucks off the ferry and over to Mott Street. They hid the trucks in an alley and put the drivers in a pigeon coop on the roof of a tenement building. They kept them there for a few hours, until things cooled down.

In the meantime, they offered the drivers sandwiches to eat and took their names and addresses off of their driver's licenses. Florie wanted to know where to find them, just in case either of them decided to do some squealing at any point in the near future.

As Florie and his guys were getting ready to leave, the driver who'd warned him about the truck leaned over to Florie and nervously whispered, "Listen, now that you got my name and address, well, maybe, you know, my wife just had a baby, and maybe you can throw me a few dollars, I dunno. You guys are gonna get off damn good on this score."

Florie looked at the guy with his trademark smirk and winked. When he related the story to me years later (Florie only began to talk about his life as it was nearing its end), he said he mailed the guy fifty bucks in an envelope from his slice.

A couple of months went by and one of Florie's ferry heist recruits got pinched on another job and negotiated a plea bargain with the feds. They wanted to know what else he'd been up to recently, and before long he ratted out the ferry-jacking crew. He became a cooperator and star witness, and Florie and the four others faced an indictment on 375 counts of interstate hijacking and kidnapping. On the day Florie's truck driver testified, the guy actually perjured himself to protect Florie.

"Are those men in the courtroom today?" he was asked.

The driver pointed to Florie's four other associates and to each in turn said, "Yes, that gentleman was there." He got to

Florie last, looked him over, and casually dismissed him: "Nah, that guy wasn't there."

Despite the driver's account, though, there was still enough evidence against Florie to convict. He was sentenced to fifteen years in federal prison.

I was heartbroken when Mommy broke the news. It wasn't difficult to sense the desperation in the air that day. Mommy had been sobbing all afternoon and Daddy was as sullen as I'd ever seen him. "Your cousin Florie's going off to college," Mommy explained to me. I believed her. College was for old people, right?

Ironically, we took the same ferry across the river to the West Street Federal Holding Facility, after Florie had been convicted and sentenced. From there, he was off to Atlanta Federal Penitentiary to serve his fifteen years. I thought it was exciting to talk to him on a telephone while looking at him through the thick bulletproof glass. I don't think Florie shared in my excitement, though. He reached out his hand to touch the glass and I did the same, then he looked into my eyes as if to say, *Hang in there, kid. I'll be back.*

There was a saying in my house that went something like this: "Florie is like the tide. Florie comes, and Florie goes, but he's always there." Well, sometimes I wish it had been high tide a little more often during my formative grade school years. I sure could have used his positive influence. In the 1950s, my neighborhood was a very scary place. It wasn't highbrow like it is now, with the million-dollar residential apartments built from the ghostly frames of old factories. When I was growing up, it was mean streets all the way; kids were always shaking me down on the way to school. And not just the bigger boys; one of my most feared bullies was a sixth-grade girl who stuck me up every day for my lunch money. There was always someone or something ready to rough me up.

I wasn't a natural born tough guy. That had to be cultivated. I was little for my age and not big enough yet to defend myself. So to compensate, I developed a strong sense of survival. I did whatever it took to save my ass, be it charm them, humor them or make them laugh at my own expense. I would do anything to win over the neighborhood toughs, as well as every adult I would encounter. I played the buffoon, the clown and the gopher, and I entertained endlessly. In the end they either liked me or left me, which was fine by me.

This inherent talent and consistent practice of talking my way out of jams went a long way toward preparing me to become an actor. My main objective was to avoid a beef at all costs. Of course, if the source of the beef persistently pressed the right buttons, there was a boiling point at which I would be forced to stand up for myself win or lose. I wound up in a couple dozen fights in those early years, and every once in a while I wound up getting my ass kicked.

The odds were not usually in my favor. I was a skinny kid until I was about ten. I wouldn't finish my food, and Mommy tried everything she could to put some skin on my bones. She went as far as to get my uncle Mario to scare me into eating. He would lean over with a mean look on his face and yell, "You finish all that food right now before I sit on you!" He was a big man. He would sit there at the table with a menacing look on his face until I did just that. With Mario's help, I soon learned to love food—more and more, in fact, with every pound I gained. I ate my way right to the hefty department in less than two years.

All in all, I was pretty intimidated at that age. Being beat up on a regular basis can make you fear and suspect almost anything. I was used to being intimidated on my way to and from school and around the neighborhood. As a consequence, I became increasingly dependent on Mommy. She was always good for soothing my logical and all-too-real fears with tales of her wonderfully bizarre ones.

When I was nine, she tried to toughen me up by enlisting me in the Cub Scouts just in time for the Jamboree Camporee. It was a big countywide event including all of the Boy Scouts from Hoboken, Jersey City and probably the whole of Hudson County. Everyone was to gather together in a big football field at Stephens Institute of Technology, which is still renowned as one of the great technical institutes in the country. The jamboree began on a Friday night and ran for an entire weekend of campfires and cookouts and good old-fashioned Cub Scout fun. We would pitch tents in the large football field, which happened to be an entire three blocks from my house.

I begged Mommy to go. It was especially important to me because I would be out on my own for practically the first time. I had always wanted to sleep in a tent, and besides, I was looking forward to a weekend without Mommy breathing down my neck. Mommy agreed to let me go and came up with the seven-dollar fee, and even went so far as getting me the uniform with the short pants and that really fancy yellow Cub Scout scarf with the little bear-cub imprint.

There were a lot of kids there on the football field, and a lot of them I knew. We pitched the army tents on Friday afternoon and I was feeling incredibly independent and grown-up. The fun lasted all of about four hours, until the lights on the field went out and it was time for bed.

I had never slept all night without my parents beside me. By midnight, I was faking a stomachache and whimpering about wanting my Mommy. By 1 A.M., my whimpering had become a sharp, high-pitched yelp. "Mommy! I want my Mommy!" I screamed, wheezing and blubbering nonstop.

The other kids in the tent started waking up.

"Jesus Christ! Who's that?"

"Who else? It's fuckin' Pantoliano."

Three blocks was a long stretch for the umbilical cord.

They finally called Mommy, and she had to come and get me at three in the morning. She crossed the field in her slippers and a large flapping housedress, with a cigarette to light her path. "Joey! Joey! Where the fuck are you?" she called, following my cries to my tent. She crawled in, found my flashlight, clicked it on and held me. "All right, all right, it's all right, hush now," she said softly as she cradled me. "Mommy's here. Your Mommy's here. It's okay, baby. Let's go home now. Daddy's already making you a nice big sangwich."

"Thank Christ!" yelled one of the other kids in the tent beside me.

Mommy snapped her head in his direction. "I heard that,

you little sumanabitch, and I know where you live. You want me to bury you in that sleeping bag?" He didn't say another word. Neither did anyone else for that matter.

Soon I was snug and warm in my own bed, back with Mommy and Daddy. So much for independence.

After that hopeless display, I had to prove to the kids in the neighborhood that I was just fooling around that night, that I had a million reasons for wanting to go back home that had nothing to do with Mommy and Daddy. Even though being with my Mommy and Daddy had absolutely everything to do with it. But the other kids didn't need to know that.

I took one such opportunity when I was riding my bicycle with some friends later that week and had fallen off unhurt. As I was lying on the corner of Sixth and Monroe, I smiled at them and told them, "Watch this." I began to scream loudly, as loudly as I had wailed for Mommy the weekend before. "Ahh! My arm . . . I broke my arm!" I was doing my best fake cry and apparently had done a pretty good job, because a guy came up to me on the street and looked gravely concerned as he offered his help. I was weeping and wailing breathlessly. "I fell off my bicycle! I broke my arm! Ow!"

He went to hold my arm and asked me, "Is this where it hurts?"

"Yeah, yeah. That's it. Oh my god, it hurts, it hurts." I had the guy convinced. I began to believe it myself.

"Where do you live?" he asked.

I didn't want to tell him my real address so I stumbled. "I live . . . I live . . . I live on Four . . . Fourth . . . Fourth, and ah . . . Jefferson."

I could hear my pals chuckle as he walked me over to a random building that I'd picked out, and then I told him I could get home from there. And I walked through the front door of the building and hid there until he walked away.

As impressed as my friends were with my performance, I was even more so. I realized that playing the role of the helpless victim was a surefire way of satisfying to near-perfection my endless list of needs and wants. On the coattails of my fake bicycle injury success, I began to go through a phase that took my bullshit artist instinct to new heights. I aimed my skill toward alleviating that stubbornly incessant source of angst in my life: PS 9. It had become impossible for me to stay on track with the curriculum. My fourth-grade teacher had taken away my reading books for the entire year because I couldn't keep up. "Dick and Jane" were certainly no friends of mine. I was ashamed that I couldn't read, and I hated the idea of going to school and being ridiculed by all the kids that could. To avoid it, I decided it was time I got sickly.

"Mommy! My stomach hurts!" I screamed from under my sheets before breakfast. "It hurts real bad! You gotta call the doctor. I think I'm dying. I'm dying, I tell you!"

"Don't you start with me. You ain't sick. I can tell by lookin' at you. Now, get the fuck up!"

"But, Mommy, my stomach! It's eatin' the rest of me up, I swear to Christ!" I was aiming for the illogical, because I knew with Mommy that's where I'd strike gold.

"Where does it hurt? There?" She pressed hard. "Does that hurt?"

"Owey, owey, it hurts bad." I knew I had her.

"Jesus Christ. Monk! He ain't kiddin'!" she called out to Daddy. "Joey's sick. We gotta take him to the hospital."

There was nothing like using Mommy's Old World paranoia to my benefit.

"Oh, my poor baby," she cooed as she placed the back of her hand on my forehead to check if I had a temperature.

I never did. But my charade always worked like a charm. When we arrived at the hospital, they put me in a wheelchair and wheeled me into the emergency room. Everybody's eyes were on me. Mommy was walking along beside me, yelling at the interns and patients to get out of the way. An elderly man in a hospital gown, wheeling an IV stand hooked up to his arm and using it to support himself, had the misfortune of blocking our path. "Hey!" Mommy called to him. "Mr. Death! Can you wheeze your way to the morgue any fucking quicker? I got a sick kid here! Get the fuck out of the way!" Mommy said with a cigarette dangling out of the side of her mouth as she patted me on the head gently. "Don't worry, baby, we're almost there."

Moments later, they wheeled me into my own private room without even doing any paperwork. "How's your tummy, sweetie?"

"It's eating me alive!" I was thrilled. I had my very own room. Something I never had at home. No Castro Convertible couch for me. Only crisp white clean sheets, and they changed them every day! Boy, was I in heaven. Pretty nurses were spoiling me rotten. I didn't have to go to school. Ice cream three times a day. On top of everything else, I got sympathy from the aunts and uncles. Aunt Dannah snuck me in homemade cookies, just the medicine my stomach required.

Then came the big bonus news. I had to stay a few more days. I became the mascot of the hospital ward, the only kid in a ward full of adults. I started making rounds with the nurses. They called me "The Sunshine Boy" because they said I brightened up their day. With the mad onslaught of attention, as popular as I was, Mommy still stayed beside me at the hospital all night.

The doctors diagnosed my condition as a mysterious chronic digestive ailment called "nervous spasms." Bingo! Now it had a name. The scheme continued on and off for that whole school year. I felt like I was living every kid's fantasy. Periodically, there'd be something I was trying to avoid at school, be it a test, a mean teacher or a pesky bully. Whatever it was, the "nervous spasms" would conveniently kick in when the problem arose. I was the best little bullshit artist in town.

About the sixth or seventh time I rolled out the spasms, the unthinkable happened. "Put him in with the rest of the sick kids," Mommy said. "Let him see what it's like to really be sick." I guess she had gotten wise to me and had them place me in the children's ward. No more privacy, no more big-shot "Sunshine Boy," absolutely none of the perks at all except for the ice cream. But how was I supposed to enjoy ice cream surrounded by a room full of sick kids, some of whom couldn't even hold their own spoons? The jig was up. Mommy had me right where she wanted me. I guess I had underestimated the wit of a fellow con artist.

They put me in a room with about twelve other kids. A boy next to me was severely burned. Having been in a fire accident, he was all wrapped up, and I was mortified by the thought of the terrible things that must have befallen the poor kid. I was embarrassed at myself for pretending next to someone who had no choice in the matter. He was authentically and maybe irreversibly messed up.

Mommy had taught me a lesson I'll never forget: If you got to avoid school, go for the fake fever trick, remember to keep that warm wet rag handy for those surprise motherly checkups and stay home. If anything, do it out of respect for that kid who wishes he were sitting in a classroom.

The minute I got to the ward, I told Mommy and the doctor that I was ready to go home, but the doctor insisted I stay overnight for observation. So I gave him something to observe right then and there as I jumped up and down and made an ass out of myself. I was desperate. "Look at me!" I said, bouncing in the air with my arms flailing. "I ain't sick at all. I feel better. Let me outta here!" Mommy smiled at her small victory. She could have been vindictive and forced me to stay as punishment, but she didn't. I like to think she was actually impressed that I had pulled it off for so long.

Hence, I was miraculously healed from that point on. I headed back to school and higher learning.

We moved to 701 Adams Street after being evicted for lack of payment at Monroe. Mommy and Daddy were heavy into the loan sharks at the time and were losing everything they earned. Mommy was practically giving all her grocery money away every night to the nearby church. And she thought she wasn't religious. She was playing sixteen cards at a shot by then. Every time she hollered "Bingo," she'd inevitably blow her meager winnings the next day on the numbers.

Mommy picked her numbers out of a dream book. The dream book assigned a number to images in dreams. She demanded that everyone in our house tell her their dreams at the breakfast table. So in the mornings we would wake up and Mommy would ask eagerly, "Okay, who had a dream? What did you dream?"

If Daddy had dreamt he had a bloody nose, Mommy would declare, "Blood! That's good!"

She'd get the dream book out and look up the number. Blood might be 147. Then she'd give her bookie a call. "Jerry! It's your favorite, Mary. I wanna play one-forty-seven for the week. Fifty-fifty combo."

Meanwhile, while Mommy was busy gathering winning numbers, Maryann and I were eating a breakfast consisting of coffee cake and milk. We would be revved up on sugar and then go bursting off to school on a high. It was something like the reverse Atkins Diet. Pack up on carbs, forget the protein and ditch the fruits and vegetables. Around ten-thirty, we'd crash and burn.

Halloween was always a big deal for me because I got to dress up and act like a complete idiot and nobody flinched. One Halloween my friends and I came up with a plan. Starting at the end of September, on our way to school, we would walk by the chicken store on Fifth Street between Adams and Jefferson. It was the only store I knew that sold live chickens. In the summer you could smell the young chickens for a three-block radius. They had cartons of twenty-four eggs each stacked outside. On our way to school, we'd stop by the store and play chicken with the owner, excuse the pun. When he wasn't looking, we would clip the eggs. We averaged about four a day for about four weeks.

We stored them at my friend Angelo's grandfather's backyard. Angelo's grandfather had lost his sense of smell and could barely leave the house, so it was the perfect storage facility. The eggs would sit there and rot in the sun for up to thirty days. Finally, on Halloween day, we'd use them for our annual Halloween egg fights with the other neighborhood kids, and the occasional innocent house or bystander.

Egg fights eventually evolved into cornstarch and water balloon fights. We'd stuff our stockings with cornstarch to hit each other with. The cornstarch would seep out of the sock and leave a mark on you, like an urban poor version of paint guns nowadays. If you got wet from an exploding water balloon or got a white cornstarch mark on you, it meant you went into prison on the sidelines, until somebody from your team replaced you. As we got even older, we traded the water balloons for bleach balloons. Now, if you got hit with one of them, you ruined your clothing. You weren't allowed to wear white either. And we didn't stop at bleach. The next evolution in our Halloween fights was in the form of a newly invented hair-removal spray called Nair. We'd run after each other and try to spray the hair-remover on each other's head. The next day at school, you'd see kids walking around with clumps of hair missing. I've cursed that game ever since; of course, without it, I'd never have needed to develop my own line of Merkley headgear hats to compensate.

As much fun as the Halloween street games became, once upon a time in 1958 it was still all about the candy. The past summer I had gone to see the circus at Palisades Amusement Park and had witnessed the antics of the great Emmett Kelly, Jr., the famous hobo tramp. I was fascinated by him. For months after I was anticipating Halloween because I was gonna dress up as Emmett Kelly. Mommy was excited about helping me with my costume. At the time, she wasn't concerned with any racial harassment overtones of the blackface she painted on me. I just told her I wanted to look exactly like Emmett Kelly and she complied. She got a broomstick and made a bandanna out of a handkerchief purely for show, and I tied the bandanna around the end of the broomstick to make a hobo bag. The four corners were stuffed with toilet paper and old rags.

But between me and a bag full of candy stood a very imposing hurdle: Jamesie, a tough little black kid in my neighborhood who was a known Halloween candy robber baron. He'd proven his reputation to me the previous Halloween, having shaken down my Halloween crew of trick-or-treaters and taken all of our candy bags. This year I decided we'd fight back. I put together a "posse" of all of my young cousins and neighbors. I sat them down and gave them a brief but inspiring pep talk. I had been inspired by watching John Wayne motivate his guys at Iwo Jima in a film I'd seen that week on *Million Dollar Movie*.

"Now look," I started, "if we stick together, Jamesie can't

take our candy, because he can't take all of us if we all fight back, right? There's six of us and only one of him. United we stand, divided we fall!"

With that battle cry, we set out on that Halloween night to score as much candy as we could carry. First we hit the apartment buildings up and down Park Avenue, and then we went over to Bloomfield and Adams Streets. You could go anywhere in those days without your parents having to protect you, save for the Jamesie factor and the other bullies.

Sure enough, Jamesie showed up just as we hit Fifth Street and Park. He jumped out in front of my crew from behind a tree, pointed his index fingers with thumbs up in gun formation and shouted, "This is a stickup! Give me your candy!" He was very theatrical, I had to hand it to him. I felt like he and I could have been one and the same, like De Niro and Pacino in *Heat*. However, from my perspective, Jamesie had fallen onto the wrong side of the fence.

I was ready to take him, and I got into fighting position. I put my fists in the air and then looked behind me to make sure everyone was poised and ready to rumble. They were already halfway down the block and running fast. I was left there all alone to face my arch Halloween nemesis.

"Hand it over! I said this is a stickup!" he shouted again. Jamesie was probably nine years old at the time, but he was bigger than me, and I was scared shitless.

"Fuck you. You ain't getting my candy, no way. Leave me alone," I said.

Jamesie paused, unsure of what to make of this skinny little blackfaced Italian runt with an attitude. He was used to being feared, and his victims usually complied immediately with his demands for candy. "What you say, motherfucker? I'll bust your motherfuckin' head, man."

At that point I was petrified. I was gonna have to do something fast, or risk losing my candy and maybe even an eye. In one hand I had my huge bag of candy that I had spent hours collecting. In the other hand I had my broomstick-turned-hobo-stick. I'll never forget what happened next. As Jamesie approached, I swung the hobo stick hard and cracked Jamesie across the left side of his head with it. As if in a Peckinpah movie, I saw my hobo bag fly off the broomstick in slow motion and land on a tree branch. Jamesie grabbed his head in pain as he went down hard on the sidewalk. I was already running when I heard his head hit the street.

I was a tough guy for all of thirty seconds, and now I freaked out at what the consequences would be. My "Hero Joey" persona quickly dissolved into a miniature hobo blur, running as fast as possible to the nearest shelter. I had my stick in one hand and my shopping bag of candy in the other. As I ran down Fifth Street, past Clinton, past Grand, past Adams, right into my cousin Kelly's building, the candy dropped piece by piece out of the bag, leaving a trail the whole way. When I got to the fourth floor, I had about three pieces of candy left in my brown paper candy bag. Louise, Cousin Kelly's wife, answered the door. She was like a second mother to me. I was crying and panicked. I would have run home had it been closer, but it was a block farther away.

"Jesus Christ, whattsamatta with you?" asked Cousin Louise as she swung the door closed behind me. I'm sure I was a sight to see, with my Emmett Kelly blackface paint running from the sweat and tears pouring off my face and down my neck. "Oh my god!" she said. "Sit down. You look like you seen a ghost! What the hell are you supposed to be for Halloween anyway?"

I was too frazzled to answer. Frankly, by that point I'd forgotten.

That Halloween was one of the first times I played a tough guy role, even if only for a fleeting, adrenaline-charged moment. It was a moment I would relive for weeks, right alongside the fear of running into Jamesie again.

Three months later, I was at Fannie's, the local candy store on Adams between Fourth Street and Fifth. It was the place we kids always hung out. Fannie was a great lady; loving, boisterous, playful and helplessly mischievous. She always wanted to feed us. In short, she was all of the wonderful Italian maternal qualities rolled into one. Her daughter, Margaret Ann, was a good friend of mine, and growing up, we always played marbles and kick-the-can together.

I was playing the pinball machine when Jamesie walked in. I could see him out of the corner of my eye. The day I had dreaded since Halloween had finally arrived, and my moment of reckoning seemed a certainty when he looked in my direction and stared. I was a dead man.

I'm not sure if it was the obligation to stand my ground, my complete and utter fear for the kid or the great game of pinball that I didn't want to abort, but I just stood there as Jamesie approached me.

He walked up to my side and watched me play for a

minute or two. I wasn't sure if he recognized me, or if maybe he had and was just trying to make me squirm in my pants before he jumped me.

My game ended and I looked up at my score, pretending I was nearsighted and squinting to see clearly. I figured it was a decent attempt to elicit some pity from him. Then he spoke. "Hey, good game, man."

Whoa. "Thanks." I nodded my head and tried to play it cool.

"You got a nickel so I can play?" he asked me.

I was safe. I guess he hadn't recognized me without my blackface.

I dug deep down into my pocket, handed my only remaining one over and stayed to watch his game. He didn't beat my score, and I thought that might set him off. It could be the end of me yet. As soon as his game was over, with his hands still resting over the flapper buttons on either side, Jamesie catapulted himself off the pinball machine backward in a cartoon-like motion. As he turned to leave, he gave me a quick nod and said, "Thanks, man. I'll see you around," and he left the candy shop and ran across the block and out of sight.

I shook my head and chuckled. I remember thinking, "I like that guy," and wanting to have someone there to turn around and say it to. But nobody saw the ultimate Halloween bully and I trade a game of pinball.

He'd always been the quintessential "bad apple" in the neighborhood, but here I was actually charmed. He was still a bad guy in my eyes, he'd probably try to steal my Halloween candy again next year, but he was likable in spite of that. I think he was on to something, that Jamesie.

I saw a little of myself in my Halloween nemesis and sympathized with the kid. I myself was a mixed bag of tough guy aspirations and charismatic intentions. Both my parents were charmers, after all. But only one of them was anything resembling a tough guy.

Driving to Cousin Patty-boy's house one Sunday with Mommy and Daddy, I was sitting in the backseat of the car listening to them yell at each other the entire way. We pulled into the DeRiso driveway and Mommy rushed out of the car and looked around the front lawn until she picked up a two-by-four. She ran toward Daddy as he got out of the car and started swinging. She made contact a few times, and each time I thought she was gonna knock him dead. She wasn't swinging lightly. I expected Daddy to fight back at any moment, but he never did. She kept screaming, "You sumanabitch," right there on the lawn with the whole DeRiso family watching, and he kept taking it. He actually laughed through it all.

I couldn't understand why he just took it like that. I loved Daddy, and like any kid, I wanted him to stand up for himself. But he never fought back against Mommy, as violent and vicious as she could get. Mommy was always the instigator. She only played the victim when it suited her purpose.

Though he didn't feel it was particularly necessary to stick up for himself, Daddy always stuck up for me. I was outside on the street playing with a kid from school one afternoon when the kid turned and threw my ball down a sewer. Margaret Ann ran and told my father, who was nearby having coffee with Fanny at the candy store. He came over, took the kid by the shoulder and said quietly, but firmly, "You, my friend, are gonna go down there and get Joey's ball." The intimidating look on Daddy's face was all it took for the kid to comply. I was used to Mommy being the one to throw an evil glance and get results, but this rare occurrence pleasantly surprised me.

The kid whimpered, "I can't lift the lid."

"Oh, don't you worry," Daddy told him sternly. "I'll help you with it." He walked over and lifted the cover, then he picked the kid up and turned him upside down and held him by the ankles with his head down in the sewer until he was able to get ahold of my ball. Daddy lifted him up and out, took my ball and sent the kid running home, pale as a ghost.

There was no doubt in my mind that Daddy would come to my aid whenever I needed it, but Mommy was the one who usually happened on the opportunity to lend a helping smack, word, tug and shove, often all at once.

As with most things about Mommy, she usually went overboard, and ended up doing things for me that I should have learned to do by myself. Even when they had nothing to do with protecting me. At Adams Street we had these little go-carts that we made from orange crates and two-by-fours with a roller skate. You'd nail the roller skate on the bottom, then lean on it and push away. Of course, I didn't know how to make my own and didn't actually have to muster the gumption to figure it out. Mommy stepped in and hired two kids down the street that were skilled at the art of go-cart making to build one for me. I had a great-looking go-cart when they were done, but I felt slighted. Half the fun of having the go-carts was being proud that you built the thing and it worked and then showing off your skill. There was really no fun to be had hearing Mommy ask the kids to do mine.

That's not to say I didn't appreciate her involvement every once in a while. In second grade I had an old teacher who would smack me around from time to time. She was ancient enough to have done the same to Mommy's brother Uncle Pete when he was my age. I was asked to read out loud to the class one day and kept stuttering through my reading as usual, and rather than helping me sound out the words, she walked up to my desk and slapped me hard on the back of my head. I was mortified. No adult had ever been physically aggressive with me like that except Mommy, but what else were mothers for if not the occasional slap. I went home crying and told my mother what had happened. She grabbed me by the arm and stormed out of the apartment, straight down to the school to confront the teacher.

When we got there, the mean old lady was at her desk grading papers. I was a little intimidated by the situation and the very likely possibility of an ugly clash, so I hung back and watched through the glass door to the classroom. Mommy got right up in the teacher's face, with her index finger raised, and speaking in a voice that was both menacing and eerily subdued, she said, "You hit my brother. You smacked him around and my mother gave you a beatin'. Now you're doing it to my kid? Nah, I don't think so if you know what's good for you. Don't you ever lay a finger on my son again." Her eyes must have said it all. I never got smacked in that teacher's classroom again. I never got called on either, for that matter.

Throughout most of grade school, my pals and I had a

community-sponsored baseball gang. We would play after school almost every day. The big thing with the ball team was to buy car coats at Guisemeyer's. They were cloth coats with leather sleeves, and they were expensive at twenty bucks, but I wanted one badly. You'd get it embroidered with your baseball team logo on the back and your name in cursive on the front. My parents eventually had heard enough about the jacket and decided it was in their interest as much as mine to buy one for me so I could shut up about it already. When Mommy walked in with the jacket on a hanger and I saw "Joey" written across the front left, I felt as if I'd just been recruited to the major leagues. I ran straight for the jacket and threw it on. I think the arms actually touched the floor. She had gotten the extra-extra-large size so I could grow into it. Apparently she was expecting me to blossom into a generously proportioned ogre before high school. I looked in the mirror and wanted to cry. It was supposed to fit snugly around my waist, but the bottom of the jacket hung below my knees. The friggin' thing was wearing me. She eventually sewed the end of the sleeves up to the elbow and said she'd let them out as I got bigger. But the fact was, I looked like a total asshole huddled inside my plus-size jacket. All the kids made fun of me when I finally wore it out, but Mommy insisted, "They'll be jealous when they've outgrown theirs and you're walking around a handsome young man with yours."

"It'll never fit me, Mommy!"

"You'll thank me later when you've grown into it, I promise you."

I opted to avoid ridicule and stuffed it away in my closet. I dreamt years later that the jacket escaped from my closet and went on a rampage across New Jersey, consuming several small children in its path before being apprehended by Newark police. My jacket was indicted on two counts of first degree murder and is currently serving two life sentences in a New Mexico federal prison. Oh, and the jacket still wouldn't fit two of me today.

I felt bad that they'd spent the twenty bucks on something I'd probably never use again, especially since we were living by candlelight every other month at 701 Adams. We'd managed to keep the phone line working with only brief interruptions as Mommy's Monroe Street scam reincarnated at Adams Street, along with the consumer identities of several recently dead Hudson County residents. I'll admit, it was fun to watch the same phone serviceman come in one month and say, "Hi, Mrs. O'Brien," and then come back two months later and say, "Hello, Mrs. Gonzalez." Of course, he was a little slow where it counted upstairs. But it worked to our advantage, and he never left without a little café con leche with a splash of Irish whiskey to perk him up.

Despite the constant need to skirt the system in the name of working electricity and functioning telephone lines, somehow we managed to always have plenty of food on the table. Having Mommy's good friend working as the checkout girl at Foodtown certainly helped. We'd go to Foodtown with a grocery list a mile long and never spend more than five dollars at a time. She'd ring it all up, but charge us ridiculously low prices for every item. Twenty-seven cents for a leg of lamb, pot roast at ten cents a pound, fifteen cents for a five-pound bag of oranges, a package of Vienna Fingers cookies for ten cents. The Marie discount was anywhere between 50 and 90 percent of regular supermarket prices, depending on her quick math to determine how close we were getting to their agreed upon five-dollar maximum.

Mommy did most of her other shopping out of the trunk of a car. Almost everything in our house, whether clothing or furniture or any of our tacky decorations, our birthday and Christmas presents, our silverware and our Christmas trees, was swag (stolen without a gun). The whole town seemed to run on swag. It was an efficient system; whatever you needed was probably parked on a corner somewhere within a ten-block radius. The system groomed you in the art of the back-door discount, and you always got a special deal on it just because you were *you*. Everybody seemed to make out well except for the particular consumer product company whose shipment had been casually reduced in half somewhere between Elizabeth and Hackensack.

Everything in Hoboken, including swag, was sold on time. If you wanted to buy your wife a pair of earrings that were a hundred dollars, you'd go over to Trapani, the town jeweler, and he'd put your name in a little tin file box with the amount you owed him and he'd let you take them home. Every month you'd pay him something like ten bucks and he'd take out your file card and knock off ten bucks from what you owed him, until it was paid for, usually interest free. It was a system based on trust and gossip. If you defaulted on your payments without working out some kind of deal first, every shopkeeper and swag artist in town would know about it the next day and you'd end up having to do all your shopping in Jersey City or Bayonne. Besides, everybody knew where everybody else lived. There was nowhere to hide.

I've always craved attention more than I probably should, and I've never really been kept in the wanting. My family fed it to me in spoonfuls, and Mommy in particular made sure that the rest of the world around us did the same. The ultimate platform for a proud mother to showcase her pride and joy in Hoboken was the St. Anne's Church King of the Feast Parade. It was the highest honor you could bestow on an attention-hungry kid like me at the time. It usually went to the children of active public figures, but Mommy had pulled a few strings through her connections at the local Democratic headquarters and had gathered support for me while going door to door registering voters during election season. I was picked out of all the kids that belonged to that church.

Mommy took me to get a tuxedo at Guisemeyer's, where my cousin Bill from my father's side was the manager. She insisted on me having tails so I could look "just like Liberace at the piano."

Bill said he could do that.

I sighed.

"What can you give it to the King of the Feast for?"

"Well, Aunt Mary, I'm going to rent it to you at my cost, which is rent. Six dollars for the day."

Mommy flinched. "Six dollars! I wanna rent the fucking thing, not buy it!"

"It's the best I can do, Mary."

"For Christ's sake, Bill, I thought you was going to give us a break."

Bill offered to put me in a winter tuxedo instead for four dollars.

For the love of two dollars, I was stuck wearing a thick, heavy wool tuxedo for an outdoor festival I was to parade at for hours in the middle of August.

Mommy had secured the only convertible in Hoboken to drive me and the Queen of the Feast, Margaret Ann, around town, so there was no escape from the glaring sun, near hundred-degree temperature and 100 percent humidity. We sat on the back of the car and went all over Hoboken. I had a king's hat and crown on, which was made of papier mâché, golden cardboard and folded fake paper velvet. The whole thing probably cost around thirty cents and didn't do anything but aggravate the situation for me.

I begged Mommy to let me take my jacket off but she refused.

"You're the king! The king wears the jacket!"

I begged her to remove the entirely criminal hat and crown.

"You're the king! The king wears the crown!"

There was no point in arguing with the Queen Mother.

We drove all over Hoboken at four miles an hour. I was in the car with Margaret Ann, and Mommy walked alongside us with one hand on the car and the other hand waving. She was every bit the ham that I was, perfectly at home in front of the crowd. There was music, and fireworks being launched from just outside the car by the seven-fingered fireworks guy and hordes of people crowding the streets. Old women were walking down the hot streets barefoot to do penance to their patron saint. They pinned money and jewelry from their deceased loved ones onto the saint. There was so much money hanging off this saint it was making me sick with jealousy. I was sweating profusely and getting light-headed from the intense heat and glare of the sun, and the only thing my mind could focus on was all the ones, fives and tens fluttering from beautifully colored ribbons and all in arm's reach. If I could just lose the jacket, I could make a run for it. I'm the freakin' Liberace king—they should be pinning the money to my wool tuxedo. That saint sure had it good.

As king, I was also denied the incredible food that lined the procession, from the sizzling Italian sausage with peppers and onions, clams on the half shell, hot scungilli, veal and peppers, hot dogs and calzone, to the fried zeppolis thrown in brown paper bags and tossed in hot oil and powdered sugar. As I stared at the crowd, I was hoping one kindhearted soul would understand what the longing in my eyes was for and toss me at least one stinkin' zeppole. But they just waved at me and smiled as if I were just another pinned-up patron saint. Some called Margaret Ann and me by name, others just whistled and hollered, "Go, king and queen!"

I looked over at Mommy and her gleaming face. She'd turn to me periodically to tell me how handsome I looked, then she'd look back at the crowd and wave. Though my papier mâché hat had melted by the time we arrived at the end of the procession where all the games and rides were stationed, and though my body was trapped in a cocoon of steam and heat, at the end of the day, if I had eaten nothing else, I was feasting on Mommy's pride. These were our people, and their affection was as thick as the air. I was secure in Hoboken's embrace. I could do no wrong, as long as the spotlight was mine.

—4—

503 Madison Street

Fatty Pants

In our neighborhood, when you went to a wake, instead of giving flowers, you gave to the "a-boost." The a-boost was a basket used for collecting cash contributions to help the family of the deceased pay for burial costs. Most often, a family member would be stationed in the back of the room whose job it would be to mark in a small book the names of contributors and amounts given.

At the funeral for a local shop owner, I was in the back of the room with Mommy when she suddenly stopped chatting with the woman next to her, turned to me and screamed, "Jesus Christ! What the hell's the matter with you? Put that back. Put it back!"

"Wha—?" I acted like I had no idea what she was talking about. Mommy had caught me swiping money from the a-boost basket. The temptation had been too great, the usher hadn't been paying attention and the money in the basket was staring at me like complimentary candy mints at a wedding. I knew it was wrong and I figured I was in big trouble. But Mommy had other plans in mind, and they didn't include teaching me right from wrong at that moment.

"Give me that, you little sumanabitch," she said as she grabbed my wrist and forced my hand open to find two five-dollar bills.

Mommy turned back to the usher. "Sorry about your loss, Micky. Here's your five back, and put us down for another five," she said as she sequentially placed the two bills I had swiped back into the basket and then took hold of my hand and walked me toward the open casket. "C'mon, Joey, let's pay our respects."

She hadn't taken any money, she had just claimed someone else's contribution for her own. It was her way of showing respect within her means. Micky, the usher, didn't appear to catch on; he just smiled and said "Thank you, Mary" as we walked away. Mommy could always think on her feet and when she saw an opportunity arise, she always took it. She was a real go-getter.

By the time I turned ten, we'd been at 701 Adams Street for five years, which was pretty much a record for us. But it was time to paint again and my parents had hit a little upswing financially. That is to say, Mommy had hit the number on a combo and Daddy wasn't losing as much as usual at the track. Things were going great for the time being, and we took advantage of that window of opportunity. The move was actually an old reunion of sorts. We wound up at 503 Madison Street, only a block east and two blocks south of our old place at 202 Monroe. I'm not really sure why that was such a big deal at the time, but there was celebration in the air, and the truth is, sentimentality found its way into and out of our household more frequently than any of us cared to admit. Our old neighbors from 503 Madison merged with our new neighbors to form an extended family.

Our new place was a two-family, two-story apartment house directly on top of a garage. Our apartment was a railroad flat. The first room you walked into was a nice-sized kitchen with a separate room that housed a stove. Our bathroom was tiny, with only a shower and no tub. I slept in the living room, while Maryann and my folks had the two bedrooms. All of our windows on the north side looked out onto the rooftop of the garage. We used the rooftop to play and run around on. In the summertime we'd have dinners and Sunday barbecues up there.

A former mayor of Hoboken lived in our building at the time. He'd been at a college in the Midwest and after graduation was returning home to live in Hoboken. He and his friend bought a car there for $300 that ended up being a lemon. His plan was to drive it back to Hoboken with the guys and sell it at a profit. Mommy saw the car and liked it. He thought he was going to be smart and sell it to her for $450. She offered to give him $250 up front and pay him fifty bucks a month to make up the two hundred she owed him. He thought he had his $150 profit in the bag. He obviously didn't know who he was dealing with. The additional two hundred never came, and he ended up losing fifty bucks on the deal. After numerous attempts to collect it, he forgave her debt when Mommy threatened she'd put me and Maryann to work to earn the extra $200;

he'd always liked us kids and ended up taking the loss graciously. Meanwhile, Mommy turned around and sold the car to an acquaintance across town for $475. The bright side was that Mommy taught the future mayor something about Hoboken economics he never would have learned at his fancy college.

Somehow, Mommy managed to create the illusion, at least for me and my sister, that even though we were dirt-poor, we weren't really all that bad off. The glass was always half-full, even if it wasn't your choice beverage. In fact, she managed to make us feel fairly middle-class, or at least working class with four-star dining. She was an incredible cook. Her cooking always had a unique zest, like her personality. She mixed her ingredients as she mixed her terms of affection. Of course, she'd call me "little fuck face" or "sumanabitch" or "you little cocksucker," but just about as often "honey" and "baby," and they were all equal terms of affection. They became endearing to me.

Mommy and Daddy hadn't yet told me about the birds and the bees when my friend Ronnie Richards came upon the information from kids at school. They told him all about how babies were made, and he beat my parents to the punch by passing the news on to me. Apparently the stork had nothing to do with it. "Your father takes his dick and sticks it in your mother's twat, and then shit comes out the end of it. And they call it 'fucking,' " he informed me. "And that, my friend, is how babies are made."

I was stunned. I was disgusted. How is this possible? Mommy and Daddy would never do anything as sick as that! I couldn't get it out of my mind. Even if Mommy wasn't always kind to Daddy, I knew they cared for each other deep down. This was all far too revolting.

When I came back from school that day, I couldn't stand to look at either of my parents. I couldn't believe that they'd be involved in this abominable act. Mommy had a little shrine on our bureau with Jesus Christ on the cross, a bunch of saints and a Christian monk. That night I was so freaked out that I took them all and put them on the kitchen table, lit a candle and prayed to every last one of them that what Ronnie told me wasn't true.

"What's the matter with you?" Mommy asked when she walked in and saw me. "What in God's name did you do?"

"*I* didn't do anything."

"Well then what the hell are you praying for? Maybe you should run it by me before you talk to God about it."

I explained what Ronnie had told me.

Without a second thought, she told me, "Ah, Joey, my poor baby, it's not like that at all. Mommy and Daddy hugged each other and God came down with you and then with Maryann."

I would have to break the news to Ronnie. I believed Mommy with all the faith I could muster. Between Mommy and the Catholic Church I was well protected from the reality of the birds and bees, for now anyway.

The Catholic Church had a strong influence in Hoboken. There was one church for every six bars in the city, so nuns were almost as common as drunks on the streets. We even had Franciscan monks from St. Anne's walking our streets—sandals, brown robes, ropes and all. Suffice to say I didn't have to walk far to confirm Mommy's account of the birds and the bees.

When we moved to Madison Street, I had to change to Public School 8, which was just across the street from us, and was forced to repeat the first half of second grade in keeping with the new system of half-grades there. My performance at PS 9 hadn't qualified me for grade 2B, so I got left a half year behind. It was a failing struggle to catch up. Mommy was frustrated by my inability to move forward in school, but she only made it harder for me at times.

Her frustration confused me. "How come you can't fucking learn this?" she'd scream over my homework. "You stupid sumanabitch, you're taking after your father, I can see that."

I wasn't sure why I didn't understand things, when Mommy made it clear a boy my age should be getting them. She would try to help me with my homework while we ate dinner. When Mommy got frustrated, or when she got angry, she would hit herself, scratch herself and even belt herself in the head. She did it on numerous occasions. We stopped our frustrating homework-over-dinner routine one night when, in reaction to Mommy hitting herself, I took the plate of macaroni and meatballs she had cooked for dinner and broke it over my head. I stood there smiling with macaroni and meatballs and ceramic covering my face. She had the nerve to call *me* crazy. If I couldn't do my homework correctly, hey, at least I could entertain.

I couldn't read, study or do my homework. I just didn't know how, and I wasn't getting any extra help at school. At parent-teacher night, my teachers would tell my parents, "He's not a stupid boy. He's just lazy."

At the start of fifth grade, I asked my teachers if I could sit in front of the class because I felt it would improve my chances of getting a good grade. I quickly found the faulty logic in this plan. The teachers figured I was eager to participate if I had asked to be seated in front, so at the beginning of the year they would pick on me to answer questions all the time. By the third week, they were all convinced I was mildly retarded, and they didn't bother me for the rest of the year. One teacher politely moved me to the back of the room where the two other "dumb" kids sat.

One of their names was Poupi Rea. Poupi is one of the most successful guys in Hoboken now. He actually bought the old school building, PS 8, and turned it into a condominium. His living room today used to be our homeroom.

But back then, all we knew was that everyone called us "dumb" or "lazy." Eventually, I just stopped caring about school and gave up. As far as I was concerned, there was no point. It just wasn't my thing. There was nothing in school I had an aptitude for. I felt like someone had forgotten to clue me in on the key to school way back when in kindergarten and I was forever out of the academic loop.

To add social insult to academic injury, I was building a reputation for having my Mommy fight my battles for me. If somebody hit me and I came home with a bloody nose, Mommy would find out who it was and retaliate, which usually involved a good smacking, scolding or not-so-nice conference with the kid's parents. My reputation was sealed for a while by an incident with Rabies, the token crazy kid in town, who was so named because of the drool that constantly dripped from his mouth. Rabies and I got into a sound-off trading insults. He'd slobber something like, "Your mother's like a birthday cake—everyone gets a piece."

And I'd reply, while wiping his stray spit off my face, "Your mother's like a railroad track—she gets laid all over the country."

It started out as a verbal battle, but it quickly escalated into the physical realm.

His fist hit first, "Bam!"

My fist replied, "Boom!"

His came back with a "Sock!"

Mine recovered with a "Smack-Crack!"

He proceeded to beat me up to the point where I almost lost my eye. He punched my eyelid shut and he held me down on the ground and punched me again so hard my eyelid almost opened up again. He had his knees on my shoulders as he continued his assault. To save myself from certain blindness or death, I pretended that he had knocked me out cold and became limp while barely breathing. The kid had genuinely worn me out, so it was an easy act to pull. A circle of children had formed around us at the schoolyard, and some were cheering for my rabid opponent, some for me. But at his apparent knockout, everybody got quiet. Rabies was scared he'd seriously hurt me and he backed off and started walking away. As soon as he did, I laughed out loud. It was a last-ditch effort to look tough despite the circumstance.

When it was all over, a friend helped me walk upstairs to my apartment. I was a mess and Mommy was horrified. She screamed, "What happened?"

"Nothing."

"You tell me who did this to you."

"Nobody."

She grabbed my friend and she slammed him up against the wall. "You tell me, you little sumanabitch. Who did this to my son?"

He caved in under the pressure. "Rabies."

She was confused. "What the hell are you talking about? A dog did this to my Joey? I'm calling Popeye!"

"No," my friend corrected her. "That's his name—Rabies."

"Mommy, please don't," I pleaded as she grabbed the broom she had been sweeping with and went downstairs, with her other hand taking my friend by the shirt collar. I followed them downstairs, begging her to stop all the way.

"Mind your own fucking business, Joey!"

"This *is* my business!"

"Not anymore," said Mommy. Once outside, Mommy took the broom and smacked the head of it as hard as she could against the fence rail and knocked the head of the broom right off. What was left was a daunting stick with spiked splinters at the end of it. "Now, *which one is he?*" she said with a predatory sneer.

Upon seeing Mommy with the imposing stick in her hands, all the kids quickly complied and pointed to Rabies in unison. He looked up and started to whimper. She ran over and pinned him on the ground with her knees on his chest, using the same method he'd used on me minutes earlier. She said, "You little fuck, if you *ever* touch my son again, I'll fucking kill you." I'm sure she meant it too.

I was horrified. I walked around for the next month with a big black eye so that every stinking bully in school could recognize me as the kid whose Mommy yelled at Rabies, and they all wanted to try their hand with Mommy. The only one who left me alone after that was Rabies.

By the fifth grade, Joey Pants had stepped down and Fatty Pants had taken his place. I was ten years old and getting fatter by the meal. I probably had a thirty-six-inch waist at five-foot-three. Some kids in the neighborhood began calling me "Fatty Pants." I had overheard an adult at school use the word "rotund" when she referred to me, and I cried when I asked Mommy and she told me what it meant. "It means you're eating well and you're healthy."

"How do they know?"

"They don't, 'cause you know what it really means?"

"What?"

"It means you're a fat fuck. And I still love you."

Letters were arriving every week from Florie in Atlanta, and Mommy would read them aloud to the family. It was a big ritual for us. I remember being impressed that the words "ATLANTA FEDERAL PENITENTIARY" were stamped on the corner of the letters. I was pretty sure this wasn't the name of a college. He'd send us pictures of him and his pals on the prison tennis team. They all looked so happy, as if they had just come back from an invigorating match at the country club and were off to spend the evening sipping martinis and flirting with the moguls' daughters. Florie would write five- or six-page letters single-spaced in tight cursive. Who knew there was so much to talk about in prison. He'd tell us about running the prison library and would summarize all the good books he'd recommend. He'd thank us for sending him provolone, sopressata and salami, and inform us that his "boys" enjoyed the Christmas fruitcakes.

In October, a month after my tenth birthday, Aunt Millie, my father's closest sister, was in the hospital dying of cancer. Mommy was going to take me on the bus into New York City, to the Port Authority bus station, to get my first pair of glasses, and then we were going to visit Aunt Millie. It was a real outing for me and Mommy to go on the bus and through the tunnel. I loved seeing New York City and how big it was. The crowds of people, the big buildings, the hustle and bustle were overwhelming, but inspiring. The shiny new Port Authority bus terminal was like our first shopping mall. I was diagnosed by the optician as being nearsighted and was given my first pair of prescription eyeglasses. I remember feeling really proud and grown-up when I got those glasses. I was finally able to see better. I thought I looked sharp. Maybe now I could finally read the words on the chalkboard at school and salvage my academic reputation and my confidence.

Daddy had worked his way up to become the foreman at the Standard Brands factory. I remember the smell of coffee on him when he'd come home. He must have rubbed coffee grounds all over himself, because from what I heard he was never there.

Daddy and his boss at Standard Brands, Larry, loved the ponies and they couldn't get enough. Larry was Daddy's white-collar boss, executive senior vice president of operations. Soon, Aqueduct Racetrack, the "Big A," would be closing for the winter and they'd come up with any excuse to get there. Daddy would punch in at work, spend a couple of hours on the factory floor, then go upstairs to get Larry in his office. Daddy would drive Larry to the track to try to get the first four races. Daddy and Larry would usually get back to the job before closing time, around four-thirty, just in time to clock out.

Mommy told me we'd be able to pay for my eyeglasses because Daddy had a good tip on a horse that day. The horse was called Four Eyes. We all got a big kick out of that and thought it made sense. Daddy knew we were going to get glasses that day and played it on a hunch and bet on Four Eyes. At the race, Daddy was watching his horse come around the bend for the finish line. Normally a mild-mannered man, Daddy would, in contrast, become completely crazy when he bet. He loved the rush. This particular day, he was yelling and screaming at the top of his lungs. "Come on, Four Eyes! Come on you lazy fucking bastard! MOVE! Come on! You can do it! GO!"

The hunch was right on—Four Eyes won the race. We would be able to pay for the eyeglasses after all. The announcer was still going on about the underdog Four Eyes when Daddy grabbed his arm, staggered and then grabbed his chest. In a flurry of flying tickets, he collapsed onto the floor. His ticket floated off into a sea of many others.

When we got home, we got the terrible news of Daddy's heart attack. There was a note on the door and we got a phone call from Larry saying Daddy was in the ambulance being rushed to St. Mary's Hospital.

Maryann and I were in the waiting room downstairs at St. Mary's fifteen minutes later. Because it was a Catholic hospital, all the priests and nuns were very strict, and created an abnormally stern, antiseptic atmosphere. There was a very firm rule that no children under the age of eighteen were allowed on the ward floors. Mommy was able to sneak Maryann, who was four, and I up intermittently to see Daddy. When the nuns weren't looking, I would put on a pair of pajamas and a robe and walk past like I was a patient.

Daddy's room and the visiting area were packed because all of the relatives were already at the hospital visiting Aunt Millie on the cancer ward below. They took turns from floor to floor visiting Aunt Millie and Daddy.

When Maryann and I finally got to Daddy's bed, he was gasping for breath through an oxygen tent and grimacing with pain. Mommy sat in a chair up against a wall under a "No Smoking" sign exhaling a thick stream of cigarette smoke. She looked worried.

That was the end of Daddy's job at the factory, which meant more than no more free coffee—it meant a different era for Daddy.

And it also meant that we were dead broke. He stayed in the hospital in critical condition for three weeks. The doctor had been sure he wasn't going to make it. The heart attack put Daddy on 100 percent disability.

The night after the heart attack, I went over to Patty-boy's house. Patty's mom had a sewing machine in the basement, and we went down there that night because I wanted to make Daddy a present. We took some fake leather material like vinyl, and I sewed some kind of a weird thing that I considered a shoe holder, so that Daddy could hang it on the doorknob and put his shoes in. Daddy said he loved it, but when I prompted him, it was clear he didn't know what the hell it was I had made him.

By Easter, Aunt Millie had died. The doctors were telling Daddy that he had to take extra care of himself. He couldn't do any extraneous exercising, but they suggested he slowly walk up the stairs backward instead. Take two at a time and rest a minute in between those steps, and then on to the next. This was the extent of the physical activity Daddy could handle. He couldn't play with me as he'd done before, he couldn't take long walks, and he couldn't throw a ball. We were all afraid his heart was going to stop any minute. All he could do was walk backward up the steps, two at a time, and rest. It wasn't exactly a bundle of fun for me to participate in, but I'd stand there and wait with Daddy as he'd rest between steps. He couldn't talk much for the first month or so, so we'd just stand in silence in the stairwell contemplating life, death and the ridiculous activity that passed for doctor's orders.

I was not taking Daddy's new condition very well. I was bored, worried and at a strange age for this type of thing to happen to my Daddy. At one point, I actually resorted to burning chickens on our pancake griddle on the kitchen stove. Well, I only did it once, but I've never forgiven myself for it. There was a little poultry shop down the street from where we lived. It was the same poultry shop where we stole the eggs for Halloween. It was actually a slaughterhouse for chickens, where you could get fresh-killed birds for soups and stews, and fresh eggs, as well as turkey. For Easter that year, Mommy bought my sister and me a basket filled with live baby chicks. They were adorable, fuzzy little yellow chirpers. Poor little Maryann, who was only four, almost had a heart attack herself when I showed her how I made the little chicks dance. I'd turn up the heat on the griddle and put them on center stage. "Fatty Pants and the Chickies Live in Hoboken" was not a pleasant show in the slightest. I had reached rock bottom.

At fifty pounds overweight, I was no longer enjoying the leeway I had once had with other kids as a scrawny runt with a charming attitude that more than compensated for my junior size. Now kids were chasing me because I was an extra-large with no room to spare, let alone for charm. I was at the playground one day with Patty-boy when two black girls hanging near the basketball court yelled at me, "Hey, I think that kid just swallowed the basketball" and they started chasing us. We ran scared straight into the building and didn't look back.

My self-esteem was not in tip-top shape. I'd given up on school, still unaware of my dyslexia, and I felt like I couldn't learn anything for the life of me. Daddy was lying in bed helpless and restless, and Mommy was taunting him, as if his heart attack had been just another thing he did to spite her. Daddy was fifty and down for the count. Mommy was beginning to go through her "life changes," which made her mood all the more volatile. Things, in short, were falling apart all around us.

We needed a savior. Amazingly, we got one.

—5—

310 Jackson Street

Hurricane Florie

She was gorgeous. She was heavenly. She was not a day over eleven. Her long, fine hair danced on her head without a care in the world as she ran toward me. It was the color of orange Fanta, the same color as the brightest leaves lining Madison Street in the fall. She was wearing a St. Anne's navy blue and yellow plaid skirt, with a blue sweater over her yellow blouse and matching navy blue knee-high socks right down to her black buckled loafers. Her name was Lois and I was pretty sure she didn't know I existed. But here she was, calling out to me as she ran from the other end of the block, "Joey! Hey, blue eyes!"—just like Mommy always called me (except when Daddy was around, because of the Sinatra issue)—and I could have sworn there was a circular spotlight following her. I had no idea what she wanted from me, but she was approaching quickly and wasn't slowing down a bit, so I opened my arms wide to catch her. Then in slow motion she passed me and just kept running. She never lost eye contact as she turned her head and said in a voice that sounded like hers but seemed to come from an amplifier rigged to the city's public address system somewhere above my head, "It's yours, blue eyes! On the corner—hurry up!" I could hear the pitter-patter of her loafers fade away as she disappeared around the corner. "What's mine?" I said to myself. At that moment, another spotlight, or actually more of a searchlight this time, illuminated a huge, jam-packed bag tied at the top with a thin rope and sitting at the opposite corner next to the curb. I ran over to the bag and untied the rope eagerly, opened it up. Yes!—twenties, fifties and hundreds, filled to the brim. It's a moneybag! I'm fucking rich! Rich, I tell ya! And it's all mine!

"Joey . . . Joey!"

My precious moment of moneybag delight is punctured by the sound of a voice in the distance calling my name. And it ain't Lois this time. It's Mommy. "Joey, it's time, honey."

I ignore her and bend down and pick up my moneybag in my arms. I grab the rope, tie the two ends together and make a loop, my Cub Scout training finally coming in handy. I strap the moneybag over my chest like a knapsack. With that, I extend my arms away from my body and start rotating them forward, my arms going faster and faster, lifting me off the ground. Higher and higher, looking up to the night sky. It's not effortless; I've got to keep my arms rotating, but it's a rush like no other. Three stories above the rooftops now, over PS 8, where I go to school, and I know that's just about the maximum height I can reach. But I'm fine with that. It's a killer view and I'm safe and sound from anyone trying to take my—

"Joey, let's go, you little sumanabitch!"

Shit. I love this dream. It's a recurring dream. I know if I wake up I'm not gonna have the money. Flap harder, flap harder. Just keep flyin'—

"Joey, wake up and help your father. Chicky and Pattyboy are coming to help too."

Back in bed. What the—?

"Daddy's got a truck outside already. C'mon, honey—"

I barely let her finish before my skin greens and my hair frizzes out. "FIVE MINUTES!" my Lou Ferrigno counterpart screams as I throw a pillow in any direction I can.

Mommy doesn't waste another second. She does the Jerry Bruckheimer hero-with-a-mission over to the freezer, where she keeps the only weapon capable of defeating the Incredible Sulk—dangerous if used recklessly, painfully effective if handled with skill. It was enemy number one to the precious snooze and about to rob me of my precious riches. It was the Mop-a-Doola, straight from the deepest, darkest pits of hell-frozen-over.

She kept it in the freezer. She would run the frozen wet washcloth under the faucet to loosen it up, just enough that it would remain ice-cold. And then, she would do the unthinkable.

"HOLY SHIT!" Jumping up, I'd rip the coldest, wettest scrap of pure torture from my face and throw it to the ground, and through blurry eyes I'd see Mommy hovering above me, smiling at me with the eyes of a recently crowned champ.

"Rise and shine, you lazy bastard. Give Mommy a kiss good morning."

She won. The Mop-a-Doola was more than any mortal kid

could handle. My moneybag was gone. Welcome to the real friggin' world. "Shit."

It was a recurring dream, I had it all the time growing up. The circumstances were always different, but they were variations on the same theme. Catholic girls, Martha Raye, a street dog—something always pointed me to my moneybag. Sometimes I just found it sitting on the street or in the house and I knew it was mine. But somehow I was always aware in the dream that it was only a dream. I could never get the full satisfaction of really thinking I had come into all this money. Reality always kept a light on, and I always had that sense of dread that I was going to have to wake up without my moneybag.

But soon the frustration waned and the recurring dream gave way to our unavoidably recurring reality. It was moving day again. Not just any ordinary moving day, mind you. The summer of 1963 was coming to an end, and we were movin' on up, right to the projects. Mommy had finally caved in and applied for welfare. She had become the sole provider in the eyes of the state, and the undisputed matriarch in the eyes of the family, and without Daddy's full income, we had simply run out of options. It was a big deal for her, since she had always been stubborn about accepting any help from anyone. She was wholeheartedly against charity aimed at her and her family, and the government was no exception. But things had gone from worse to much fucking worse, and she eventually bit her lip, swallowed her pride and pulled some strings to get us on the fast track to the projects. Even against her own will, she always found a way to get things done. There was a waiting list eighteen months long for the brand-new project buildings on

Jackson Street. We moved into 310 Jackson Street in just two weeks. She was amazing.

She was also depressed. So was Daddy. They both hated the idea of living in the projects. I, for one, was ecstatic. Ours was a brand-new building in a sea of old, aging project buildings, twenty-one to be exact. There were four new buildings in total, and they were lined up across from each other. They were among the tallest buildings in Hoboken at the time, with ten stories of bright red brick towering over the adjacent railroad tracks. Having the train tracks so close gave the whole development that unique sense of desolation that only train tracks can inspire. It was picturesque to me, but for my parents, desolation mixed with preexisting desperation was not what the doctor had ordered.

Love and marriage went about as well together at 310 Jackson Street as a horse and an angry horde of South American killer bees. Neither psychotherapy nor marriage counseling was an option for them in Hoboken in 1963. And being old school Catholics, they were pretty much stuck with what they had, for better or for worse, till death did they part. And Mommy was definitely doing her part to make good on that vow already. Monk had an amazing ability to absorb her punches, even in his weakened state. They had been living unhappily ever after for over twenty years now, but the move to the projects had refueled Mommy's aggression toward him. I began to wonder if perhaps Daddy had actually died back at St. Mary's and the figure moping around the house was some collective family hallucination.

I hated how she ridiculed him constantly, and took every

chance she could to embarrass him in front of Maryann and me and whoever happened to be around the house. Every morning, I imagined Mommy in one corner, punching away frantically in preparation, and her trainer forcing water down her throat. Daddy would be in the opposite corner, sipping his morning Sanka, decaf thanks to his heart attack, and reading down the latest list of thoroughbred racing leaders in the morning paper, while his trainer yelled at him in utter confusion, "Yo, Monk, ain't you gonna get ready or somethin'?" And Monk answered, "Nah, she's harmless. She's just gotta let off some steam; she'll get over it. If she wants the title, let her have it."

I would be sitting at the kitchen table eating breakfast and I could just hear the ref calling out, "All right fighters, when ya hear the bell, come out fightin'." Ding-ding-ding. Daddy walked into the kitchen. Mommy didn't bother with touching gloves or any such formalities; this fight was no-holds-barred. She would just stand over the sink with a cigarette dangling from her lip, with a look of disgust that would have had the entire Chicago Outfit begging for forgiveness. "Joey, make sure you give your father some room today—God knows I would." *Centrella establishes some good jabs and a right haymaker, she's working her way in.* "I just caught him jerkin' off in the bathroom again and I'll be damned if I heard the sink runnin' after." *Eew. Centrella releases a big left hook and follows up with a hard right, nice combination.* "The least you could do, Monk, is wash up after you shame yourself under the same goddamn roof your son's gotta share with you!" *Oh boy, it's a clean right uppercut to the chin and a follow-up right to the chest, and I'd bet she's trying to finish this one before the end of the round.*

Mommy, why'd you have to go there? No offense to the songwriting geniuses Sammy Cahn and Jimmy Van Heusen, but in my house, marriage was an institution you could all too easily disparage, I don't care what the local gentry said.

Needless to say, Monk started taking refuge from the house more and more. He had stopped smoking and drinking, so the Rex Bar was out of the question. That's probably why he started taking me to the movies again. We'd go to the great old Fabian Theater on First and Washington Streets, or the Loews Paradise in Journal Square. I went to see *West Side Story* at the Fabian with Daddy and cousin Patty-boy twenty times; they kept showing it on and off for almost a year after it won Best Picture in 1962. Daddy was totally engrossed as Tony sang about Maria, and I felt he was safe there in front of *West Side Story*, safe from his Mariacella. I wonder if he'd ever imagined life with Mommy would turn out like this. I could only hope that his thoughts were far enough away from 310 Jackson Street when we'd go to the movies, at least enough to allow him an occasional dose of serenity. If you ask me, I think he was just fine sitting there at the Fabian Theater, though you could never really be sure with the Monk. He was about as expressive with his emotions as the Lincoln Memorial. He wasn't free to talk about them. His emotions were always reactive. They were never instigative, like "Jesus Christ, Joey, what did you do that for?" Instead it was "What the hell happened, Jesus Christ, ah leave me alone!" So it was great to hear Daddy laugh at the movie theater. As much abuse as he endured, it seemed that the

Monk was incredibly capable of enjoying himself when the opportunity arose.

All in all, project living was still the life for me. Mommy had landed us a fifth-floor three-bedroom apartment with black, white and red speckled square-pattern linoleum throughout the apartment. There was a little alcove that you walked into first that veered into the kitchen and on to the living room. The living room opened to a hallway at the other end where the three bedrooms were. That's right. One for Mommy and Daddy, one for Maryann and one for me. It was a novel concept. For the first time in my life, I had my own bedroom. My unjust sentence to the Castro Convertible was finally lifted, to the dismay of future chiropractors, and I was rewarded for my penance with a brand-new bedroom set. Mommy bought it all "on time." I guess she'd figure out how to pay, or avoid, the monthly bill later.

I was sleeping in a new bed, but surrounded by the familiar, if worsening, Jack Dempsey–Georges Carpentier replay at home and a familiar roster of friends and relatives that lived no farther than just down the block—Uncle Popeye, Aunt Minnie, Florie Branda, Aunt Claire and Uncle Duke McCourt, Mary Fat. In that sense, nothing much had really changed, except that I had officially become a kid from the projects, with all the entitlements it granted. I was on my way to A. J. Demerest Junior High, and coming from the projects gave me the right to be considered a tough kid. If I could somehow tiptoe my way around the whole Rabies-kicking-my-ass-and-Mommy-intimidating-him-with-a-broomstick incident. That was gonna be a tricky roadblock to my tough-kid front. But I was optimistic. I was in the projects now and played with the kids my age in the courtyard that separated the two sets of new buildings. There were kids out and about at all hours—Italians, Puerto Ricans, African Americans, Irish. And though we were still pissant grade-schoolers, my pals in the projects were like a gang straight out of the Jets and the Sharks. We would wage war against the Jersey City Heights kids, who would storm down the hill over by the railroad tracks, and we'd beat them back with rocks and sticks. Of course, they had the high ground and always beat us in the end. But that didn't matter. We'd challenge them every friggin' time.

We dressed "Nickie Newark" style. Burgundy was our favorite color. We had Guinea T-shirts, see-through socks, four-button leather jackets if you could afford them. I couldn't get one just yet, but like everyone else, my hair was loaded with hair spray and parted on the side with a hot comb. I'm sure that's another reason why I got bald prematurely. The hot combs were really fucking hot; I must have burned out all my hair follicles by the time I hit puberty, but that was no concern of mine then. No, back then, I just had to make sure that the sides of my hair came up on a sharp angle, pre–Dr. Spock. We didn't do sideburns. We were only kids, but we were cool.

Having the train tracks nearby proved to be a godsend for my pals and me. No backdrop-to-desolation adult nonsense for us. In our eyes, the tracks represented opportunity. They signaled to us when the trains were approaching. And inside the train cars—therein lay opportunity. These railroad cars were stocked with beautiful things. You never knew what was coming out of Maxwell House or Standard Brands. The railroad cars were nondescript on the outside and closed and sealed with leaded straps that were easy enough to break. But if you broke them, it was a federal offense, not to mention that the railroad bulls would bust your head open before he ran you in. We'd break the federal seal, slide it open and start throwing stuff on the ground as the trains were moving—Lipton tea, coffee, cocoa, Spam. Sometimes Levi Strauss would grace us with his jeans. You never knew what treasures lay hidden in those railroad cars. There was everything from ladies' underwear to baby socks. Whatever it was, we'd carry it off and we'd sell it door to door like a pack of testosterone-treated Girl Scouts with their thin mints, minus the cute outfits. We'd sell it to the little mom and pop stores; we'd sell it to our neighbors; and we'd keep some for ourselves and for our families. The railroad tracks were a sure bet, and the neighbors came to rely on us for some of the basics. We were performing no less than a highly valued service to the project community.

We weren't all about committing federal offenses in the name of public service, however. There were no Robin Hood intentions anywhere to be found when we repeatedly scammed the neighborhood pizza deliverymen. Nah, we were just looking for a cheap thrill and a free meal. One of us would call, always from a different phone, and order a pie to a random apartment in the building. The delivery guy would show up and deliver the pizza, and while he was doing that, we would break into his car and take all of the undelivered pizzas. Hard to believe it worked every time, but it did. We ate a lot of pizza in those days—and the pizza guys always came back for more. There was nothing like the thrill of running upstairs to one of our apartments and enjoying the pepperoni, sausage, half–green pepper and extra mozzarella spoils.

It was while lounging around in my apartment finishing up our brick-oven baked swag one afternoon that I first heard the beautiful music that became the background soundtrack to my time in the projects. It was a faint, soothing melody, and it seemed to be coming from the hallway. As it turned out, it was coming from the emergency stairwell. The elevators on the fifth floor opened up to a hallway with access to the two adjacent buildings and a third door that led to the fire exit hall and onto the emergency stairwell, which you were only supposed to use if there was a fire or if the elevators were broken. The older black, Irish and Puerto Rican boys would go into the stairwell, about five or so at a time, and make use of the reverb haven it provided by belting out the most amazing a cappela tunes you've ever heard. They loved to sing, and the Frankie Valli style tunes would resonate throughout the entire building and into our apartments. We'd go into the emergency stairwells and listen to the older boys sing their songs. We'd sit there, while the entire stairwell stank of urine because the older boys would piss in there all the time, but we didn't care. They couldn't hear us, and we sat quietly and listened to those beautiful voices. Usually they were love songs like "What's your name? Is it Mary or Sue? What's your name? What's your name?"

The kids still ruled in the projects. But my support system of adults had grown even wider. On our floor alone, we had an assortment of friendly neighbors that would've given Mr. Rogers and his red cardigan a run for his make-believe money. Night or day, their doors were always open for me. And I made use of it often, especially when the plumes of tobacco smoke seemed to rise less from Mommy's Chesterfields and more from Mommy's ears.

In hindsight, the brief cease-fire after Daddy's heart attack had been the calm before the storm that began raging in earnest with the move to the projects. But that storm, we were already used to. We all had our protective gears lined up every day. It was second nature. I had my outlets and my means of escape, and Daddy had his. Maryann was only six, and she was still protected by the precious naïveté of single-digit childhood. But there was another storm brewing. It was a different kind of storm. They say that the worst hurricanes, all short-term damage aside, are necessary for the long-term survival and prosperity of the flora and fauna of the affected region. I couldn't agree more. This storm was no less than a Category Five, and it began its approach with a phone call from Atlanta one particularly humid Indian Summer day in 1962.

I had come home from school and gone straight to the courtyard. Mommy called me up for supper. We sat down to the table and the phone rang. I ran to pick it up. "Mary Centrella, please."

"Who is it?" We didn't hear the Southern twang very often in Hoboken, New Jersey, and I was intrigued.

"This is Carl Hansen calling from Atlanta Federal Penitentiary. Is your mother there?"

Without another word to Mr. Hansen, I pointed the handset in Mommy's direction. "It's Atlanta."

Daddy looked up from his pork chop.

Mommy didn't say a word, but her face said it all. Surprised, nervous, mortified—all wrapped up in a wide-eyed piercing stare straight toward the phone. Had she been gifted with Superman's powers, she would have melted that telephone with heat-inducing lasers from those eyes. Mommy wasn't a pessimist, but she was a worrywart extraordinaire. Florie must be dead. Or maybe severely injured in some prison uprising. Maybe he killed someone and he's gonna get the chair. She picked up the phone and it visibly shook in her hand. "This is Mary," she said as her mouth wrenched into a tight, wrinkled mass of lip. It was how she protected herself from bad news; I'd seen it before. ". . . Uh-huh . . . Uh-huh . . . A-ha." In a single motion, the tight protective seal undid itself and her lips widened into a radiant and utterly breathtaking smile. I swore I could hear angels singing somewhere above her, and I wouldn't have blinked twice if a brilliant white sunbeam had suddenly flashed through the kitchen window and illuminated Mommy and the newly canonized phone. "Yes," she said to Carl Hansen in an effortless exhale. "Yes, absolutely. Yes, I understand. Understood. Yes, that's okay. Thank *you*, Mr. Hansen."

We all stared at her as she returned to the table. She said nothing and looked at no one. This moment didn't involve us. This was all hers. Still smiling, she helped herself to some macaroni and took two bites before she realized the three of us were still staring. I think the smile became a smirk at that moment. "Cousin Florie's coming home . . . from college. It's official. He's coming to live with us. Next Saturday."

Florie was well into his fifties at that point, and I knew damn well that "Atlanta Federal Penitentiary" wasn't followed by an "and University." But that's how it was referred to in my house. Mommy and Daddy both knew I knew where Florie had been "studying" all these years, but I guess they felt it was in my best interest if they didn't outright say words like "in the can" and "locked up" and, God forbid, "prison" in front of little Joey. It might corrupt me. Of course, calling my father's mother a "fucking lousy cunt" was par for the course, but that was different in Mommy's eyes. She probably didn't even realize she cursed the way she did when she did. She usually looked possessed whenever her temper elevated to the "fucking cunt" level anyhow, and who knows, maybe there was some poltergeist involvement. Any bystander would have believed it. Regardless, at that particular moment I wasn't concerned with terminology. Florie was coming back into our lives.

We had been receiving Florie's letters pretty consistently, and there were indications that Florie was being considered for early release on account of his good behavior. He was the prison librarian and a model prisoner, and I'm sure he was chummy with everyone from the head warden down to the grand-theft convict and ex-pimp sharing his cell. He was that kind of guy. People looked up to him. I certainly was no exception. Florie had left quite the impression on me by the time he went off to "college." He was larger than life in my eyes, a legacy and a legend. The memories I had of Florie were the happiest of my childhood up until that point. When he had been around, I was the king of the world on top of the refrigerator; Mommy was always happy and things were good. The fires of everyday battle were put out in his presence, and so it was unavoidable that the thought of him coming to live with us inspired an instant burst of energy in me as I sat at the dinner table. I was excited. It was like the President of the United States himself was coming to live with us.

And still there was a haze surrounding the excitement I felt, but I wouldn't have been able to put my finger on it then. In the days ahead, as Cousin Florie's arrival approached, something like a vague sense of dread became ever more present, and whether I was projecting it on Daddy or I was picking it up from him, Daddy was no doubt at the center of it. He'd been as visibly cheerful right after hearing the news as the rest of us were. But during the course of the following week, as the tension in the house began to build with all the preparations for Florie, it became apparent that Daddy was afraid of something. And despite the thrill of anticipation, so was I.

I'll never forget the following Saturday when we drove to JFK Airport to pick Florie up. Mommy and Daddy, Maryann and I, and Aunt Tilly. It was the first time any of us had ever been to an airport before, and it felt like we were on our way to pick up a member of the royal family. It was a big day for the family and, needless to say, nerves were on edge. Mommy was in the backseat with Maryann and Aunt Tilly; I was up in front with Daddy. Mommy screamed at him nonstop all the way to the airport.

"You're driving too slow!"

"Jesus Christ, Monk, whaddya trying to do? Kill us?"

"Turn here!"

"Turn there!"

"Where the fuck did you learn how to drive?"

By the time we got to the entrance tunnels to JFK Arrivals,

we were half an hour late. We parked the car and ran in to the gate, and right past Florie. He spotted the family and followed us for a couple of seconds before he snuck up behind Mommy and grabbed her. She turned around and screamed out his name, and they hugged and kissed. I don't think I ever saw Mommy that happy again for the rest of her life. Daddy went up and gave Florie a big warm hug, followed by Aunt Tilly, and then Florie ran up to my sister and scooped her up in his arms and gave her a big kiss. Maryann hadn't been born until after Florie went to college. I stood there and watched in awe as Florie was reunited with the family. The legend came to life as he worked his rounds of hugs and hellos. He looked like a million bucks, which would be more like ten million in today's money. He had on a brand-new sharkskin suit. Everything was new. Apparently he'd stopped off somewhere in Atlanta and bought some clothes. A new shirt and brand-new shiny Italian leather shoes, a hand covered with gold rings—he was an incredible sight to see, with that wild smile in his eyes and that devilish grin. And he kept looking right past me.

"Where's little Joey?" he finally asked.

I jumped up and down and yelled, "I'm Joey! I'm Joey!"

He ignored me. "Hey, Mary, where's little Joey?"

"I'm Joey! I'm Joey!"

Finally, he looked down at me and said, "Who's the fat kid?"

I was crushed.

"Hey, Maryann, where's your brother? Did this fat kid eat Joey?"

It broke my heart. "I *am* a fat fuck," I thought to myself, "a fat twelve-year-old no-good lump of shit. And Florie hates me." I was thirty pounds overweight at the time, but I hadn't given it a second thought until that moment. I wanted to crawl into a suitcase and be carried off on the next Pan Am flight to the South Pacific, never to be heard of again.

And then Florie broke into a huge smile, and though he didn't even try to pick me up, he gave me the biggest bear hug I had ever had. And he looked in my eyes and said, "It's great to see you, kid."

I decided right then and there at JFK that I was never ever going to be fat again.

And at that moment, a new and improved Joey had already stepped in to take control. We hadn't even left the airport, but the winds of change had arrived, and his name was Florie.

—6—

310 Jackson Street, Part II

Who's Your Daddy?

Florie wasted no time getting back into his old life. He'd barely wrestled his pearly white dentures loose from the Carlo's cheesecake Mommy got for his welcome back party when he dashed off to Hester Street in Little Italy early Sunday morning to meet with his old family mentor, Joe King. He came back with three new suits from Lymie's on Fifty-seventh Street, two jackets, five pairs of slacks, three pairs of Florsheim shoes and three elegant fedoras, brown, blue and gray, in their hatboxes. He'd been back from Atlanta less than twenty-four hours and already he was loaded.

He eventually established somewhat of a routine. He'd spend his days across the Hudson, and his evenings, well, he spent plenty of them across the Hudson too. He was home for dinner at least a couple of nights a week, though, and he usually had breakfast with us in the morning. Florie was sleeping on my old digs, the Castro Convertible couch in the living room. It was quite the irony, actually, a guy of such clout and elegance spending his days romping around with the big boys in the big city and coming home to crash in cramped quarters in the projects on two ripped, drooping cushions laid atop a frame that was barely roomy enough for a boy of twelve. But it wasn't a cot in Atlanta, and that's all that mattered for now. The funds were funneling into Florie's pockets, and we felt the change at home immediately. Enter stage left: the green. Exit stage right: the blues.

Not that anything in my house could ever be that black and white, or green and blue for that matter, but the first few weeks after Florie's arrival sure made it seem that way. Things got better around the house financially speaking. The bills were actually getting paid for once. And this was lucky when it came to getting food on the table, because Marie, Mommy's friend, had moved on from her post at the Foodtown cash register. I'd gone from a wardrobe of hand-me-down clothes from my cousins to a fistful of hand-me-down bills from Florie. Twenty-five here for a new pair of shoes, twenty-five there for new pants and a shirt to wear under the Italian knit chocolate-brown Oleg Cassini sweater he gave me. He even gave me a hundred bucks so I could finally get my four-button leather jacket. I was able to brave the Jersey City gangs in style.

Mommy was wearing new outfits to church bingo, and though Daddy generally steered clear of Florie's handouts, he was enjoying the temporary breathing room that having Florie around gave him. Mommy's attention was diverted, and because the cash was flowing, she had one less excuse to blow up at Daddy. The sudden onslaught of Chinese food in our diet probably had a lot to do with the good humor in the house too. Nobody ate Chinese food in Hoboken back then, and Florie was taking us into Manhattan at least twice a week for the stuff. We were the cream of the project crop standing proudly next to our four-foot flaming pu-pu platter trophies. Oh yes, Florie was taking care of us from the get-go.

It was no secret that Florie was connected. In fact, his status as a known New York wiseguy was, for better or worse, pretty much a badge of honor for us. Florie was not the norm for Hoboken. Hoboken belonged to the legitimate, hardworking, blue-collar family man who slaved his day away either at a local factory or on the docks and in a good week brought home just enough dough to keep ends on the verge of meeting, and to pay off his bookie if he was lucky. In that context, Florie stuck out like a thirty-six-ounce medium-rare porterhouse at McDonald's. He was money. Not that there wasn't enough corruption all over town to make for a dozen sequels to *On the Waterfront*. But Hoboken didn't typically see the fruits of its corrupt labor. It was a source, not a sink, of the business. The glitter and glamour on the front end of mob life was as far removed from everyday reality in Hoboken as Hollywood Boulevard was to Washington Street, and having Florie around was really the closest thing to having a movie star living with us. He was well known and respected, and his celebrity status raised our own status somewhat in the community. The kids at school knew that I had mob connections at my house now, and it did wonders for my self-esteem. A New York mobster in the house had serious cache for a twelve-year-old.

His connections were certainly no secret, and his immediate reinstatement upon his return made it clear that Florie intended to be back in the game full-time. The mystery at the time lay in the actual source of his income once he returned. The rumors abounded. Some in the family figured that Florie had taken the rap for the ferry heist six years earlier and was now collecting his generous payoffs. Others believed the payoff stuff was a smoke screen Florie put up because he didn't want anyone to know that he was back in the business, as obvious as it may have been. We were curious, but knew well enough not to ask.

Florie and the pals he'd bring home were well trained in the delicate art of pulling the see-through wool over our eyes. It was easy enough to assume they were doing quite well for themselves in the trucking and garment industries while dabbling on the side as landscape artists. That would explain the shovel Florie kept in his trunk. These businessmen were dedicated to their trades, and if there was ever a lawn that needed some tending, God help them if they weren't the first ones on the job, and the best dressed gardeners that money could buy. And really, how brilliant that they all shared a quirky taste for deer hunting in the woods off the brand-new turnpike after sunset, and late-night fishing under the Pulaski Skyway. No wonder they got along so well. I mean, if you're ever going to have a chance of catching anything in the Hackensack River, it's got to be late at night, right? Nah, we knew better, but nobody ever mentioned it in the house—*ever*. It was an implied understanding, on both our parts. I may have thought I knew what he did, and I may have been right, but I didn't know that for sure, and I would never have been able to prove it in a court of law. Every one of us was a potential material witness, and by not discussing his business he was protecting us as much as he was protecting himself.

I learned all this quickly, with an exercise in tapped-phone etiquette thrown in. Mommy sat down with me one day to explain that our telephone was tapped " 'cause they're keeping an eye on Cousin Florie, those bastards that wanna take him away again." Oh, those bastards. You could actually hear a clicking sound every time a call connected, so I don't think she was just being paranoid, for once. My cousin had "done nothing wrong," of course, but I wasn't to speak about him over the phone anyway. He lived here and worked with his cousins in Fort Lee, and that's all there was to say about it.

I never knew for a fact that Florie had killed anyone himself, but I certainly thought about it a lot. I have a feeling it was hard to avoid in his business, as busy as he might have been planting violets. I do know that he had trouble sleeping through the night. You couldn't help but hear him moaning in his sleep almost every night. He'd wake himself up every time, along with anyone who hadn't already been woken by the last outburst twenty minutes earlier. His moans became a constant backdrop to the night in the house, as sure as cricket noise must be to folks in the suburbs. It was clear that whatever he was doing during the day was haunting him at night. No prepubescent Peter-Panning high above Hoboken with a moneybag for Florie. If his nightmares were anything as chilling as the sounds he made while he was having them, the ghostly reminders of hidden demons echoing through the living room and creeping ever so determinedly into our bedrooms, I can only pity him. Then again, he was sleeping on the Castro, and that was a nightmare in its own right.

Florie hadn't fallen into his line of work by random coincidence. As a young boy of eighteen, he'd never flipped through the Sunday paper and circled in red the help wanted ad for "GOOD $$, BAD KARMA, WILL TRAIN." There was never a choice in the matter for him. His father ran a mom and pop heroin shop out of their one-bedroom apartment on Mott Street in Little Italy. His father, Joe Isabella, was as striking a physical presence as Florie, I'm told, minus forty or fifty pounds. Apparently, he was awfully fond of his product by the time his first and only son was born. Granted, back in 1911, the junk was still officially legal, though it's doubtful that Daddy Joe's client roster ever included the pharmacists and doctors that were required to prescribe narcotics in those days. In 1923 the U.S. Treasury decided to ban all legal sales of narcotics, causing a serious boom to street business, since addicts became forced to buy from illegal dealers like the Isabella family. As business soared, Daddy Joe needed help, and he enlisted the aid of young Florie.

At twelve, Florie found himself selling the heroin his father was preparing at home. He'd wake up in the morning, eat his breakfast in the kitchen and watch his grandma, uncle and pop cutting the imported smack on the dining room table with cotton stuffed in their noses to avoid inhaling too much of the stuff. Grandpa Joe didn't always wear his cotton. They'd put it in little brown jars topped with corks and pile them on the floor underneath the table. After breakfast, Florie would stuff his own nose with cotton and help Grandma wrap the goods in brown packing paper tied with white string, and then he'd go off and make drops up and down Mott Street, making friends in high and low places along the way and getting to know the charming folks he'd be doing business with for years to come.

By the time the 1924 Heroin Act became law, making the manufacture and possession of heroin illegal, Florie's criminal fate had been sealed. He was a teenage local pro and had established a solid reputation in Little Italy and Chinatown. Joe had made enough money by then to buy a small bridal shop on Elizabeth Street in an attempt to go clean, but it was too late to sway young Florie away from the business. He took over for Pop and went into business on his own. Florie's future had already been cultivated on the picturesque opium poppy fields in northern Burma, refined in a makeshift straw-roofed refinery on the outskirts of Shanghai and sold to the ambitious young turks in dimly lit back rooms between Canal and Broome Streets.

He wasn't a made man, but Florie had worked his way up as close as you could get without actually ever getting there. He became tight with Don Vito himself. Vito Genovese had been incarcerated on related federal narcotics violations back in 1957, and Florie had taken care of him in Atlanta. Had Vito been released, Florie would have been made soon after. But he saw it all anyhow, top to bottom. He'd partner up with different guys on and off, and over the years he'd built himself an extensive and quite eclectic crew of associates. His pals would come over to Jackson Street all the time, and I'd hang around watching the wiseguys smoke cigars, drink screwdrivers and shoot the shit with Cousin Florie. I looked up to Florie, and by association, I looked up to his friends. I was captivated. All the guys that he brought home were nice, charming and funny, and they all dressed well. Someday, I'd think to myself, I'm gonna be just like them. I didn't know any better. It was face value for me and I was in awe.

My father Monk volunteered to join the armed forces in World War II at the age of thirty-three. He was the epitome of the greatest generation. He served his country selflessly and wore his honor quietly. Florie was probably locked up in jail at the time. As his own breed of soldier, Florie wore his five-hundred-dollar brand-name suits proudly and his flashy gold rings with everything but modesty. You couldn't have found two more vastly different men on the street. You certainly would've been hard-pressed to find two more different men sharing the same immediate family in the same three-bedroom apartment in the projects. And not to mention, the same leading lady.

Daddy must have known—it was obvious to anyone who knew Mommy well enough—that she had more than a cousin's share of love for Florie. But Monk had had over twenty years now to consider his wife's feelings for her cousin, and all those years must have wrung out any jealousy he ever harbored. He had always seemed calmly resigned to the fact that his wife just didn't adore him as she once may have at those community youth dances years earlier.

Having Florie in the picture was hardly anything new either. The three of them shared a long history. Florie and Mommy were third cousins on the Centrella side. His mother, Lizzie

Isabella, my Grandpa Gus's first cousin, ran the bridal shop on Elizabeth Street. Mommy used to go there all the time as a little girl and would spend hours tagging along with her older cousin as he helped his mother at the shop. Aunt Lizzie was a second mother to Mary after Grandma Mamie died, and years later Mommy would visit Aunt Lizzie every Sunday and take care of her as she grew ill while Florie was locked away.

Monk and Florie went almost as far back. They were the same age and ran in similar circles growing up, and though Florie grew up on Mott Street in Little Italy and Monk on Madison Street in Hoboken, they were good friends. Daddy would spent his weekend days in the 1910s and 1920s with his pals from Hoboken on the streets of Little Italy mixing it up with the local youth. The two communities inevitably overlapped, as Italian-American families tended to be spread between Little Italy and Hoboken, and there were always cousins on the other side to visit.

The three of them remained close all along, through their teenage years, through Monk and Mary's early infatuation, through their bumpy courtship and dysfunctional marriage, through the time me and Maryann came along. Mommy adored Florie through it all.

Between Grandpa Gus, his old-country tradition and Florie's come-and-go lifestyle, with fifteen years of accumulated jail time even before his latest prison term in Atlanta, I don't think Florie and Mommy ever considered marriage an option. But the status quo at 310 Jackson Street was making it pretty clear that Mommy had the whole damn cake in her hand and was eatin' away at it too, and quickly. The current living situation had certainly raised some eyebrows, especially on the Pantoliano side of my world. I never really thought about it, despite the obvious signals. A kid doesn't want to have to process the romantic element of a parent's life in his consciousness, even if he's capable of it. I don't think I was capable of seeing Mommy as being in love with anything besides her little Joey, a good wager and a fresh pack of cigarettes. At least not until it was forced upon me.

A little over a month after Florie showed up, I began to sense a change in the dynamic of the adults around me. It was my first lesson in the laws of gravity: What comes up must come down. After a brief high that came along with the excitement of a new face around the house, with lively dinners and tall tales and a constant stream of relatives coming to welcome Florie back, my parents' mood once again began to sour. The carnival was picking up and moving to a new town, and Mommy was back in the unfortunate habit of shooting the Monk down any chance she could get.

Daddy had always been the one to throw a little salt over any drama she created. Mommy had a knack for encouraging heaviness in the air, and Daddy had a knack for injecting some much needed lightness to counteract it. But the equation had changed, and Florie was around to take care of that now. Daddy was still in recovery, and didn't seem to have the energy to vie for center stage, or even to play a supporting role as he had in the past. Instead, he was receding inward and keeping to himself more than unusual. I don't think his depression had much to do with Mommy's run-of-the-mill aggression or her feelings for Florie. There was more at stake here than Mommy's heart alone. He couldn't have been blind to the way I was hanging out at home more these days for a chance to spend time with Florie when he'd come back from the city. There's no doubt Monk could sense my admiration for Florie.

He would have been the first to admit Florie's unsurpassable charm. He knew better than anyone that Florie's presence was as tangible and striking to those around him as the alligator shoes he wore. He walked into a room and you were usually distracted from whatever had occupied your mind a second earlier. You wanted Florie to notice you because you felt good if he did. You felt good if he liked what you had to say, and you'd choose your words accordingly. Monk was no stranger to this. He'd been friends with him long enough to know the effect Florie could have on a young, impressionable kid like me. He couldn't compete with it. Especially not after the heart attack; it was too physically demanding for Daddy to be playful with me.

Florie himself had developed emphysema from years of smoking three-and-a-half packs a day, but you'd never have known it at the time. He was energetic and entertaining, a stark contrast to Daddy, who was literally just trying to stay alive at that point by keeping diligently to his exercise routine and keeping mostly to himself. He certainly wasn't radiating the vigor that a twelve-year-old feeds off of.

Good or bad, the comparison was there for me to make, however subconsciously I did it. And between Florie and Daddy, and even Mommy for that matter, Florie definitely took the cake. He was the one I was looking forward to seeing every day now. Daddy wasn't ignored, but his silver-haired friend was swiftly eclipsing Daddy's day-to-day role in my life.

Private arguments between Mommy and Daddy were taking place more and more frequently, usually in covert locations in the house, without subtitles to decode the Italian they got carried away in. I have to think that whatever came out of them didn't make the skies any clearer for Daddy. Mommy knew his weakest points, and that's where she always attacked. I'm almost certain any inferiority Daddy may have felt, Mommy amplified, and any fears about his role in this family she solidified as best she could. I could imagine her pitting Monk against Florie with every bill paid in cash and every new shirt I wore, painting the situation with a spin of Discovery Channel basics: A competing male demonstrating more virility and showmanship has entered your territory, Monk, and he's challenging your dominance—as if there was a challenge, Mommy might add. Whatever antics she may have used, Daddy was a smart man, and I'm sure he'd seen the bad moon rising bright as day and smelled the trouble finding its way over to Jackson Street long before Florie's plane landed at JFK.

So he did what any sensible man would do in the situation. He took a vacation.

Some of Daddy's friends, including Patty Prince of the original Hoboken Four (the very first quartet that Sinatra sang with), had been talking about staving off the approaching cold weather and heading down to Florida for three weeks at the end of November. Daddy was hesitant at first. He'd never vacationed apart from the family before. God knows Daddy needed

Mary Centrella, my mommy.

Florio Isabella (Cousin Florie).

Dominick "Monk" Pantoliano, in uniform —my daddy.

Daddy later in life, with a picture of me in the background in the NBC miniseries *From Here to Eternity*, emulating the photograph of my father in uniform when he was younger and off to war.

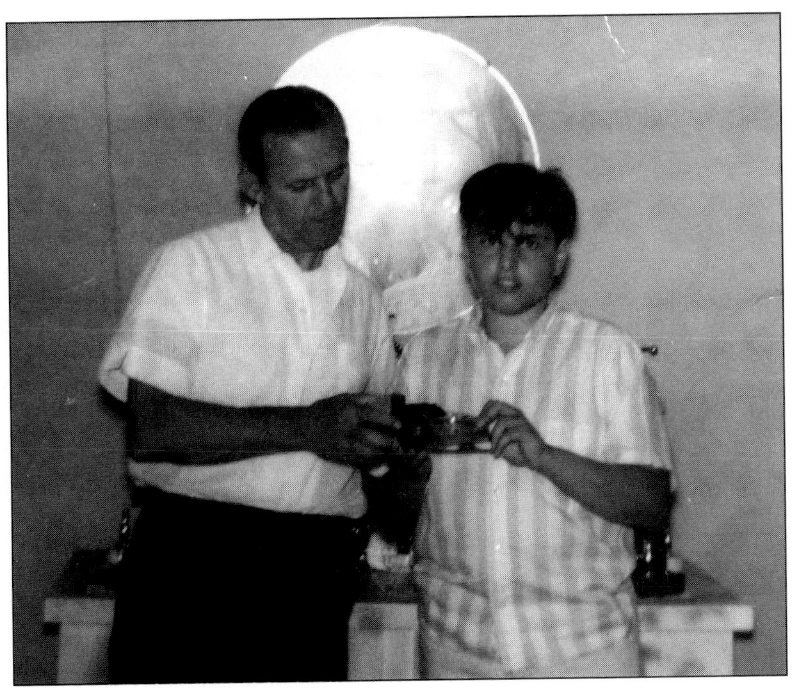

Me with Daddy before Florie came home.

Florie comes home and I begin to lose some weight.

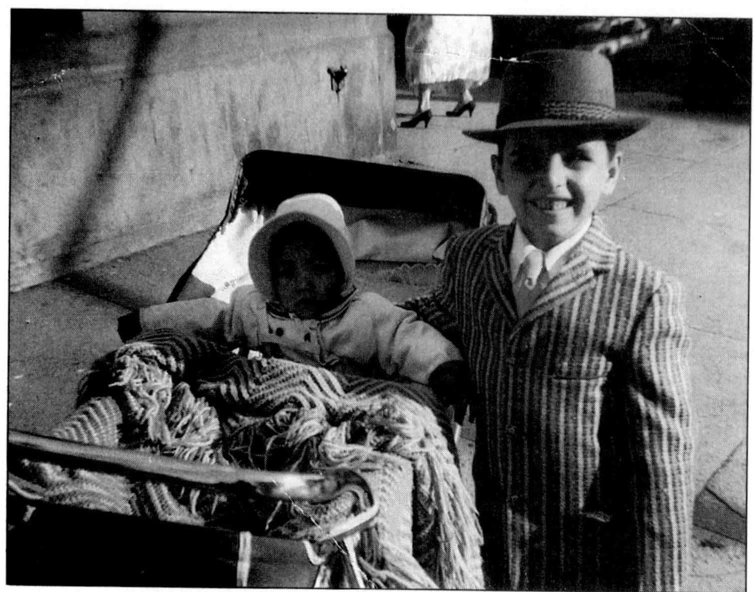

Me with my sister, Maryann, in her baby carriage.

Daddy, Grandpa Pete, and Uncle Popeye.

Me in my four-dollar winter tuxedo—I'm King of the Feast.

Mommy and Uncle Pete, her brother, circa 1921.

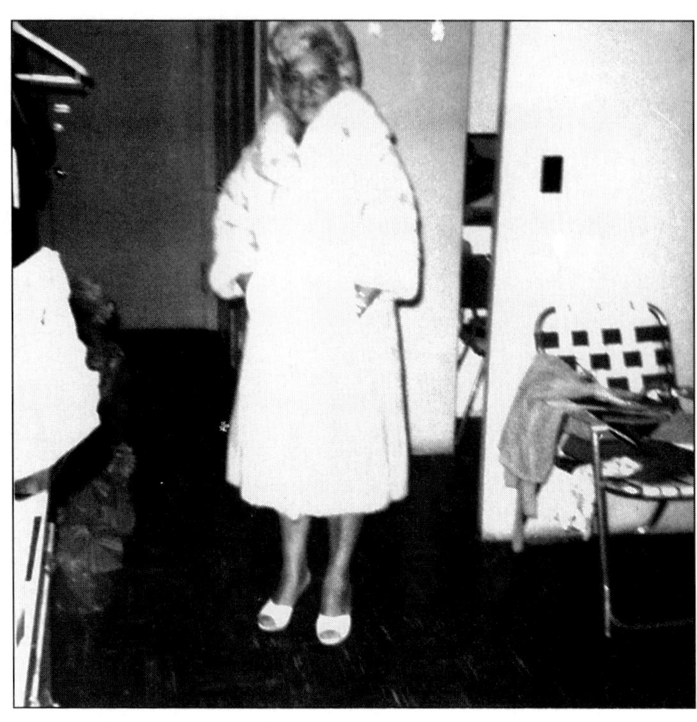

Mommy in the mink coat, a Christmas gift from Florie.

Daddy and Mommy in front of their new TV.

Easter Sunday, how we loved to dress up.

Florie and Mommy, in her favorite turquoise dress, on their way to a wedding.

School dance—1969.

One of the many Sunday family dinners.

a proper vacation. Florie knew too, and he insisted Monk take his pals up on the offer. He even went so far as offering him a thousand bucks to pay for the trip. I don't think Florie had any ulterior motives here involving alone time with Mommy. Florie had been an eyewitness to some of Mommy's worst outbursts over the last several weeks. I think he was afraid she was going to give Daddy another heart attack and kill him. "Get out of here for a little while, Monk," I heard Florie telling him after dinner one night. "It'll be good for you. You need it, pal." It was nothing but an act of kindness out of compassion for an old friend. Monk took him up on the offer.

Daddy left at the crack of dawn on a Wednesday morning. He came into my room and startled me when he sat down on the edge of my bed. "Take care of your mother for me, Joey. I'll miss you." He leaned over and hugged me, and I think I managed to tell Daddy that I loved him before I fell back asleep.

Wednesday afternoon, I scored big after school on the train tracks with Cousin Patty-boy and some kids from the building. We'd hit the Lux soap mother lode. The last time we had come across the Lux car, the neighborhood moms had gone crazy for it. To this day I'll never understand the level of excitement we elicited out of those women for a bar of soap, but we'd been able to charge them supermarket prices and we'd made out big. By the time I left to get groceries with Mommy across the street at Foodtown, I was two dollars and forty-five cents richer and wiped out from the rush any decent train robber must feel after a day's work. Of course, I made the mistake of bragging about my winnings to her just as I was pushing the grocery cart with Maryann in tow over to the checkout line.

"Two dollars and forty-five cents, Joey? Not bad. That'll just about cover it. Hand it over. I gotta check your count." Nice timing, Joey. Florie may have been helping out, but why take his money if she could take mine? Besides, she'd probably spent his cash at bingo already today.

"C'mon, Mommy. You gotta?" This was hard-earned cash after all.

I noticed her lip start to curl up and pull her left nostril up with it as she exhaled from her cigarette. That sneer was a sure sign that something had set her off. I could see the wheels in her head as she got revved up. "It's *your* dinner, Joey. Besides, you can blame your father, that no-good sumanabitch. He left us broke." Ah, of course. The old standard. Some women at the line had overheard and were staring. Mommy blew a stream of smoke their way. "Daddy left us. That no-good rat bastard dirty dog. If it wasn't for Florie saving our lives, we'd be out on the street, you know. You know that, don't you?"

She was my mother, and I was supposed to believe her. But he was my father. Ain't I supposed to trust him too? "Daddy's on a vacation, Florie told me so."

"You know why he left?" She ignored me and continued. "You wanna know why your Daddy left us? 'Cause he thinks that I'm sleeping with Florie, that's why. He thinks your Mommy is a fucking who-wa!"

I noticed the young woman at the cash register staring up at us with a startled look on her face. The woman in the front of the line started coughing. She looked disgusted. Another woman next to us started shaking her head, but I think she was enjoying it, because she was smiling. Mommy was never one to be discreet.

"The truth is Florie's done everything for this fucking family. Your Daddy's never done nothing. Not a goddamn thing. He's a no-good sumanabitch, you hear me?"

Mommy stared at me as if she expected me to say something. I heard her, all right, but I just looked up at her and shrugged my shoulders. I wasn't convinced yet.

"He abandoned us, Joey. He left me with thirty-two cents in my pocket!" The cashier was shaking her head now, and the woman next to us in line seconded her, shaking her head and saying "how could he" as she looked over at Mommy. Mommy was winning them over. But she wasn't going to be satisifed until she got a sign from me that I was with her on this one. And it was working. After all, everyone else was agreeing with Mommy. Except for the lady who'd been in the front of the line—I think I heard her mumble "lunatic" under her breath as she left with her bags. Still, I started to seriously consider that it was Daddy's fault my winnings tonight were being confiscated, and I started shaking my head too.

"If it wasn't for Florie, we'd be begging on the goddamn street like fucking gypsies. They'd have kicked us outta there by now. That Florie's done everything for you kids, and don't you ever forget it! You think Daddy cares about us? That rat-snake bastard. Where is he now? On his way to Florida to bang some five-dollar hookers and with Florie's money no less. What did he ever do for us? Ha?! What?! Nothing, that's what."

The cashier and the woman in line nodded. So did I, and

then I made Mommy proud, topping it off with my own "Sumanabitch." That's right, now I was angry. The master had taught me well.

I had aced the test and it was time to move on to the next lesson. Mommy looked up and took a long, hard drag on her cigarette, and then looked back in my direction and let out a long, high-pressured exhale. The stream of smoke blew right between me and Maryann, and I could imagine little miniature Mommy figurines forming out of the smoky swirls as they left her firecracker-cannon mouth and danced around my head, taunting me with what was coming next. "He ain't your real father, you know."

If she had wanted my attention, she had it tenfold now. My heart dropped to the ground. "What do you mean?" I asked.

Mommy was calmer now. Victorious, really. Her audience was wide-eyed and frozen. "Monk ain't your father," she said, and paused for dramatic effect. She always did that before the clincher. "Florie's your real father." BANG.

I suddenly felt sick to my stomach. First, the stab from the thought that Daddy wasn't my Daddy. If Daddy's not my Daddy, then who the hell's my Daddy? Then, in an instant, the twist of the knot and the guilty pang of excitement. Florio Isabella Superstar. My father? It was too much to handle and I started to tear up. So did the cashier.

Then Mommy looked back at me. "I figured you were old enough to know."

My ears were ringing. As old as you think you are at twelve, I didn't feel old enough anymore, not for that.

Her mission accomplished, Mommy decided to cut me a

break as she approached the register to pay. "Count out fifty cents, honey, and you keep the rest. I'll make you a yummy lasagna and it'll be worth every penny." I wiped my eyes dry with my right hand and reached in my pocket with my left, trying to fight back the urge to cry as I pulled out a handful of change from my spoils.

She took two quarters and the cashier patted my head. "You'll be fine, Joey," the girl said. "Florie sounds like a decent fella." She was trying to make me feel better. I looked up at her and said nothing, too captivated by the tiny men she had standing on either shoulder. That was Daddy on the left; he was dressed in a tight red suit with a pitchfork in his hand and horns on his head. The one over on the right, in the flowing white robe, floating halo and wings, that was Florie. His whiter-than-white teeth sparkled as he winked at me and smiled wide.

"Let's go, Joey," Mommy said.

Florie was still over in New York when we sat to dinner later that night, and it was just Mommy, Maryann and me, and a meat lasagna that would have fed an entire floor of freshly clean Lux-scented project families. I couldn't eat a bite of it.

"Ain't you gonna have any lasagna, honey? C'mon, eat up before it gets too cold."

The lasagna got real cold that night.

I spent days reasoning the whole thing out in my mind. I couldn't think of anything else. I'd sit in class and stare at the chalkboard and watch the words on the board blur and rearrange themselves back into the teacher's perfect cursive handwriting, except now the board read, "Florie is your father."

I'd come home and go straight for my room, lie down on

my bed, stare at the popcorn ceiling and just think. I have blue eyes. Florie has blue eyes. Mommy and Daddy have brown eyes. I'd think, Florie's father's name was Joe too. Joe Isabella. Mommy used to talk about him all the time. She must have named me after him, and she's been lying to me all these years with that whole St. Joseph's load of crap. To think I even get off for school on St. Joseph's Day just so she can keep the lie going. Wow. Maybe Daddy did leave us. Why should he care? I bet he knows too. Maybe he's known this whole time . . .

Mommy had slammed me with a semi truck loaded with doubt of the most piercing kind, and I was left confused and disoriented. I was praying to God to make it all make sense, while I was reveling in my new reality—all at the same time.

Part of me wondered if I might get a hole in my chin like Florie had when I got older.

After having spent five weeks getting to know Florie and becoming comfortable with him, I was suddenly thrown into another period of adjustment. I couldn't look at him in the same way now. He'd talk to me and I'd space out, engrossed in the possibility he was talking to his son. I was even a little embarrassed to be around him. Everything he did and said now had more gravity to it, including what I knew about what he did for a living. Before, it had been a step removed, like he played the role of a gangster on TV but didn't really live that way. Now it was personal and ever so real. Florie was a bona fide tough guy, as real as they get. He probably busted kneecaps for fun and kept a collection of the front teeth he had punched out over the years. Maybe he even glued his dentures together from that collection and that's why they looked so real. I would imagine what he could do to me if I ever got out of line. His very presence now, his charm and his humor, his dashing manner and intense stare, his air of wisdom and insight into the world, his legendary life stories—all of it became even more imposing. I guess I became a little afraid of Florie—no less in awe of him, but a little afraid.

I inevitably began to pay much more attention to his relationship with Mommy. I had never wanted to imagine her being romantic or sexual with Daddy, and I had no easier a time imagining her that way with Florie. But the thought inevitably hung around like a bad zit every time they were home together, and it made me uncomfortable. Maybe they weren't sleeping together now, but they may have in the past, and even that thought was too much to handle. I tried my damnedest to get that ugly thought out of my head.

Long story short, I was a bit screwed up at the time. Halfway to the halfway house.

Two-and-a-half weeks went by like this. It was Saturday morning a week before Christmas and I was watching *Abbott and Costello Meet Frankenstein* in my mother's bedroom. I heard a knock on the door and then a fumbling of keys. I figured it was Florie; maybe he'd forgotten something on his way to the city. Then I heard Mommy's voice rise to a pitch I hadn't heard since . . . Christ, Daddy's back. Florie had told me that Daddy was supposed to come back on the following Tuesday. I was hoping he wouldn't. I didn't want to see him.

I tiptoed over to the entrance of the hallway to have a peek. Lo and behold, it was Daddy, and the short, stout and chummy

Patty Prince. They looked a lot like Abbott and Costello standing there in front of Mommy at the doorway. I chuckled at the scene, at Abbott and Costello look-alikes shocked to their socks, with nowhere to run as Mommy yelled at them. For a moment I forgot about everything Mommy had told me about Daddy. Daddy had probably offered Patty a sandwich or a cup of coffee upstairs and hadn't anticipated running into Bela Lugosi in drag and on speed. I wanted to run over and hug Daddy. But I just stood there and listened.

"What the hell are you doing here?"

"What are you talking about, Mary?"

"What're you coming early for? You think I'm fucking Florie?"

"What? For Christ's sake, will you stop already?" Daddy's eyebrows were lifted permanently upward and pulled taut as he defended himself against Mary, making the furrows on his forehead look like the ripples in a lake after a speedboat had just ripped by.

"I know what you're thinking," Mommy charged on.

"What? I ain't thinking nothing! Patty decided to drive back a couple of days early. He was my ride."

"I ain't no fool, Monk. I know why you're here. I know about that son of yours in Germany. And I know about all the who-was! You ain't never gonna fool me, Monk! Never!"

Patty took a step back, but didn't leave the scene. He stared at Mary and Monk in turn with his chin down and the look of someone patiently waiting for the punch line. I was waiting for the punch line too. I had heard Mommy's bit about the "who-wa" he supposedly fucked in Germany and the half-brother I supposedly had. (When Ralphie Cifaretto called his girlfriend a "who-wa," he was imitating the way Mommy said it.) That story I had never believed until now. It hit me hard and I ran to the door and yelled out, "Thanks a lot! I hate you for leaving us!" With that, I grabbed the Styrofoam candy cane Christmas decoration hanging on the wall next to the door, slammed Daddy right over the head with it and dashed off to the stairwell. I could hear Daddy as I ran, calling to me, "Joey, come here! Come back, Joey, come back!"

I thought I woulda gotten him good, and he would have fallen to my arms and confessed that I wasn't his son and that in fact he wasn't off to Florida but to West Berlin to live with his other family and that he never meant to hurt me and would I please forgive him and come visit him as soon as I had a chance and he could take me around the Breitscheidplatz and buy me some *kurze hosen* and *kniestrumpf* so I'd fit in with all the German kids.

I didn't know where I was heading, but I knew the courtyard was a good start. I sat down in front of the basketball courts and started to cry. When I noticed a couple of kids heading over to play ball, I picked myself up and went to the Laundromat across the street, where Maryann had been this whole time. When I walked in, she was standing on a plastic chair so she could reach the table where she was folding our clothes. She was adorable and looked so innocent, and I remember wishing we had different parents that day so I wouldn't have to cry in front of her. But I felt the need to tell her the situation. I walked over to her, and wiping the tears from my eyes, I managed to tell her, "You better go home—really bad fight. Go home, Maryann." And then I ran off again, still shaken and crying. I ran, still not exactly sure where I was headed. I just had to run. And before I knew it, I had run right up to Uncle Popeye's building.

"What's up, Joey? You don't look so good."

"Mommy and Daddy are getting a divorce."

"What're you talking about, kid?" he said as he closed the door behind me.

"They're getting divorced." I don't know why I put it that way exactly. But that's what came out.

He put both his hands on my shoulders and leaned down so we were eye to eye. "That ain't ever gonna happen." I could hear Abbott and Costello coming from the TV set in the living room and synchronized chuckles from cousins Beaver and Edward. "C'mon, sit down with the kids and watch some television."

I walked past the kitchen, where Aunt Minnie was feeding baby Louis. "Hey there, Joey. What's wrong?"

"Kid's had a rough day," Uncle Popeye offered.

"Is everything all right . . . with your mother?" Aunt Minnie asked, assuming Mommy had a hand in my mood.

I shook my head. "Nah."

Aunt Minnie exchanged a quick glance with Popeye and then looked over at me and grinned. "You hungry, Joey? I'll make you a sangwich."

"Sure."

I went to sit on the couch with Beaver and Edward, and Popeye joined us a couple of minutes later. He wasn't dog catching on Saturdays, and the four of us watched Chick and Wilbur run from the monsters to the soundtrack of Uncle Popeye's recurring symphony of snorts and cackles, followed without fail by a repeating hack-and-cough crescendo. He was amused, and that was just what I needed to be around. There's nothing more consoling than an amused Pantoliano. I stayed at Uncle Popeye's the entire day.

The sun was setting over Jersey City when I finally left Uncle Popeye's. Mommy had finally tracked me down and was frantic on the phone when she told Aunt Minnie to send me home. As I walked back, I was feeling guilty for slamming Daddy with the candy cane that morning. I think I really wanted to hit Mommy, but I hit him. I always ended up hitting Daddy when I was upset, and he never laid a hand on me. He was so gentle with us, and we always beat him up. Mommy had taught me well, and I was angry at myself for it right now. I started to think about all the possible scenarios for my new life. Me and Maryann might live happily ever after with Florie and Mommy, or Maryann and I might live in cramped quarters with Daddy and his sisters. Of course, I also imagined Florie out of the picture and us living just with Mommy and Daddy again. My heart was split and I was confused. I knew I didn't want Florie to leave, whether or not he was really my father. I had never brought the question up with Mommy after she first dropped the bomb, maybe because the possibility existed that she'd been lying and she'd tell me, and I don't think I wanted to know for sure. Guilt, sadness and anger made me confused. It obviously wasn't just about not knowing what to believe, or not being sure who my real Daddy was. I wasn't sure who I *wanted* my Daddy to be.

When I got back, Mommy yelled at me from her bedroom,

"Come in here, Joey." All of her clothes were laid out on her bed and she was packing a suitcase.

"Where you going, Mommy?"

"Same place you're going, Joey." Ashes from her cigarette were dropping all over her clothes and the bedspread, but she didn't seem to care. She was on overdrive and barely folding her clothes as she stuffed them in her suitcase, hell-bent on breaking a record for speed packing. Apparently I didn't understand just yet. She stopped and turned around. "Don't just stand there, Joey. Grab your suitcase and pack your clothes. We're leaving!"

"What?"

"Just do as I say and hurry up!"

And I did as she said.

Mommy took me and Maryann, and we walked out onto the street with our suitcases in hand as the cold rain turned to snow, walking from Third Street to Fourteenth Street and then across seven blocks to the Fourteenth Street Diner on Park Avenue. We waited in front of the diner for Florie. He was coming to pick us up on his way back from New York. The three of us stood out there with our three suitcases and our soaked coats as the wet snow poured down, and we didn't say a word for the twenty minutes we waited. I think maybe Maryann said she had to pee—that was it. Even Mommy was uncharacteristically silent. I'll bet a box of Fluente's that she felt as guilty as I did as we stood on that corner listening to Nat King Cole urging us over the public address system to have a merry, merry Christmas.

Florie picked us up and we went right back home. So much for packing up all our clothes and lugging our suitcases for eighteen blocks through rain, sleet and snow. Mommy's fine eye for dramatic effect never ceased to hit the mark. Daddy slept at Aunt Rosie and Aunt Dannah's on Sixth Street that night, and the adults made their arrangements the next day. Daddy agreed to move in with his sisters.

It was not until Christmas Eve, five days later, that the reality of Mommy and Daddy's separation finally hit me. Cousin Kelly typically hosted the feast on Christmas Eve, but he felt uncomfortable inviting Mommy over after her ordeal with Monk, so we ended up at Aunt Tilly's for the grand Feast of the Seven Fishes. Only Aunt Tilly, me and Maryann, Mommy and Florie, Uncle Pete and Aunt Louise, cousins Patty-boy, Cosimo, Phillip and the other Mary Ann were there to enjoy the *baccalà*, frutti di mare, *sògliola* with hot peppers and sweet peppers, stuffed clams, fried calamari, shrimp in white wine sauce with linguini and zuppa di pesce. For the first time ever, the Pantoliano side of the family wasn't there. All seven fishes were alone with the Centrellas.

Mommy had a brand-new turquoise dress on and her hair was done up in that lacquered beehive style that made her look something like Audrey Hepburn in *Breakfast at Tiffany's*. She looked beautiful. She seemed younger than her forty-nine years. She had a gleam in her eye that I didn't recognize and was in good humor all through dinner. You could tell she had lost some weight. For anyone older than fifteen in that room, the signs were as clear as Vegas neon, and let me cross myself quickly before I venture to guess that Mommy was being satisfied in ways she hadn't been for years. Either that, or she was in love.

We weren't done feasting when Florie and Mommy got up to say goodbye. I was crushed that they were actually going through with it. She'd arranged for Aunt Tilly to watch over Maryann and me after dinner because they had apparently made better plans for the rest of their evening. I'd been secretly hoping all through dinner that they were going to back out at the last minute and stay with the family. Mommy came over to me and gave me a fat kiss on the cheek and said, "Have fun, honey. Don't stay up too late," and then Florie followed with a pat on the head and a "Merry Christmas" and a twenty-dollar bill stuffed into my pocket. They were off to New York City for a night out with their friends and a midnight show at the Copa. I got to hand it to them—it took some balls to pull that one off in front of the family, on Christmas Eve no less. But off they went, leaving the whole clan in the dining room dead silent for a good seven seconds after the door slammed closed behind the jolly couple, most definitely a record for any Centrella event before or since.

And then the talk came. These were the kind of people that had no problem talking about you to your face; it was the way things were done. But the seven fishes had been met with good cheer despite the news on everyone's mind, and I think everyone had either forgotten about Mommy and Florie's plans or, like me, had expected them not to go through with it. Mommy and Florie hadn't given anyone a chance to bring it up. They left, leaving three-and-a-half species of fish still uneaten on the table and leaving us with our mouths wide open.

Aunt Louise was beside herself, pissed beyond belief that Mommy had "passed over the Monk" after all he'd been through, and livid that she had the gall to throw him out and keep Florie. Tilly chimed in that "You can fool some of the people some of the time, but you can't fool all the people all of the time." I'm not sure what she meant by that, given the situation. Mommy couldn't have fooled a pygmy chimp the way she wore her heart on her sleeve, and she knew it. Still, every adult Centrella at the table joined in ripping on Mommy. It was the first time I had heard anyone talk publicly about the Florie situation, and the first time I had heard anyone talk so poorly about Mommy. Even Uncle Pete, the one Centrella who reminded me more of a fun-loving Pantoliano than some of the real Pantolianos, and who usually stayed away from sticky situations, had his two cents: "It just ain't right. How could she do that in front of the kids? It just ain't right."

Meanwhile they're doing this while my sister and I are sitting at the table, as if we're invisible. It hurt. They kicked the cushy rug of childhood naïveté right out from under me. I knew they were right, and that made it feel that much more terrible. I felt deserted by her; I was angry about her suddenly deciding to live for herself. And I was really angry about what she did to Daddy. In my heart I honestly believed that I would never need Mommy again. I made a Christmas Eve vendetta promise to myself that night, that I would never need her again. It was the first night I slept straight through without yelling for Mommy.

Meanwhile, Mariacella and Florio danced the night away, oblivious to my self-proclaimed coming-of-age moment. They had cocktails at '21,' dancing at the Rainbow Room, the big bad sound of big band swing at the Copa. Florie couldn't have been nearly as graceful as Daddy with the Peabody back in the day, but having Mary around to lead must have made him look halfway decent at least. Lord knows she could swing like the best of them.

Mommy and Florie came to pick us up in the morning. Her beehive hair looked more like a blind bird's nest, and she was still wearing the turquoise dress, only it looked a bit wrinkled under her brand-new mink coat that Florie had recently "acquired" and apparently given to Mommy for Christmas. She looked like a professional prom date. "Jooo-eeey, hon-eeey, give Mommy a kiss. Merry Christmas, my love." Yeah, Merry friggin' Christmas to you too. We went back home and opened up the Christmas presents with Mommy and Florie. Then Daddy showed up at noon and took us to Aunt Rosie's. I spent the rest of Christmas Day with Daddy and Maryann at Aunt Rosie's house. We were officially making the family rounds. Nobody was digging the situation, least of all me and Maryann.

Mommy and Daddy never lived together again. In hindsight, it was the best thing in the world that could have happened to the Monk, and I thank Florie, and Mommy for that matter, every day for forcing the opportunity on him, wittingly or not. I'm convinced it saved his life. They announced their separation to the family on New Year's Eve, but they were never legally separated. In fact, they remained married till death did they part. They had just done away with the whole "to have and to hold" bit.

As March approached, Daddy had made the decision to return to the Sunshine State and settle down there for a while. We had barely seen him over the last two months, and he called and said he wanted to come by Jackson Street to say goodbye to us before he left. By this time, Mommy had insisted I refer to Florie as "Daddy" and I willingly complied. As much as the situation with Monk hurt me, I was still living under a layer of doubt about who was my real Daddy, and I still enjoyed entertaining the possibility that Florie could be the one. At the very least, it made the reality of my present situation much easier to swallow.

I was watching television in Mommy's room, nervously anticipating our scheduled meeting with Daddy—the Monk, that is. It was just the two of us. Mommy had left at eleven-thirty in the morning with Florie, a half hour before Monk was supposed to arrive, telling us, "I don't want to see him." I was genuinely pissed at her, less for her cowardice and more for the fact that she left me to deal with the inevitably uncomfortable situation while she went tomato picking in South Jersey. It was years later that I realized you couldn't pick tomatoes in February in New Jersey.

At 11:57 A.M. we ran down the five flights of stairs to meet Daddy at noon at the Foodtown just across the street from the project building. I was as eager to see Daddy as Maryann was, but as soon as we walked out and I saw him standing in front of the Foodtown in his brown overcoat and hat, I tensed up. He was waving at us, and Maryann let go of my hand, crossed the street and ran into his arms, screaming, "Daddy! Daddy! Daddy!" I watched him pick her up over his head and hug her tightly and kiss her and pet her straight brown hair while I stood perfectly still, one foot on the street, one on the curb. When I saw him start to walk over to me, I tensed up, putting my hands in my pocket and looking straight down. He sensed my hesitation and stopped just before the near curb. "How are you, Daddy?" Daddy liked to call me that.

"I'm good," I answered in my best Lawrence Tierney tough-guy, which I'm sure sounded nowhere near as tough out of a twelve-year-old as I thought it did.

"Come over here."

"No."

"Come on, give your Daddy a hug."

"I don't wanna."

"What's the matter?"

"Nothing."

"Then come over here!"

"No!"

"Why not?"

"You ain't my father!"

I might as well have kicked him in his false teeth. He turned pale and stood motionless and silent and stared into my eyes for what seemed ten minutes but was probably more like half a second. I didn't know what to do, or how to take it back, so I just stared back. I was on the second step of the stairwell, so we stood eye to eye, and he reached out and gave me a backhand across my face. It was so unexpected that I fell to my side and rolled down the last two steps to the ground. He immediately picked me up and held me and started crying. "I'm sorry, Joey, I'm sorry! You okay, Joey? You okay?" I was fine. But that was a moot point. Florie and Mommy happened to be coming up Jackson Street at the very moment Daddy decided to hit me for the first time in my life, and they got a clear view of my reflex dramatic lurch over the bottom steps. Florie jumped on the brake, leaped out of the car and went straight for Daddy. I saw him coming and got in front of Daddy to protect him—it was my natural instinct; I didn't want Florie to hurt my father—but Florie was in such a rage he didn't even notice me and started punching Daddy with me in the middle. They got in a full-on fistfight, and I was catching a lot of the punches because I was literally stuck in between the two of them.

I could hear Maryann start to cry as she backed away from us, and Mommy screaming from the car at the top of her lungs, "Stop it! STOP IT!"

"You son of a bitch! I'll kill you!" Florie was screaming as he threw punch after punch, spit flying out of his mouth.

"Wait! Stop! Stop it! Stop!" Mommy's voice seemed to be getting more distant. But she continued to yell from wherever she was heading.

"What the hell do you think you're doing! He's my son!" Daddy yelled back to Florie as he returned his punches, fists colliding.

"What the hell are you doing, smacking the kid around like that? I'll fucking kill you," Florie yelled.

"He's my fucking son, you understand me?" Daddy yelled back.

"Stop it! STOP IT!"

That's when I noticed she wasn't telling them to stop fighting. Florie had put the car in neutral without thinking about the slight incline on Jackson Street, and the car was rolling at procession speed down Jackson Street with her in the passenger seat. It was Mommy's personal parade, but there were no saints to be found. Instead of waving her hand as she had for the King of the Feast parade, she was raising her fists and screaming, "Stop it, you motherfuckers!" Florie and Daddy noticed just as I did and finally released me from between them. The three of us started racing down Jackson Street toward the car and Mommy while it was passing a group of kids in the playground who were looking on in amazement. We managed to grab the back bumper, but the car was too heavy and it was pulling us with it as it rolled down Jackson Street. I fell for a second, but Daddy held on, while Florie managed to jump headfirst into the front seat. He jammed the brake with his hands and then maneuvered the rest of his body in through the window and around the steering wheel and stopped the car halfway into the intersection of Second Street.

Had Groucho Marx been buying a container of milk at Foodtown, you can bet this would have been his next movie. Meanwhile, Florie was yelling at me in front of my father because I had been trying to protect my father. He was furious. I had done what came naturally to me and now I was caught in the middle of two fatherly instincts. As soon as the car stopped, Mommy started freaking out and insulting Florie, despite the truly heroic save, and Daddy slowly walked back over to where I was picking myself up off the gravel. Maryann ran up to

Daddy and held on to his waist, still sniffling. We walked over to the intersection and stood standing on the corner listening to Mommy blast away at Florie in the car. It was the first time I had heard Mommy get this crazy on him, but I wrote it off as an exception to the norm. She'd just been scared helpless moments ago, after all.

I think Daddy knew better, though. Rodgers and Hammerstein couldn't have written a better libretto for Daddy at that moment than the poetic justice ringing ever so gently in his ears. With his children on either side of him and his eyes closed, he listened to the sound of sweet Mariacella on fire: "Florie, you motherfucking idiot! You sumanabitch, you almost had me killed, goddammit . . ." Her voice reached crescendo and then trailed off into the distance again as Florie drove past us to park the car. Ironically, the sound was terribly comforting.

Daddy never again mentioned what I had said to him earlier. It's as if the episode with Mary and Florie in the car had somehow calmed all his nerves and reassured him that everything was going to be okay, that he still had a son in me despite Mary's attempts to cut him out of the picture. He may have even felt pity for the old friend he was about to leave behind for a while. He knew his wife's abusive manner wasn't an isolated phenomenon directed only at him, but would eventually show its face to any adult male close enough to her in life. For all the novelty of fancy dresses and nightclubs and wads of cash and pu pu platters, the "honeymoon" period was bound to give way to the reality of life with Mommy one of these days. We had just witnessed a sneak peek.

I know for a fact that Daddy still loved Mary despite everything. He adored her quirks, her lively spirit and the near-asphyxiating love she gave to her children, her nieces and nephews and her young cousins. She was adored by them all. And he didn't blame her for the way she was; he had always pitied her for the childhood wounds that would never heal. But he knew damn well that he had had enough for now. Daddy hugged me for a long time before he said goodbye, and I'm sure he could tell by the look in my eyes that I was sorry.

Meanwhile, in the span of less than a minute Daddy had been fighting, running and playing tug-of-war with two thousand pounds of Detroit's finest like the best of them. The doctors later swore he might as well have signed his own death certificate, that it was a miracle he was still around after all that. God was saying, *Thank you, ol' chap, for taking care of my little girl for so many years, but I got a new sucker for the job now. Go along and head south now. You can borrow the keys to that condo I keep on Collins Avenue in North Miami Beach. Job well done, Monk.*

Job well done indeed. Daddy or not.

—7—

1431 Eleventh Street, Fort Lee

Goodbye, Paradise

I have two photographs taken of me in front of the same circular mirror next to our door at 310 Jackson Street. In the first I'm standing next to Daddy just weeks before Florie's return, and in the second I'm standing next to Florie about a year later. The difference is striking. In one year, I had gone from a disheveled Fatty Pants with the confidence of a rudderless dud, with a matching expression on his face, to a trimmed down, bright-eyed kid with his chin up and a fine Oleg Cassini sweater to match his new, polished state of mind. It is the most telling pair of photographs I have collected. They sing the prelude to the rest of my life.

Florie's presence, now a year and a half strong, had made us all seem like things would forever be moving forward, past our poor roots to something better, a place where you could remove all the candles from every room without fear that they'd be needed to illuminate our nights at the next shut-off date. I was finding a hope in Florie that I hadn't gotten from anyone else in my life before. Not only was he going to take care of me, but he was going to show me the way, because he seemed to understand me like Mommy and Daddy couldn't. Mommy had always made me feel special, in the ways only a mother can. Daddy had always shown his unwavering love for me through the toughest times. But what Florie was giving me was something different. Neither Mommy nor Daddy inspired me to strive for something better than the lot in life they'd been given and had handed down to me in turn. With Florie around, I had someone in my life to look up to and emulate, and this instilled a drive and confidence in me that had been lacking before. It wasn't just the new clothes and wads of cash lying around the house, though that certainly helped. It was the new sense of entitlement he gave me. "The world is yours, Joey," he would tell me. Maybe there was something for me out beyond Hoboken's city limits; big things, maybe. But he'd make sure to remind me that I wouldn't find those things by following in his footsteps. "Do as I say, not as I do."

But for the time being, that something would be Fort Lee, New Jersey.

The push out of Hoboken began the Sunday afternoon that Florie brought Maryann and Mommy into New York City with him to visit a partner of his who went by the name "Ralphie." One of the provisions of Florie's parole had been that he was not to leave the state of New Jersey without permission from the parole board. He'd technically been violating his parole with every trip made across state lines to work or play in Manhattan. As they sat down to dinner with Ralphie and his wife and daughter, two plainclothes cops showed up at their door. They'd been monitoring Ralphie for months and were carrying a search warrant. They searched through everything in the house, from Ralphie's box spring to Maryann's plastic baby purse.

I had just gotten through with dinner at Patty-boy's house when I got the frantic phone call from Mommy. Mommy was whispering, a habit she had picked up after eighteen months of having our phone tapped by the FBI. I guess she figured if you whispered they couldn't hear you. "Get the mink coat out of the house now!"

"What's going on?" I asked, automatically in a whisper.

"They're gonna search the house. Just get it out, goddammit!"

I grabbed Patty-boy and we got on the New Jersey Transit #21 bus to Hoboken. I forced him to come because I was afraid of getting jumped while carrying a fifteen-thousand-dollar mink by myself. When we got to 310 Jackson, we got the mink and stuffed it in a Foodtown paper bag, then we covered the bag with cereal boxes and soup cans to hide the coat. We managed to get the coat to Aunt Tilly's in Cliffside, putting it up in her attic for safekeeping, away from federal hands.

Meanwhile, upon searching Ralphie's bedroom, the detectives came upon half of a joint that Ralphie had smoked before his guests arrived. Being with a known felon in the presence of an illegal substance, in addition to being on the wrong side of the Hudson River without prior permission, was enough to get Florie on a triple violation of parole. "Looks like Atlanta's getting their favorite librarian back," one cop said as they cuffed

Florie and Mommy and placed Maryann's baby purse in a plastic bag for possible evidence. Florie had about seven years left on his original sentence, and he would have probably served them out had it not been for the stash of one hundred hundred-dollar bills Ralphie kept in the kitchen, inside a package of Domino fine granulated sugar. They were able to cut a deal with the two detectives. Five thousand dollars sweet cold cash for each of them and no handcuffs or jail time for everyone else. And Maryann got her purse back.

When the detectives finally left, Florie and Ralphie shared a long sigh of relief and a bout of nervous laughter, but Mommy kept uncharacteristically silent. Flushed and shaken, she turned to Florie and spoke as calmly as she could. "I'd rather be broke than live like this, so either you get out of this life, or get the fuck out of ours."

Florie attributed Mommy's ultimatum to her frazzled nerves and hurried her and Maryann out of Ralphie's and back to Hoboken before any other words could be shared in Ralphie's presence. I don't think Florie ever expected to hear that from her, considering her family had benefited the most from his lifestyle. I don't think Mommy ever expected to hear that come out of her mouth either.

Florie was no spring chicken, and he knew he was pushing into his fifties and that the next jail cell he landed in might be the last room he'd ever occupy. Not only that, but he had a lot more to lose now than just his freedom. For the first time, he had the family he'd always wanted, and he was not eager to deny himself that. The pinch that never came about marked a change in the dynamic of Mommy and Florie's relationship and hinted at the promise of a new and unprecedented chapter in Florie's life. He would abide by Mommy's ultimatum and extricate himself from the life. But not before he could find a way to keep the cash rolling.

Florie turned to his cousins in Fort Lee, the Tropeas, to seek their help in getting into a legitimate business. The Tropeas were hardworking Italian-Americans of means. Uncle Sal Tropea owned the most prominent gas station in Fort Lee, a Texaco station on Palisades Avenue just off the George Washington Bridge. The Tropeas had done well in the gas station business, several notches in the Ben Franklin food chain above my aunts and uncles in Hoboken. They owned their homes and they owned their second homes. They drove new cars and they had boats and second boats. Florie decided he was going to take most of the money he had saved up, quite literally in his mattress, and invest it in a gas station in Fort Lee—as soon as he was ready.

In the meantime, Florie moved us out of the projects and into the "burbs" of Fort Lee, at 1431 Eleventh Street, which was a two-bedroom apartment in a big two-family brick house on a newly developed block. It was like a mansion to us, on a tree-lined street in a neighborhood that actually had a tennis court. Move over, Cleavers, the Pantolianos are coming to town.

Florie took Mommy furniture shopping in lower Manhattan, on the Bowery, and spent ten thousand dollars cash in one day. Ten thousand 1966 dollars, mind you. He told Mommy to pick out anything she wanted. She picked out everything she wanted, covering every room in the house with Spanish-Mediterranean style furnishings. In the living room, we had a long velvet couch with gold trimming and red velvet matching chairs covered in see-through plastic. We had a series of ultimately gaudy gold lamps held by large naked women, with all the frills you'd find today in a country flea market. The dining room got a Spanish-made oak table with fancy scrolled legs and eight matching chairs. Above the table hung an Italian glass chandelier with an aquatint that Mommy had always dreamt of having. A glass-top table painted in gold leaf would finally replace the fold-up card table for the nightly games. Her bedroom was a white antique set with frilly painted flowers. Maryann was sleeping on a canopy bed. Everybody seemed to luck out furniture-wise except for me. Once again, I was stuck on the couch. At least this time it was velvet.

As far as our furniture was concerned, we fit in perfectly well with upper-class Fort Lee life. That was about the extent of that comparison.

The Tropeas became an ever-present extension of our family, as if we had suddenly acquired an entire new branch of our extended family without the formalities of a wedding involved. We had moved into Fort Lee in July 1966 and immediately began visiting the Tropeas down at the Jersey shore for weekends in Ortley Beach. Summers with the Tropeas were markedly different from what I'd been used to in Long Branch, from the fancy bottles of Rolling Rock and Heineken replacing the cans of Schlitz the adults were drinking, to the water-skiing that replaced mosquitos-repellant surfing.

Florie rented us a bungalow at the Lucky K, across the street from Uncle Sal and Aunt Mary Tropea's place. While we had a dock on the lagoon behind our bungalow large enough to park a boat, we were missing the actual boat. But we spent most of our time on the Tropea boat, fishing around the inlets on Barnacle Bay and riding, while being pulled by the dinghy, on big inner tubes that Uncle Sal would bring from his gas station. Ortley Beach was on the "A" side of Seaside Heights on Barnacle Bay and was thus considered upper middle-class. Long Branch was out.

Patty DeRiso used to come down to the shore with me a lot. As crazy as I was about Florie, I'm not sure Patty-boy felt he was all that special. He used to stand up to Florie's disciplinary talk more than I'd seen anyone do. Florie didn't seem too happy about not having a fan in his son's best friend. One day he grabbed him by the arm and said to him, "Listen, you little prick. You're gonna learn to respect me whether you like me or not!" And Patty-boy learned, quickly I might add, to at least act like he respected him. In the end, Patty-boy warmed up to Florie and would love him as much as I did.

The two of us were clowning around, and we went into a storage bin that belonged to the owners of the house we were renting. We found a couple of sets of boxing gloves, and we were in the backyard by the lagoon shadowboxing. Florie had come back from the city and came out and watched us. He started laughing. "What the hell are you guys doing? You wanna be boxers now? Come on, I'll show you how to box." Over the next couple of days Florie decided he was going to train me, and he began teaching me the moves.

After a long afternoon of teaching in the sun, Florie absentmindedly walked right through the plate glass patio door at Uncle Sal's place. Even though he could have gotten killed, he only walked away with a bunch of scratches and razor-sharp cuts on his nose and cheeks. He was sober, and it had just been a mixture of exhaustion and, we joked, maybe the fact that we never had glass patio doors in the projects.

His face was a bit sore from the incident, and he kept warning me to be careful and not go near his face when we would box during the following days. I tried to hit him anywhere else—in the gut or in the chest—as we would spar and he would give me pointers.

In the course of the training, I started getting better and better. So he said we should go a round and really see how good I was. "Start throwing jabs and try to catch me," Florie said.

We started sparring and Florie was throwing little jabs at me. He was encouraging me to try my best to get him. At one crucial point he let his guard down. I saw an opening and just instinctively went for it. To my horror, I hit him directly on the nose. It opened up his wounds and blood spurted out of his nose instantly. As I opened my mouth to apologize, he started yelling and punching me. He had gloves on, so it wasn't dangerous, but his temper scared me more than anything else. As he was punching me, he was saying, "What did I tell you? What did I tell you?"

I was so startled I fell spread-eagle right into the lagoon. The water was only about four feet. My sister was laughing, but Mommy came out of the house right as I fell, and she went over and got nose to nose with Florie.

She was yelling, "You trying to kill him? Stop it, Florie!"

Mommy fished me out and dried me off. Florie came over to me and said he was sorry, but that he had lost his temper. "There's a certain amount of trust that's involved in sparring," he said, "and I told you not to hit me in the nose."

It was always an adventure when Florie's rarely seen temper crept to the surface, and it was a reminder of his limits. As much of a father as he was to me, there were limits that he had established throughout his life, and I needed to stay on the safe side of them. With both my mother and Florie, there was always a climate to test, before you knew what to push and how far. Needless to say, I have used that barometer I developed in my childhood throughout my life to keep me out of trouble. The larger-than-life tempers of my mother and stepfather honed my acting skills on a regular basis.

When Florie let me go shark hunting with him two weeks later, I knew I'd been officially forgiven. It was the first time I really felt like a man and not a kid. Mommy didn't want me to go, but I begged her.

Florie took Mommy aside and told her he thought I was man enough and that she should let me go out with the other men. It was the first time that Florie told Mommy that I was "man enough" to do something. I have always appreciated that moment when Florie stepped in. Not only did he stick up for me to Mommy, but he indirectly told me I was a man and that let me know he respected me. It helped me respect myself. I tend to doubt that Daddy would have stuck it out against Mommy's wishes.

On the shark trip there was me and all of Florie's friends, Uncle Sal Tropea, Sal's three kids—Ronnie, Johnnie and Bobby—Sal's brother Sonny, Sonny's son Joey and Cousin Curly "The Jeweler." We all rented a big fishing boat with a captain and crew and went about three miles out to sea. Even though we were supposed to be "fishing," a lot of the men brought rifles and guns. When I asked what else they used the guns for, most of them said for deer hunting in the wintertime. Cousin Bobby was unique in the group because he brought the bow and arrow he used to hunt with.

For lunch everyone had packed big submarine sandwiches and several cases of beer in huge coolers. The captain didn't have enough water for all the people on the boat. It was understood that you were supposed to bring your own. Our group, not being typical shark hunters, or fishermen for that matter, hadn't really thought it would be necessary to bring water of their own to drink. So for the entire trip we were all drinking beer and eating hero sandwiches. I was excited about drinking beer with the men. There were a few things that didn't live up to the fantasy we had had about shark fishing. Not only was everyone completely dehydrated, but I don't think we ever counted on the amount of time it would take us to get out to the sharks. It took us about three hours just to get out to the designated fishing area. By that time we were all feeling drunk and sick, and had terrible sunburns.

When we finally arrived, the crew on the boat and a bunch of us kids threw ground-up fish carcasses and guts into the water to attract the sharks. It was truly disgusting. After the dead fish and blood stewed in the waves for a half an hour or so, everyone began dropping lines into the water.

It took a while, and as any true fisherman knows, patience is the key. However, as novice fishermen, we did not know this, and we soon became bored while waiting. Some of the men with guns started shooting at the seagulls that were ducking down to the deck in hopes of landing a crust of our old sandwiches. The majority of the landlubbers had no clue what to do with themselves out on the water.

An hour and a few dead seagulls later, Florie, Uncle Sal and Bobby caught two or three sharks, seven-footers. The captain brought one of the sharks to the side of the deck and said, "Stand back." As soon as everyone had done so, all of the guns began firing at the poor shark. For a long time its mangled body flopped around the deck, until it became still. By the time everyone stopped shooting, the fish had nineteen holes. Finally, they put him in a box. With an amused expression, the captain gave me a hunting knife and told me I could try to skin it. It was extremely difficult to even pierce his skin; it felt like sandpaper.

The day had begun as beautiful with clear skies, but as it progressed, the waters became rougher and a storm was rolling in. The rougher the waters, the more unsteady the boat became. Ronnie and Joe Tropea, who were seventeen and eighteen at the time, started getting seasick, and everybody started laughing at them. Florie was teasing them for being sick. About ten minutes later, he had to join them as they leaned over the rail. All three were sick and green. I would have to say the highlight came when Florie puked out his top denture into the water.

One of the crew saw the denture floating in the water and was able to catch it with a net. Florie was too sick to be grateful.

He went to lie down, and I began to tease him exactly the way he had been teasing his two cousins. He got so mad he started trying to grab me, saying things like "You little son of a bitch if I catch you I'll feed you to the fucking sharks." I was definitely over the limit.

Uncle Sal finally saw the breaking point in Florie's temper and said, "Leave him alone, that's enough." Florie's bad temper could have had all sorts of unsettling ramifications. Luckily for me, he shifted his attention away from me and started trying to finagle his way off the boat and onto shore.

As he held his stomach and struggled up the deck, Florie headed toward the captain of the ship. His approach was generous at first. He offered the captain five hundred dollars cash to turn the boat around and take it back to shore early. The captain refused the offer and said their time wasn't up yet and there were other people on the boat who had paid their money to fish. So Florie, desperately sick and pissed off, resorted to habit. He put his rifle to the captain's throat and said, "You take us back or I'll blow your fucking head off." Ah yes, the only true, foolproof form of persuasion Florie knew.

It was effective. The captain turned the boat around and we went back.

Even as Florie was trying to get out of the life, he didn't really understand how to function without his wiseguy survival skills. Florie hadn't been back into New York since the near-pinch at Ralphie's, but he still had forty thousand dollars left after the furniture shopping spree on the Bowery. That was more than enough to buy a gas station, and would leave plenty to spare for maintaining the lifestyle we were slowly becoming accustomed to. In those days, a single-family home with a view of Manhattan went for seventeen thousand dollars, so forty thousand dollars was a lot of cash to have lying around. Florie couldn't put the money in the bank, because men like him couldn't use banks. There was an inherent mistrust of organized financial institutions. Banks were for the stealing of money, not the storing of it. There was also the issue of having a legal record of his financial property, and the absence of any legal means with which he had obtained that property. He didn't want to leave the cash in the apartment in Fort Lee where someone might break in and steal it while we were away at the shore. So he took the cash wherever he went, including Ortley Beach. He kept it stuffed between the box spring and the mattress at the Lucky K.

After dinner one evening, Mommy and Florie were taking a nap in their bed before a poker game at the Tropeas' across the street. Mommy and Florie would often sit and smoke cigarettes in bed together in the morning when they'd wake up, in the afternoon after a nap and in the evening after dinner and before bedtime. Cigarettes were an integral part of their lifestyle. As they woke up and got ready for the card game, they put out their cigarettes in an ashtray sitting atop the bedspread. When they got up, a lightly smoldering cigarette butt was knocked onto the bedspread. They were just sitting down to a card game at the Tropeas' when Maryann came screaming from the bungalow. "Fire! Fire in Mommy's room!"

Florie jumped up from the table and yelled, "Holy shit!" Everybody jolted out the door and started running across the street, but Florie insisted, "Don't worry, I got it, I got it." The forty thousand dollars cash under the bed was his little secret and quite likely on its way to becoming his charred secret. The last thing he wanted was for anyone to know about his money. Everyone stood on the lawn as Florie rushed in and instructed me to stand by, near the hallway.

The bedroom was full of smoke, but it was still a little source fire. He held the mattress up and stuck his hand beneath it to feel around for the money. The coils from the box spring were red hot and he kept branding his hand and yelling with pain. Finally he found the money. He began desperately grabbing wad after wad of unprotected hundred-dollar bills wrapped in paper bands and throwing them into the midst of the hellish, smoky atmosphere in the hallway, eight, nine, ten at a time. I was stationed in the hallway to catch the money and stuff it in a bag. Once he'd saved it all, he was able to put the fire out by throwing pans of water onto the bed. We wound up buying a used replacement bed with some of the salvaged money. Rather than break his and Mommy's habit of smoking in bed, Florie just began to leave the cash in the suitcase he'd transported it in.

Even though his cash was intact, there were still no gas station purchases in the works by the time the summer was over. It was time to start the ninth grade at Fort Lee High.

I was fourteen and in a new school. I didn't mind it, even though I was the new kid. The first thing I had to do was refurbish my image. When I lived in Hoboken, I was considered a fat, overweight goofy kid. But when I moved to Fort Lee, I created the Hoboken tough-guy image, because everybody knew about the reputation of Hoboken. It was a change from my old reputation that had been partially based on the Rabies fight. I knew for a fact that I didn't want Mommy fighting my battles now.

I created a new image, and Florie was right behind me on it. He was always showing me the ropes and teaching me how to stand up for myself. He said he was going to make a man out of me yet, even if it killed him. Always a man of his word, he got a little carried away after one of my first fights at school.

Because I was the new kid, I became the target of a particularly serious bully in school. His name was Steve and he hated that I was new but already perceived as the Hoboken tough guy. One day he started picking on me and I was trying my hardest not to react. I tried to charm him, reverting to my old Hoboken ways, while avoiding confrontation. But he was so relentless in his taunting that I finally gave up and took a shot at him right there in the school hallway in between classes. Steve pushed me back and slammed me up against the lockers. A teacher suddenly materialized and broke up the fight.

Between notes in class and messengers, we made a plan that we were going to meet up after school to finish up what we'd started. For extra "insurance," Ronnie and Joey Tropea gave me their senior class rings to wear so I could inflict major damage if necessary. I was ready.

The school bell rang and served as the fight bell. There was a lot of excitement that the new kid was going to be in a fight, and by the end of the day half the school had gathered in the schoolyard. Steve and I immediately started whaling on each other. The kids were surrounding us, cheering and jeering us on. I took everything I had and used Florie's boxing instruction to take a strong first hit at Steve. It was the same punch I'd got Florie's nose with. To my surprise, I caught Steve, accidentally, across the bridge of his nose with the ring.

I had broken his nose. I knew it. I heard it break, and blood spewed from his face. Within a few minutes it was all over both of us. We were both terrified, and ran like hell in opposite directions.

After my amazing victory, I was walking with my cousins, headed for home. They were patting me on the back and telling me what a great fighter I was. I was on top of the world. Out of the blue, Florie pulled up in the used Dodge Dart he'd just bought. He always picked me up from school, and when I wasn't waiting at the usual meeting place, he had started driving in the direction of home looking for me.

He saw the blood all over my shirt and freaked out. "What the hell happened to you?"

"Nothing," I said.

"Don't lie to me. What happened?"

"I got into a fight."

"Who did that to you?"

I said, "No no no. I caught him in the nose. It's his blood."

"Don't lie to me," Florie said.

Ronnie interjected, "Joey won," but Florie was angry and was letting his worst fears take over. Without listening to the cousins, he had reached over into the backseat of the car and pulled out a golf club that he always kept there, along with a tire iron "in case of an emergency."

He jumped out of the car and forced the club into my fist and told me to go back there and "bash in the fucking head of whatever fuck did this to you. I wanna see this kid's head on the end of this club."

"But, but, but . . . Joey won!" Ronnie and Joey kept chiming in to my defense.

"Don't tell me he won. Look at him! He's got blood all over his shirt." Florie turned back to me. "Now take this club, Joey, and go back and finish the job. I swear, if you don't do it right now, I'll bury this club in your head myself!" He was beside himself with anger that anyone would inflict harm on me—and that I would let it happen.

I was still absorbing the true outcome of the fight. I couldn't even speak as my cousins continued to argue with Florie. "It's true, Florie, Joey won! That blood ain't Joey's, it's the other guy's!"

"Is that true, Joey?" Florie asked me, and looked me dead in the eye.

All I could do was nod my head "yes" and mumble "Uh-huh."

With that, he dropped the golf club to the ground, smiled and clasped his hands gently around my bloodstained red cheeks and kissed my forehead. I had been initiated into Florie's standards of manhood.

"Get in the car, Joey. Let's go home and find us something

to eat. Atta boy, Joey. I'm proud of you, kid. I'm proud of you."

Despite my blooming reputation as a tough guy, the transition to suburban life wasn't seamless. Mommy was already saying she couldn't stand the noise of the birds and the "fucking crickets," and the sound of the trees blowing in the wind was driving her crazy. She would never get used to them. She was actually happy when winter came, because the crickets were not around.

That winter, I got a job at my Uncle Sonny and Cousin Bobby's gas station pumping gas and changing tires. They paid me a buck an hour. That year gasoline was thirty-three cents a gallon and the car wash cost twenty cents. I worked across the street from the Horizon high rise, the most prestigious high-rise in Fort Lee. Tommy Eboli lived there, also known as Tommy Ryan. He was the big of the big, the *capo de capi*; the boss of the Genovese crime family. He had succeeded Vito, Florie's previous roommate from Atlanta. Tommy had a brother, Pat, who also lived at the Horizon. I went to school with Pat's son Tommy Jr., who visited the gas station frequently.

Because of the proximity of it all and my acquaintance with Tommy Jr., I was exposed to what a real big-shot gangster was like. It was fascinating for me because, in a way, it added to the hazy puzzle of information I had formed about Florie's life in the business. When Tommy Ryan drove into the gas station in his new car of the week, everybody would whisper with excitement. Everyone jumped to offer any type of help imaginable. He was a celebrity to us. At that time, that is what my friends and I understood to be the definition of power. In some way, we were intimidated, no doubt, but we also thought we might aspire to that kind of power and success.

Even though that power was also finite, as we would learn. Tommy was shot to death while we were at a wedding in Hoboken. We knew immediately because there were a couple of known wiseguys at the wedding. Florie and I were at the bar, and he said to me, "It's interesting that Tommy's guys are here." He meant people from the Genovese crime family. No one had gone into hiding. To Florie, that meant that Tommy's murder was a sanctioned, prearranged, understood hit agreed to between the crime families. Even though Florie had promised to get out of the life, it surrounded us, and I think this made it much harder for him to figure out a way to become straight and uninvolved.

As part of his mission to make a man out of me, the wiseguy way, Florie began taking me on his trips into Manhattan when they resumed later that year, regardless of his parole restrictions. Me and Patty-boy got our hair cut, our nails manicured and our shoes shined in Manhattan. Patty-boy was like the brother I never had. Of all my cousins, he was the one I was closest to, and we had plans to travel around the country together when we were twenty-one years old. We would argue all of the time. We'd argue until we fell asleep. Then we'd wake up the next morning and be best friends again. We were inseparable.

The barbershop Florie took us to was a fancy place on Seventh Avenue and Fiftieth Street. It was a wiseguy hangout where high profile, big-shot wiseguys would go regularly. Not only did they get certified, wiseguy haircuts and shoeshines, but they could catch up on the latest gossip of who had been made, bumped or was about to be either of the above. Florie always knew at least a couple of guys there at the barbershop. As we walked in, there would always be a few greetings of "Hey, Flo, how are ya?"

"Hey, how are ya?" Florie would answer back in the same tough yet cheery tone, in a way only Florie could do. There was a special station where you'd go and they'd put you in a robe and bend your head back and wash your hair, and then they'd give you a razor cut with a straight-edged razor. Then they'd blow-dry it with that kind of *It Takes a Thief* Robert Wagner look, which was the dry, hairspray-type of a do. In those days, it was all about the hot combs. At the time, the barbershop had so much of an aura about it, between the cool hairstyles and the wiseguys, it made me want to be a barber.

A friend of Florie's stepped up as Florie was about to pay and insisted on paying our whole bill. Florie started to thank him and the wiseguy directed him over to the corner. I found out years later what was said in that conversation. At the time I noticed that Florie was disturbed by the conversation, and I asked him what was wrong. He said, "Nothing." After we left, he was acting strange. He took Patty-boy and me to lunch at Jack Dempsey's and talked about the good old days with the champ himself. Florie's mood was steeped in a regretful nostalgia.

I found out later that the wiseguy warned Florie to stay away from Billy Paradise, because Billy was involved in a business that had not included the right made men and the wrong people had taken offense. Basically, they were giving Billy one more chance to include the right businessmen in his profits by allowing Florie to talk some sense into him. If this wasn't successful, Billy was going to "disappear." I can see now why Florie had such a difficult time leaving the pressures of the business.

Florie was still deeply involved with the life and couldn't quite disentangle himself from certain businesspeople he had always depended on. One partner that he continued to visit was a black guy named Jack. Florie would bring Patty-boy and me to his house often. Despite the connotations the label "professional pimp" may have today, Jack had a beautiful house on Riverside Drive, which was one of the best neighborhoods. Jack was a very good dresser and I looked up to him for that reason. I didn't quite understand what he did for a living. Florie and Jack had been in prison together, and they were extremely close. And he had a beautiful wife who was a prostitute. Her name was Jan and she had beautiful blond hair. When Florie and Jack talked business, I would play with Jan's little French poodle Jay-Jay. I loved it so much she ended up giving it to me one day.

Mommy was always disgusted that we visited Jack and Jan's house. When she would reluctantly accompany us, Mommy would always say to Jan, "Beautiful girl, you're such a beautiful girl. I can't fucking believe . . . What the fuck are you doing? You're so beautiful. What are you doing, being a prostitute? I don't understand this, you could have whoever the fuck you want." I didn't understand what a prostitute was. I always thought Jan was like an angel.

Florie was still hanging with the same people and postponing the final step of getting out of the life by buying a gas station. One day the phone rang on a Sunday morning and it was Cousin Georgie from Brooklyn. He wasn't as chatty as normal and promptly asked, "Joey, where's Florie?"

"He's over in the kitchen."

"Get him on the phone, please." I gave him the phone. I couldn't hear Georgie, but I could see Florie.

Florie had a strange, wary tone. He put his hand to his head and slumped over. "What? Oh God, no, no, no, no," he said, and I saw the color rush out of his face. He couldn't stand up. He just dropped the receiver and sat in the red velvet chair with a listless look on his face for a full minute. After a while, he said to me, "Get me the paper."

I was scared. I had never seen Florie like this. I ran as fast as I could to get the paper and brought back a copy of that day's Sunday *Daily News*. He snatched it and quickly opened it, and there was the headline, "Gangland Shooting," and a black-and-white photograph of Billy Paradise lying in the gutter with his car door open.

Florie just stared at the picture and then turned to me and said, "Joey, get me a drink." I went and poured him a drink. I was numb. I had met Billy more than a few times, and as I poured Florie's drink, I felt a cold chill down my back. In a way, I understood, without completely understanding, the dark possibilities that must surround Florie and his friends on a regular basis. I knew not to ask questions.

Later, I learned that Florie would no longer receive the money he'd been getting for taking the prison rap. The Sunday morning phone call message was clear. It had said: "Don't come into the city no more. It's over."

The choice had been made for him. He was out of the life. It was really over.

—8—

159 Palisade Avenue, Cliffside Park

The American (Day) Dream

Eight months in Fort Lee must have convinced us all that we were ready for bigger and better things, because as soon as an opportunity opened up to move into bigger digs, Florie and Mommy jumped on it. It was a three-bedroom, single-family brick house on Palisade Avenue in nearby Cliffside Park. Within a week of finding it, we had packed up our boxes once again and moved in. The house was brand-new, but more importantly to us, it was a house—the first one we had ever lived in. We were all thrilled. The rent was inexpensive, but you'd never have known from the looks of the place. We'd found an honest-to-goodness great deal, and I got my own bedroom out of it.

The only bad news was that I had to switch schools, and in Cliffside Park, ninth grade was still part of middle school, so it felt like a demotion of sorts. On top of that, I was building a crew at Fort Lee High and hated the thought that I'd eventually be graduating from Cliffside Park with a whole lot of strangers. I was thinking long term, but having just moved into a house, it was inevitable. Houses have a way of unleashing one's long-term perspective like no two-bedroom apartment can.

The guy who rented us the place was an Italian immigrant contractor. He had built the house originally for the Cliffside Park Pintos, whose daughter, Julia, I'd met in the ninth grade that year.

About two weeks after moving in, Julia saw me crossing over to Palisade Avenue to go home, and she ran up to me to tell me I was living at her house.

"What are you talking about?" It was the first I'd heard of it.

"That's our place. My mom and dad are building it. They own it."

Apparently, they were still involved in heavy litigation with the contractor and the house was rightfully still theirs. I went straight home and told Florie. It was the first he'd heard about it too. All the chips fell into place that same afternoon, when the contractor stopped by to let us know that the court had put a lien against him. We had to be out of our dream house in two weeks.

"Excuse me?" Florie was turning pale.

"I got no choice, Mr. Isabella. You have to move out." He looked past Florie's shoulder to a house lined with walls of boxes still unpacked. "Looks like it'll be easy enough for you, eh?"

Florie wasn't in the mood for humor. In the same movement, he picked up a box cutter that had been resting on the gold leaf table and grabbed the back of the contractor's head, pressing the box cutter to his neck. "I want every fucking dime back and you're gonna pay for the move. Right?"

The contractor couldn't get a word out. He just shook his head with his eyeballs fixed downward, staring at the box cutter under his chin.

"Good," Florie said. "Plus two hundred for the trouble you put me through."

Within a week we found a two-bedroom apartment in Fairview, the next town over about four blocks away, and we moved out a week after that. The contractor had been right about the move, though. It was a breeze.

Florie made him buy my bedroom set back too. I hadn't even gotten a chance to rip the "DO NOT REMOVE" tag off the mattress.

—9—

313 Ninth Street, Fairview

The Fairview Boys

I was the new kid on the block again for the third time in under a year, but being stuck at Cliffside Park Middle School despite the move to Fairview was plenty of evidence for me that stability was overrated. The new apartment was on the second floor of a duplex building. Below us lived the landlord, so it was important that we keep our shouting down to at least a humble roar. It was a tall order.

Daddy had been away in Florida for long enough that it had become completely natural for me to refer to Florie as my "stepfather." That's what he'd become to me in my heart anyhow.

Meanwhile, Daddy's life in Florida had given him an opportunity to heal, through a regimen of dancing, good times and plenty of women—three things he happened to be quite good with. The Sunshine State had plenty to offer Daddy, and he ate it up wholeheartedly. He was working as a bartender in the southern tip of Miami Beach, the little American Riviera known best as South Beach today. He'd probably still be alive today, dodging bikini-clad models on Ocean Drive in his walker, had he not made the mistake of having an affair with his boss Victor's wife, a sweet transplanted blond Georgian. The details are unclear, but Daddy had to leave Florida before he could say "thank you, ma'am" and ended up moving back to Hoboken. He took a place in the projects on Marshall Drive and got a job with Failla's Memorial Home, driving a hearse. Within weeks, a woman named Betty moved in with him. She became his long-term girlfriend.

Thanks to his new job, for the last twenty years of his life Daddy wore dead people's clothing. When he would go to their homes to pick up the bodies of deceased men of similar build, he would casually mention to the widow as he placed her husband in a body bag that her dead husband looked like a size 40-regular. Once she'd confirm that, he'd mention the coincidence, and more often than not, the widow would offer her husband's wardrobe without Monk ever having to ask outright. Not that he didn't occasionally. He wore plaid jackets and polka-dot shirts and thick-striped ties of every color, and whether or not they matched each other, they all matched his trusty black hat.

Much as his brother Popeye did with the dead dogs of Hoboken, Monk took liberties in his care for the city's dead humans. Monk and his coworker Bacco were waiting for the embalmer to come treat a corpse one day when they somehow encouraged each other to have a drink while they waited. Their boss, Sye, wasn't around, and neither was anyone else to watch the body, so they decided to take the corpse with them to the bar across the street. The three of them sat in a booth and the waitress came up to take their order.

"What's the matter with your friend over there?" The dead man didn't seem to be enjoying himself, with his head lying low.

"Aw, he's dead drunk. Leave him alone," Daddy replied. They had a couple of rounds, returned to Failla's and watched their drink buddy get ready for his funeral. Leave it to Daddy not to let a little death interfere with a drink and a good time.

I was genuinely happy to have Daddy back in my life on a regular basis. I didn't stop referring to Florie as my "stepfather"; I just felt privileged to have them both around. Besides, Daddy's limo was always good for a ride. On St. Patrick's Day my friends Red Donahue and Mike Gould and I were going to go to the parade in the city. Daddy came to visit me in Fairview. I asked him to drive Mike and me over to Red's house and then drop the three of us off at the Lincoln Tunnel, where we'd catch a bus going across. He agreed and we drove off to pick Red up. Red owed a big sum of money to a guy named Tubby, a big bookie in town, and the rumor was going around that they were going to give him a beating, so Red had been pretty much keeping to his house on the weekends. We decided to take the opportunity of reinforcing his currently heightened paranoia for the sake of our own entertainment, as any good friend would. When we got to Red's house, I got out and went to the door. When he answered, I told him Tubby had sent a guy to get us, that they'd grabbed us on the avenue and made us take them to his house.

"Get the fuck outta here," Red said, not buying a thing that came out of my mouth.

Until Daddy, who had been clueless to the whole plan, rolled the window down and yelled angrily, "Will you get in the fucking car?"

Red stopped smiling. He'd met my father only once and didn't recognize his voice. He looked over at me and shared a quick "Oh, shit" before he took off running down the block thinking he was running for his dear life.

Daddy was very proud of me when I clued him in, and he even joined in and gave Red a little more grief as the hearse crept ominously down the street following him, before we finally took pity on him. Everyone's got their breaking point, and Red wasn't looking so good. We did him a favor in the end, though. He worked double shifts at the A&P and paid Tubby back with interest at the end of the following week.

My whole family embraced life in their own crazy way, and the Pantolianos were particularly adept at finding the quickest route to a song, a prank, a punch line or a pointless celebration. Daddy had a ritual practical joke during wedding celebrations, most of which took place at Romano's on Fourth and Jackson Streets in Hoboken. The dinner hall would be split between the bride's side of the family and the groom's, and depending on your relationship to the couple, it was typical that one or the other half the room was full of out-of-town strangers. During the coffee and cake segment of the evening, Daddy would go over and chat with a group of women. When they weren't looking he'd place the top plate from his false teeth into an unsuspecting guest's coffee cup and walk away to watch from a distance, usually alongside a crowd of eager onlookers, as the woman realized in horror that there were false teeth in her cup.

Once you witnessed Daddy's ritual, you were indoctrinated, and at the next wedding you couldn't wait to see who Monk's next out-of-town victim would be. Daddy didn't mind the persistent taste of coffee in his mouth from countless soakings. He was a dedicated sportsman.

Unlike his brother, Uncle Popeye typically found himself on the butt end of wedding jokes. Actually, it was just one in particular. Everybody in the family knew Popeye loved to sing, and knew he liked to have people's attention while doing it. Of all the Pantolianos, in fact, Popeye was the top ham, and that is saying a lot. Popeye would get drunk and the family would all encourage him to sing. They'd beg him, "Popeye, sing 'Mala Femena.' C'mon, Popeye! Sing, Popeye, please!" And Popeye, without fail, would be warmed by the crowd's insistence and begin his rendition of Jimmy Roselli's song. Every band that played weddings in Hoboken knew the song. At the beginning of his performance you could hear a pin drop, but eventually the hum of the crowd would rise as everyone steadily increased their chatter and chuckle and ignored my uncle the male diva until, like clockwork, Popeye would blow up, throw the microphone down on the floor and scream, "Every time you do this to me, every time!" It was foolproof. Popeye was a trusting soul by nature, and that provided an unlimited source of entertainment for the family. Uncle Popeye always hoped that maybe they meant it this time and perhaps they really did want to hear him sing. Most of them I'm sure did; he had a good voice. But it was much more fun to piss him off and sit back and watch his reaction.

* * *

Just as I began to hit puberty, Mommy began to aim her rage at me. She wasn't showing me the sunny side of her personality as much. From the moment she had seen me walking a girl home from school, she must have realized I was going to be another dirty rat-bastard grown man one day, and instead of "Joey, my Joey" I became more like Mommy's "fucking pain in the ass." She turned on me, and in reaction I turned on her. Part of me felt that she had chosen Florie over me and Daddy because in her eyes we were worthless. I was bent on proving to her that I wasn't worthless, and in some sense, I may still be. (Wait until my therapist reads this.) I realize now that Mommy was just welcoming me to manhood, Italian-American style.

To piss her off, I would carry my schoolbooks in the crook of my arm like a girl. She'd get angry when I'd wear a beret backward, and so I always made sure to wear any hat I had on backward. I've done it ever since. I had originally gotten it from a Mickey Rooney movie where he played a jockey and wore his beret the wrong way around.

As for puberty, the more I wanted girls, the more shy I became around them. It didn't come off that way, though. I was voted both the best dresser and the class flirt. I think I scared the girls I got close to at first because I was too fast. I really didn't date girls through high school. In some way I even feared them, because I was convinced that, as much as I wanted them now, they'd be sure to turn into my mother.

For that reason, I didn't bring girls home all that much. I'm sure subconsciously I didn't want to facilitate the transformation. As Mommy started to become more and more demanding,

I needed more and more diversion. I figured if there were more people around, she'd lay off. My friends liked to play cards, so I'd set Mommy up with a Friday night poker game with my friends George (Tonto), Froggy Gentile, Tommy Warner and Mike Gould. Mommy would charge them all ante. Every time you anted up, it would go to the house to pay for the soda and the food she'd cook up and serve—a food and beverage charge. I'd come home from a night out at one in the morning, and they would still be playing. Those guys loved Mommy because she was a character and could curse like the best of them. No, actually she was probably better. She was one of the boys. She'd rag on the guys and break their balls and they were crazy about her.

In the meantime, I was still working on my tough-guy rep. Every time I had moved into a new neighborhood, there was another clique of friends. When I was hanging out in Fort Lee, there was the Fort Lee clique. On Palisade Avenue there was cousin Patty DeRiso and Rich Pepe, Jerry Carderelli and the Sonalano twins. Then when I moved to Ninth Street and Fairview, I hung out with the John's Pizzeria guys. My m.o. was that I accumulated a lot of acquaintances but just a few friends.

The Fairview Boys had one of the toughest reputations, and we were feared. One of the reasons I probably liked the Fairview Boys the best was that everybody regarded them as the most lethal, technically dangerous tough guys around the neighborhood. That wasn't saying much, though. We had a reputation, but we had no real assets to back it up. But nobody knew that. That's the beauty of public relations. Among the guys were the ones I just mentioned at the card game. There was also Red Donahue, Tommy's brother Robbie Warner, Eddie Prey, Crazy Rizzo, Mike Lachowitz, Sammy Abotti and Joey Fiano.

One Friday night hanging out with the Fairview guys we were drinking in a friend's garage and planning to go to a dance in another town. Upon our arrival in the schoolyard, outside of the school gym, we were inquiring about the action of the evening. What's it like in there? What's the girl:guy ratio? Pretty much all of the essentials. A friendly guy was answering our questions politely and describing the party to us. Out of nowhere, Crazy Rizzo caught him broadside. While the guy was talking, Rizzo decided to piss all over the guy's pants and shoes. The guy was shocked and furious, but alone, so he ran off.

We knew we were looking for trouble, and just in case, I had torn off an aerial antenna from the hood of a car and turned the broken end like a hook and shoved it down my left pant leg. When trouble came calling, my plan was to use it like a whip. In the meantime, I couldn't bend my knee because of the length of the antenna, so I had to walk with a limp. Froggie and I were somewhat plastered.

About forty-five minutes into the dance, the kid that Rizzo peed on showed up with his friends, about half of the Leonia football team. Eddie was holding Froggie and me back from fighting. Froggie was about four-feet-ten-inches tall and weighed about eighty-five pounds soaking wet. He had me in the middle of us, like a sandwich. Eddie was telling the guys, "You don't want any trouble with us. We don't want any problem. Listen, we're sorry. Our friend's an asshole. We just want to have a good time. So let bygones be bygones."

The football team agreed. Eddie let us go, and they let their guard down. With that, Froggie whaled off and gave one of the guys a punch in the head. It turned into a free-for-all on the dance floor. The fight was in full force. In the middle of the floor I hit the ground. A guy jumped on top of me and I was about to protect myself, but the guy was not hitting me. And for the life of me I couldn't figure out why. Finally I rolled out from underneath and discovered it was Froggie, who was out cold on top of me. I was trying to get the antenna out of my pants but I couldn't. It's a good thing I wasn't able to, because I would have had a major weapons charge on my record.

Meantime I picked up Froggie and put him over my shoulder. I tried to carry him out. As I was sneaking out through the basement, two teachers grabbed me by the collar. They pinned me by the arms and they grabbed Froggie and held us for the Leonia police department. The teachers told the cops, "These are two of them." One of the cops grabbed me and Froggie and separated us. He put me in a police car and said, "Wait here."

The cop went back to start picking up other kids, and I stayed in the car waiting. Then I realized that I was not handcuffed and the car was not locked, so I jumped to the other side of the car, opened the door and ran––straight into a fence. I got up and climbed it. I realized as I hit the other side that I could have walked right through the fence; there was a big gate right next to where I had climbed. Now I was by myself and I looked to hail a cab. I couldn't. I finally got a city bus. I wound up safe in Fairview while everybody else got arrested.

Not too long after I had a little trouble with Crazy Rizzo

myself. At John's Pizzeria I was in Florie's car and it was about ten o'clock and I was going home. I was pulling out of John's parking lot and Rizzo was there, in front of Florie's car, holding a cup of Coca-Cola like he might spill it onto the hood of the car. There were a couple of girls in front of John's and he was trying to impress them. Florie always kept his tire iron underneath the seat on the driver's side in case of trouble. So when Rizzo stepped in front of the car with the cola, I was thinking, "If this fucking kid does anything crazy, I got the tire iron."

So I go to him, "What the fuck are you doing, Rizzo?"

And he says, "What do you think?"

"Don't do it, man."

"What are you gonna do about it?" he taunted me.

"C'mon, it's my stepfather's car."

But now he was tiptoeing toward me, and he held the Coca-Cola farther over the hood of the car.

"Rizzo," I yelled, "I swear to Christ don't do it."

He stated laughing and pouring the cola all over the hood of Florie's car.

I jumped out, and he went for me, and I had the tire iron in my hand. We just went at each other like two bulls locking horns, each grabbing the other. He saw the tire iron and tried to wrestle it from my hand, but I hit him in the side with it.

He kept trying to get the tire iron. I knew if he did he was crazy enough to bash my head in. So it became a fight over the tire iron. He bit me underneath my right arm. A crowd arrived, and we wound up on Anderson Avenue, in the middle of the street. Cars started screeching to a stop and traffic was building up. Somebody was trying to break up the fight, and I got put into a headlock. The same guy had me in a headlock with one arm and Rizzo in a headlock with the other. He took the tire iron away from both of us. At this point I realized the guy had only one arm; the other was a stump ending at the elbow. That's the arm he had me in a chokehold with. This guy was strong.

By now the cops were coming. It was a free-for-all and we were trying to run away. Rizzo started taking off down the street. The cops jumped out of a car and grabbed him. I leaped underneath a parked car in front of John's Pizzeria. The cops were breaking everything up looking for me. They finally put Rizzo in the car and took off.

John, of the Pizzeria, who hated Rizzo, took me in the back so that the cops wouldn't find me. I'm back there with his son Dino, who as a young boy had put his hand accidentally in a meat grinder and lost four fingers. Dino would walk around with a sock on his hand. I don't know why he just didn't use a glove. To Dino's chagrin, Rizzo would always tease him about it.

I began to think about Rizzo and how he had been arrested and I wasn't. I started to feel guilty about it, so me and Mike Gould walked down to the Fairview Police Department. It was about four blocks away. I went in and told the cop I was looking for Rizzo, who was sitting there with cuffs on. He looked at me and I looked at him, and I told the cop, "I'm the other guy you're looking for."

The cops kept us there for another half hour or so and then let us go. We go outside, and immediately Rizzo and I finished it. We duked it out fair and square this time, no tire iron involved. We were both so exhausted from the previous fight that it lasted all of two seconds. After which we both drove down to the local hospital to get tetanus shots, since I had opened him up with the tire iron and he'd bit out a chunk of me. That's what friends were for.

Tonto, as my friends and I called him, was a tall, good-looking, half-Cherokee half-German-American. One of the many jobs that Tonto had in the past summers was at an arcade in Palisades Amusement Park. We called him Tonto because he was half-Indian. Tonto was a trusted employee, and so he had all the keys to the jukeboxes and the pinballs and all of the games of chance in the arcade. He showed up one too many times late, and the lady who owned the joint fired him. But he had a copy of the keys made before he had to turn them over. Now in the summer, two or three times a week, he would deal one of us in as the lookout, then go into the arcade through a window at one or two in the morning and empty each coinbox halfway of quarters. If he only took half, his boss would be less likely to notice she was being robbed. It worked. We would get out of there about one hundred dollars in quarters on a good day. The lookout would get a 35 percent cut.

With friends like these, you wouldn't think I had much time or hope for school, but underneath the surface and the chaos, my dreams and hopes began to jell somewhat and take shape. Like Sinatra sang, I was going to "follow my secret heart." I was scared about my inability to read. I knew it would be an impediment in my life. Later on, in my senior year, I would discover I was dyslexic and had a third-grade reading equivalency. I was uneducated and ill-prepared. But I had encouragement. Florie would always tell me if you put your mind to it, you could do anything.

I began to seriously consider acting as a way out of the life I knew. I never mentioned it much; I wouldn't think of it. I wasn't ready to yet. I was embarrassed and felt I might be speaking too soon. But, though my options were limited, I was pretty sure this was something I wanted to do.

One of the Fairview Boys I had an especially dynamic relationship with was Joey Fiano. He was a little spark plug of a kid, all of five feet, eight inches. He had sandy hair and freckles. His father had been born in Italy and started with nothing when he came to New Jersey, but eventually he'd opened a successful little grocery store on Anderson Avenue across from John's Pizzeria.

He was one of my best friends, but having said that, I also had a real good time busting his balls. It was a competitive relationship and it was fun. Fiano had a really short temper that matched his frame. Our relationship was similar to that of Mommy and Daddy's when she would get Daddy all riled up. Like Mommy, I was the instigator. He'd try to keep the peace like Daddy, but he'd always end up blowing his stack, like Daddy would occasionally as well. That's what I loved and that's what Mommy loved too; it was when we knew we had won. That's probably why I had a kinship with Fiano; I got to exercise a relationship I had seen growing up in my house for years. I'd get Joey Fiano until he popped. Once he popped, I had won.

He had a Ford Falcon convertible that we all drove around in. He fancied himself the smartest kid in the group, and he had every right to. He had high SAT scores and was college-bound, unlike the rest of us. And he was very ambitious. The rest of us didn't know what we were doing with the rest of our lives, even though I had a secret but far-fetched hope. But Fiano, he had plans. I never knew what they were, but you knew he had them and was probably every bit capable of achieving them.

Fiano and his father seemed to have the kind of relationship that I had with Mommy and that he had in a friendship way with me. It was very argumentative and abrasive between them. They were too much alike. On the contrary, his mother was quiet and reserved. But the old man was a hardworking Italian who had worked hard to get his citizenship. He spoke broken English and I think that embarrassed Joey. Joey had three younger siblings, a brother and two sisters. One day, out of the blue, his father dropped dead of a heart attack. It was a huge shock to everyone. His mother was completely distraught. She had relied on her husband her whole adult life. A week after burying his father, Joey's mother passed away. This kid had a week earlier been insulated by a middle-class family, and now he was an orphan with three younger siblings to take care of.

Like many seventeen-year-olds, he could be a little self-centered. But he proved otherwise. His aunts and uncles were figuring out what to do with the kids, and Fiano put his foot down. They were his brothers and sisters, he said, and he was going to take care of them.

His dreams of going to college were shattered because he'd have to support his siblings. He began working during the day and attending night school. His youth was taken from him quite overnight, because he chose to raise his sisters and baby brother and take care of them. He felt it was his duty. He had become a man by giving up his youth, and I will never forget his strength of character. I've always thought about his example when faced with difficult choices since. I learned that when you're young and one of your friends' parents dies, that death defies reality as much as it defines it. It makes you sharpen your priorities. Perhaps subconsciously, it made me start focusing a lot more on how I was going to make my own way in the world. Life wasn't always going to be about going out and drinking and getting into fights. Not, at least, if I had half a brain.

In the maelstrom of those adolescent years, even now it's difficult to figure out which pebbles of experience made an especially noticeable dent. But I know that Joey Fiano's experience was one of them. He represented the values of an Italian-American youth whose love for his family overrode his self-interest and became paramount in his life when the need was greatest.

But lest I stray too far from the path of relentless messing around and goofing off, a precious commodity of youth, I'll tell you about going to the first football game of the new season. This was about six months before Fiano's father died, and Fort Lee High was our big rival. We were going to play on their turf in Fort Lee. The football field was down the block from where we lived on Eleventh Street, where Florie used to play tennis.

Fiano's father gave us his fruit truck. We decorated it with the Cliffside Park colors of red and black. We had banners and we had some of the cheerleaders with us too. After the win, we were celebrating and rubbing the victory in everybody's noses down Palisade Avenue in Fort Lee. Some Fort Lee kids in a convertible Camaro pulled up alongside us and started yelling at us and giving us the finger. We were doing the same to them. Crazy Rizzo was drinking from a Coca-Cola bottle, and he threw it at the car. A cop car saw him do it, and they went after us and arrested us. They brought us to the Fort Lee police station and were questioning us. When it was time for the cop to question me, he took me in a little room and said, "What's your name?"

And I answered, "Patty DeRiso."

"Where you from, Pat?"

And I gave him my cousin's address. At that point Patty-boy was living with his sister Mary Ann and her husband, Dominick, and wasn't at the game at all. I didn't think there was any way he could get in trouble. The cop asked for my phone number, and I was trying to think ahead and thought Mary Ann and Dominick should be working, there wouldn't be a problem. There were no answering machines in those days. I gave him my cousin's phone number.

The police finished having their fun with us and were about to let us go when these kids in the Camaro showed up and said they wanted to press charges. Instead, the cops arrested them too.

I forgot to warn Patty-boy, and he got the beating of his life. He had gotten home from work to a slap from his twenty-two-year-old sister.

"What happened?" she asked.

He was clueless.

"You got arrested!" she continued.

"No, I didn't!"

WHACK. "Don't fuckin' lie to me! The cops called and told me you were all fuckin' arrested."

"What the fuck are you talking about?" Patty-boy denied, utterly confused.

WHACK. "Don't you curse at me! You went to the football game?"

"What football game?"

WHACK. And so on and so on that night.

For a long time Patty-boy couldn't understand why he had gotten in trouble; it was a complete mystery to him. I for one never had the balls to tell him. But the strategy worked liked a charm, and from then on any time I got in trouble I'd say I was Patty DeRiso.

Things at the time were tensing up with Florie's money situation. He had completely stalled on the gas station idea, and his prospects for earning money anywhere else seemed to be diminishing. Forty of the original last fifty grand he had made from his previous life had, in six short months, vanished at the track. They could have bought a house, but they never did, for unknown reasons. The potential for high returns on investment at the track was just too tempting. Florie was too passive about finding work in the legitimate world. He never felt it was the right time to take over the gas station because he was probably too afraid he'd run it into the ground. Ultimately, he wasn't making money outside of the criminal life because he simply didn't know how to. He didn't have the same tools to work with. The way Florie saw it, if he couldn't bribe, and he couldn't threaten, and he couldn't get vendors to give away their wares for free in exchange for protection and other lucrative business proposals, what could he do? He didn't know how to run a business that was based solely on that poor sap's game "supply and demand." Economics meant nothing to him. To throw money at the ponies seemed safer than to throw money at three gasoline pumps and hope for the best. And he was too proud to use the Tropeas' experience in the business to help him start his own. It had been his original plan, but he never seemed to be able to follow through with it. It made him feel vulnerable.

It was the end of the month, and we went to the track as a family. For us, going to the track was like going to the theater. It was a big occasion. Mommy and Florie would get all dolled up. They washed the car, and we drove down on a warm Saturday afternoon to the Big A. Florie had gotten a tip on a horse, and he bet the last seven thousand dollars he had. When we went to the track with Florie in the old days, we used to go to the clubhouse, which cost five dollars more. But now there was no clubhousing; we were on the bleachers with general admission.

Florie's investment didn't pan out. His horse came in third. He banged his head against the steel support beam and started blaming God for all his misfortunes. I knew I was witnessing Florie at his all-time lowest.

"JESUS FUCKING CHRIST ON THE MOTHERFUCK-

ING CROSS! YOU COCKSUCKING BOWLEGGED MOTHERFUCKER!" he shouted as he banged his head over and over again.

My own finances, however, happened to be on a nice upswing. I had just landed a job working at Madison Avenue Coiffeurs for Men in Fort Lee. The shop was right across the street from the high school I'd spent six short months of my life in. I was going to Cliffside High, and a buddy of mine, Billy Kanig, was working at the shop as a shine boy. He said he didn't like the hours and was quitting the job. I thought it might be cool to work there, still romanticizing the wiseguy barbershop hangout that Florie had taken me to in the city. Besides, it was good money. So Billy arranged a meeting for me with Carl Caramana, the owner. Caramana had the hottest hairstyling salon in Jersey at the time.

I went to work directly after school. I'd clean up and shine shoes, but I made all my big money on Saturdays and during the summers. On Sundays I would go in and do the windows. My relationship with Carl grew, and he trusted me. He gave me the keys to the salon. Old-school hairstyling was at the top of its game in those years, with the hot comb, the razor cuts and the blow-dries. Pampering yourself at Madison Avenue Coiffeurs was a really chic thing to do.

Carl's father was Hollywood Joe Caramana. He had a barbershop in Paterson, New Jersey. Father and son made hairpieces in the back of both shops. Carl put out a display and started selling goatees and mustaches. All of the rich guys would come in to Madison Avenue from the Horizon House, this high-rise building overlooking Manhattan. I shined Buddy Hackett's shoes and a few other wiseguys', and they were all big tippers. My friends would come on Saturdays, and I would give them facials and hot combs after work. I thoroughly enjoyed it.

I was a shine boy and being trained by Carl to do hair-styling, and I was making $175 a week. Carl would do the hair-styling shows on weekends, and my friends and I would all be hair models. Carl would pay the guys ten bucks, and they'd get a great haircut and a free trip into the city. People would come from the South and take courses on the weekends to learn how to style hair. I'd watch and learn from Carl while he taught these guys how to cut hair. Later on in New York, when I was studying acting, I would go to my friends' houses and cut their hair for five bucks. When I was a shine boy in Fort Lee, becoming a hairstylist was looking very tempting for me. I even came close to enrolling in Charlie Cabibbi's Barber College. What stopped me was the dreaded thought of being on your feet for twelve hours a day.

I hung out with my friends at the Audobon Bar on 186th Street and Amsterdam Avenue. It was a real blood bucket, which means anything could happen there. It was an all-black neighborhood dive bar filled with winos and rummies during the day. It had a great jukebox, playing some of my favorites, like Otis Redding, the Temptations, Arthur Conley, the Four Tops, Diana Ross and Aretha. It was my first introduction to soul. One Saturday after the rest of the shift had left the guys came over to the shop, and I was going to give them hot combs and style them and then we were going to go to the Audubon. A couple of the guys, myself included, didn't have IDs. In those days you needed to be eighteen to drink in the state of New York. At the time I was sixteen. To solve the problem, I borrowed Carl's mustaches and goatees and glued them on to make us look older. We were all lacking in facial hair.

We drove into the city in Fiano's Falcon. The guy at the door saw the beards and figured we were old enough and let us right in. He didn't even charge us a cover. We were having a great time, dancing and singing. My cousin Janice Pantoliano showed up. She was a senior. She saw me and said, "What the fuck are you doing with a mustache?" Before I could explain, she ripped it right off my face and half of it fell to the floor.

We got into a big cursing argument while I was on my hands and knees trying to find the other half of the mustache. I was in big trouble, considering I was underage at a bar with a half a mustache on my face. I found the other half and put it back on, but only kept my profile to the bartender the rest of the night. At the end of the night the guys gave me back their goatees and mustaches and we all went home.

That Sunday I cleaned everything up and put the mustaches and goatees back. There was a two-way hairpiece tape in the display case, so I taped the torn mustache back together. As luck would have it, several days later Carl still had not touched that particular mustache.

Then a customer came in, and Carl took it out to show him and it came apart in his hand. He looked at me and I had a guilty look on my face. Later in the day he asked what had happened to the mustache. I told him I'd borrowed it and related the whole story. He told me he couldn't have that at his shop and that he had to let me go. He fired me. I felt terrible that I'd let him down and lost what had become one of the primary sources of income for my family.

I said farewell to glamour and went straight to the A&P and became a stock boy there.

At this point in school, there were three girls I had major crushes on: Joyce Boganin, Donna Laura and Linda Germer. Linda was a dancer and a real cutie. She was the first girl I ever took on a date to New York. I took her to see *Man of La Mancha*, the first Broadway anything I ever saw. She had dreams of being a Broadway dancer and I had dreams of being a Broadway star. She got to be a Rockette later on. I liked her, but we never really had a relationship. I took Donna Laura and Joyce Boganin on dates too, but my relationships with girls usually didn't last more than eight days, or one or two dates tops. I never had a steady girl in high school and didn't go to my high school prom.

I went down to the shore that summer before my senior year, and there I met Stevie Smith. She was cute and she wasn't like the girls at Cliffside. That's because she wasn't from Cliffside at all. She was from Nutley, New Jersey. I met her down in Seaside Heights. She was looking very WASPy, not that there's anything wrong with that, just ask my wife, Nancy. She had dirty blond hair, pretty blue eyes and freckles. She had my heart going pitter-patter. We'd take long walks on the boardwalk and talk about our favorite movies.

Summer came to an end and school started and the Temptations were coming to the Copa. All of the kids at Cliffside wanted to go see the Temptations and very few of us could get in. There was a guy who handled the cigarette machines at the barbershop when I had worked there. He was half a wiseguy, and he hooked me up for the Copa. He got me two tickets.

Now I had the tickets, but I didn't have a date. I really wanted to go with Stevie, so I called her up out of the blue and invited her, and her mom let her go.

The cigarette machine guy told me to bring a lot of dough to the Copa to take care of these guys. Go right through. Don't get in line, go through the service entrance. Ray Liotta and Lorraine Bracco would use the same entrance years later in *GoodFellas*. I did it first, except with smaller bills. It wasn't quite as smooth as Ray and Lorraine's walk. These guys hit me up for cash every ten or fifteen feet. They'd say "Come with me," I'd hand them a ten, and then they'd hand me right off to the next guy, for another ten. By the time we got to the table, we were almost broke.

We ordered a full-course meal on a tabletop that was the size of a half a dollar. This guy from the cigarette machine had truly delivered. We were right up front. One of the four Temptations sang to us. It was probably good that we couldn't drink since we were minors, considering that at the end of the night we had just enough money to pay the bill. A Chinese waiter screamed at us about "Fifteen percent. No good! Fifteen percent!" right in front of everybody. We didn't give him anything because we had nothing left.

We had no way to get home without cash, so I got my last dime and called Florie up. He said he was on his way.

When he came to pick us up, I could see a longing in his eye as he stared off to the back entrance of the Copa and to a life that was receding farther and farther away from him with each passing destitute day. He asked how it was.

I told him, "It wasn't so great." I lied.

—10—

217 Cliff Street, Cliffside Park

The Great Escape

SCENE: The JP Hair Salon in some nondescript strip mall off of Route 4 near Paramus, New Jersey. Present day. A large middle-aged man of Italian descent has just taken a seat in the barber's chair closest to the door as a young receptionist in his early twenties, with decorative hair and multiple piercings around his face, places a gray smock around him and returns to the front counter. There are three customers seated in the waiting area, while two others are getting worked on by two young female hair stylists in their late twenties, one of Italian descent and one of Puerto Rican descent. Both female stylists can be heard chatting away loudly to their respective customers. A neatly trimmed JOEY PANTS in an obvious jet-black tightly cropped wig approaches the large Italian man. Joey is wearing a smock. He has two gold hoop earrings and a flower-shaped cubic zircon stud in his left ear, and two matching hoops in his right. Several gold rings, one with a large red stone, adorn his fingers on both hands, and a large gold-link bracelet hangs loosely over his right wrist. There are light traces of application on his face.

JOEY: Nice to see you again. So what don't you like about your hair?

CUSTOMER: I dunno. You're Joey Pants, you tell me.

JOEY: All right, well, you got that classic Kennedy look going, but that's getting old, isn't it? I think you're ready for a change, maybe we'll do a nice George Clooney Caesar . . . or if you really wanna turn some heads, I can give you a little midway cut and mess up your hair a bit with some gel on the way out, make you look twenty years younger, like a well-fed Italian Ed Norton, you know what I mean?

CUSTOMER: Nah, actually I have no clue.

JOEY: Ah, you tough guys are all the same. Okay, how short?

CUSTOMER: Shorter than it is now.

JOEY: You want me to cut over the ears, or leave your ears covered?

CUSTOMER: Just leave my ear intact and I'll be happy.

JOEY: I'm just gonna get cutting, then. (*JOEY takes a pair of scissors from their alcohol bath and begins cutting CUSTOMER's hair.*) So I haven't seen you in a while. How's Martha?

CUSTOMER: She left me.

JOEY: Oh, I'm sorry to hear. She was a nice gal. You're better off.

CUSTOMER: Yeah.

JOEY: Well, I don't know about you, but when bad things happen to me, I like to think that there's always a good thing on its way. Like the time I got sent away to prison thirty years ago . . . You know, I used to be a tough guy myself, did you know that?

CUSTOMER: Nah, I didn't. You didn't get psycho on a customer or anythin', didya?

JOEY (*Laughs.*) No, no. I wasn't cutting hair back then. I was hanging with a bad crowd after high school. We ended up robbing the White Castle in Cliffside Park. A shot was fired and it hit the counter guy in the arm. He couldn't flip those bite-sized burgers after that, and they gave me ten years for armed robbery and assault with a deadly weapon. But what I was saying was, I thought my life was over then. As it turned out, my cell mate and I got close, and an uncle of his died some time after I was released on good behavior, and since my buddy was still in the can, he signed over the money to me so the lawyers couldn't get to it. He tells me to hold it for him but to take enough for myself to pay for barber school, 'cause I had always talked about doing that when I got out. So I start going to barber school, and a couple of years later, my buddy's killed in a prison riot and I'm stuck with all his uncle's money. So I opened up this joint and I've been here ever since. It was like a dream come true. You see? And it wouldn't have happened if I hadn't taken the rap for the White Castle mess and gone to jail first. I mean, 'cause I never shot the guy, but I took the blame for it 'cause they had it all wrong and my lawyer—

CUSTOMER: (*Cutting JOEY off.*) That's a nice story, Joe. So you always wanted to cut hair?

JOEY: Not really. It was just the only thing I was good at. I think when I was a kid, I wanted to be an actor.

CUSTOMER: Oh yeah? And what happened with that?

JOEY: Ah, I was no good. I wasn't cut out for that sort of thing. You know, my mother used to laugh at me when I'd tell her I was going to be an actor someday. I guess she was right in the end, God bless her soul. Mothers always know best, don't they? (*Pause.*) Yeah, I'd have to leave Jersey. I could never live out in Los Angeles. I got everything I need right here.

CUSTOMER: I hear a lot of them New York–based actors are movin' out to Connecticut these days. They don't live in Los Angeles anymore.

JOEY: Connecticut shmunecticut.

CUSTOMER: Hey, you know, speakin' of actors, anyone ever told ya you look a lot like that asshole on *The Sopranos*, you know, that Ralphie guy?

JOEY: Yeah, I get that all the time. I really hate that show. (*JOEY turns CUSTOMER around in his chair to face the mirror. JOEY turns to face mirror as well, revealing the head of a red dragon tattooed on the back of his neck, with orange-yellow fire reaching up to the bottom of his hairline. It is obviously the top of a larger tattoo that extends down his back. He applies gel to CUSTOMER's hair.*) So what do you think?

CUSTOMER: Looks great, Joe. (*JOEY sweeps hair off of CUSTOMER's shoulders and takes off CUSTOMER's smock as CUSTOMER smiles in the mirror. He looks nothing like Ed Norton. CUSTOMER gets up off of chair.*) It was nice talkin' to ya. Ya always know how to lighten me up. Say hi to that little poodle of yours.

JOEY: It's a shitsu. I will. (*CUSTOMER hands JOEY a twenty-dollar bill and leaves.*) Thanks, take care. (*JOEY stuffs bill in his pocket and looks over to reception counter. The receptionist is engaged in a personal phone call. JOEY glances over to the waiting area.*) All right, next!

Life as a movie is the inevitable analogy in our cinematically influenced times. We're surrounded by big screens and small screens and wide screens and, as soon as anyone can fucking afford them, plasma screens, and it's way too easy sometimes to imagine your life as just another film in a constant state of production. I guess having been in a couple of movies myself helps, but that's not the point. The figurative director's on set around the clock, bringing the elements together to create every scene you encounter. The editors are working furiously in your brain to rewrite history as they sift through all your memories and piece together the best-looking picture and send scraps to the basement to be filed for the outtakes. Characters walk in and walk out on cue while your set designers impress you with every new town you visit. Then your accountant calls you to say your film's way over budget and brings the whole damn thing crumbling down for an entire afternoon, or longer.

When I look back to reflect on that movie, I'm often blown away to realize how easily my script could have veered off in a thousand different directions, most of which would not necessarily have warranted the most encouraging review. As the summer of 1969 was coming to an end, I was well on my way to life at the JP Salon somewhere off of Route 4. After all, I had really enjoyed that job at Madison Avenue Coiffeurs, and the pay had been great. And I had every reason to consider myself a lucky shit if I ever got to work at a place like that again.

It had been several years now since we'd been evicted from our last address in Fairview. "Excessive noise," the landlord had said when he hand-delivered our eviction warning notice at Ninth Street. Mommy had answered the door; not the best move to press our case. She gave him a taste of how excessive that noise could actually get up close and personal, and our fate was sealed.

We'd moved to an apartment at 217 Cliff Street in Cliffside Park, the next town over from Fairview. It wasn't more than six blocks away from our last address, but it was six blocks in the right direction. I had to change schools again. I moved from middle school to high school. I guess I'd been fortunate to start high school twice in the same year.

Florie and Mommy were barely making it, and the financial situation had gotten so bad that he had to park his Dodge Dart around the corner because he was way behind in his payments and had a repo man on his ass. Florie had been struggling in the straight world. The "working stiff" life had never gotten any easier for him. Their gambling habits weren't helping any either. They were eating away at every bit of headway he and Mommy made.

Remarkably, they managed to pull together about five grand, probably from loan sharks, to take over the management of the little grocery store down the hill from our apartment. We'd all go there every day to work. Me and Maryann helped after school to make sandwiches and sweep the floors. Mommy and Florie shared the day and night shifts. It worked for a while.

In no time, we got so behind in our bills that we had absolutely no credit left with our suppliers and utility providers. The coolers of deli meat, refrigerators of sodas, freezers of ice cream and the television set in our apartment all began to operate like parking meters. We had to put in two dollars' worth of quarters to keep any appliance working for the day. It was just like the old days on Monroe Street.

That was the only way we could "buy" what we needed to run the shop. We paid for the equipment on "time," literally. Once a week, a guy from the electric company would show up and empty the coin boxes. That's how we made the payments. It's the only way we could be trusted to make the payments.

You can't blame our creditors. If anything, they went above and beyond to accommodate us. It was no surprise, since Mommy was a natural-born con artist and a top-grade charmer; she always found a way to keep things moving when all else failed. The creditors couldn't trust us to pay on time, but they kept us in business at the grocery store. If only they could have protected us from ourselves.

Mommy was in charge of keeping track of the shop's checks and balances. She couldn't figure out why the cash register came up eight dollars short every day. It was driving her absolutely insane.

"Some jerk-off's stealing eight bucks from my till!" she'd bitch at the dinner table every night.

Every night, she was answered by three pleas of innocence.

This went on for weeks until Florie finally caved in and admitted to having taken two dollars out a "couple of times." But not eight dollars.

Maryann and I followed by admitting we'd both taken two dollars out "here and there." We thought we deserved it. But we swore we hadn't taken eight bucks. We'd never do that.

Mommy eventually figured out the "swindle."

Since none of us got paid, every day me, Maryann, Florie and Mommy were each swiping two bucks from the register for spending cash. Of course, Mommy thought she was the only one. We all thought we were the only ones. As far as I know, the swiping continued on all our parts as long as we had the grocery store. I know that I kept taking two bucks regularly, and since nobody was complaining, it was obvious that I wasn't alone. It was just another family thing, like Sunday night stuffed shells.

Cliffside Park High School was perched high on the cliffs of northern New Jersey, bordering Edgewater on the edge of the Hudson River below it, with the skyscrapers of midtown Manhattan just visible in the distance. It was almost picturesque. But it was still school, and that always tampered with any bucolic sentiments I may have had. More than any other time in my school life, I was really put in my place. And that place was the bottom rung of the academic ladder.

They had a system at Cliffside Park High that divided up the students by what was no less than a questionably objective assessment of their potential for success and an estimated guess on their eventual lot in life. Category One included the college-bound kids. They were the cream of the crop; the pride and joy of Cliffside Park High and of hundreds of gleaming northern New Jersey parents. They were the future doctors and lawyers and accountants and corporate administrators.

From there, the categories moved down the pecking order of society. There was the business category, which was something like the future secretaries of America. There was the trade category, training New Jersey's future auto mechanics, plumbers and electricians. I'm convinced it was a clever way of getting all the kids together in the same room who could give teachers some free advice on their engine trouble or malfunctioning A/C. And so it continued down the cafeteria-fed food chain through Category Six: the Unhelpables. Category Six was where you went when all hope for any kind of decent future was lost on you. You were either too dumb or too uninterested to be taught anything of value. You weren't worth the effort of a teacher. All that could be hoped for was that you wouldn't cause any trouble, and if you could do them that much of a favor, you'd walk out with a courtesy diploma in a couple of years.

Those of us in Category Six called it "the Sixes." And if you haven't guessed yet, that's where I found myself from day one. My academic reputation had preceded me. I'd be in a class with an official title like "U.S. History" and a teacher who'd just have you sit there quietly for forty-five minutes in a room filled with what turned out to be the toughest kids in the school, and there was absolutely no teaching and no learning going on. Nothing. We sat there staring at walls decorated with an outdated map of the United States showing forty-eight states, while drool slowly dripped out of our mouths for forty-five minutes every damn day! It was absurd. We were the dismissed ones.

All the way through junior high, teachers held a lingering flair of hope that I would break out of my dyslexic bubble and prove to the world I was smarter than my grades may have indicated. The presumption was that once I got to high school, I was too old to learn to study. Theoretically, I hadn't picked up any method to learn in school after ten years of schooling. If I ever had a problem with self-confidence in a school setting, it was made all the more problematic by having the school system officially verify my worst fears. Truthfully, I don't know why they didn't just send us home or directly to prison, where they all expected we'd end up anyway. I'm sure they had much better uses for the space we Sixes took up.

In the middle of November, posters went up around the halls announcing auditions for the senior class play that would run at the end of February. The play was called *Up the Down Staircase*. I could barely read the title, but I knew that this was exactly what I needed to be doing if I was going to take my acting bug seriously. Miss Damiano, the drama coach, suggested I try out for the lead role of Joe Ferone. Maybe she found some similarity between us and thought it'd be a good fit. As Bel Kaufman explains in her endnotes, the character of Joe Ferone is "a hostile, handsome young man with a high I.Q. but failing in almost every subject. He's been hit hard by the world outside, so hard that he protects himself against future disappointment by expecting the worst from every situation." I don't know about the other stuff, but I *was* a handsome motherfucker.

The truth is, I was crazy about Miss Damiano at the time, and as much as I was eager to get the role, I was also eager to spend time as her little protégé. She was a first-year English teacher, pretty with dirty-blond hair and blue eyes, no more than twenty-two years old.

Of course, teenage crush aside, she ended up being one of my saviors at school. She and Mr. Fredericks, who, though not as cute as Miss Damiano, had taken an interest in me where other teachers hadn't. Both had an acute sense of my self-loathing nature and the self-doubt that had been planted in me back in Hoboken and had not only been reinforced, but had grown more damaging at Cliffside. It was so rare and unexpected that any teacher would take such an interest in my cause, especially now, at the end of the line, senior year. And because of that fact, I actually took heed of what they'd tell me. I was convinced of my own failure, they would say, and it was limiting my ability to excel at something—or anything, for that matter. They were right. It's no surprise that when I told them I was interested in acting they jumped on the opportunity.

As the new decade arrived, Vietnam was revving up, along with the whole peace movement, and a lot of my friends' older brothers and a couple of cousins of mine had already found their complimentary nonstop first-class tickets to the South Pacific waiting for them at home. That past September, I had gotten my own notice to sign up for the draft. Nixon was president, and he had instituted the draft lottery. You couldn't feel removed from the Vietnam draft situation if you tried. Especially if you were eighteen and had a dick in your pants and arches under your feet, even while life around you went on like nothing else in the world mattered except that dance Friday night and the leisure suit or Beatlesque Nehru jacket you were wearing.

On the night of December 1, 1969, 366 dates were read over the course of an hour. The first hundred or so dates that were called would be drafted. So if you were one of Nixon's unlucky bastards and your birth date was anything before, say, the 115th pick, your future had been decided and you were off to Vietnam—or Canada, as the case may be. Anything between the mid-hundreds and mid-two-hundreds, and you were shitting a brick halfway between Poughkeepsie and Saigon. If the war escalated, you had a good chance of being sent away. Any number beyond that, you knew you were lucky. You had missed the boat and were damn glad about it. My number was 316 that night.

I was with Florie when they picked my number. I remember I had been in the candy store hanging out and it was time to go to dinner. He picked me up in his Dodge Dart and drove me home, and we were listening to some guy in Washington call the numbers out on the radio. As we drove through Cliffside Park on that first cold December night, it was as if the rows of houses were passing us by and we were the ones standing still. I felt a sense of relief that night, like I had been acquitted from a life sentence.

With the draft out of the way and my less than promising vision of a future military career all but vanished, I had that much more time to imagine myself leaving Jersey on my own terms. And I was doing a lot of that. After all, graduation was coming up soon and I was in the market for a way out. I was falling in love fast with the idea of becoming an actor. It was the only thing that ever gave me an inkling of motivation to do anything besides being the very talented fuckup I was. Of course, the possibility seemed as far removed as the flag they'd just put up on the moon, and Mommy would take every chance she got to remind me of that. I was stomping hard on delicate ground with her.

I desperately wanted to be in the senior class play and I was deathly afraid I wouldn't get the part, even though teachers like Miss Damiano and Mr. Fredericks were encouraging me, as was Florie back home after I told him about it. The fear made me coy on the outside. I was hiding my real enthusiasm for doing the part, and pretending I didn't care about getting it. It was the Centrella part of me in action: Expect the worst, not because you hope to be pleasantly surprised, but because the worst is bound to happen.

But in this case I had good cause to worry. I couldn't read the friggin' script. I'd find out two months later that I had a third-grade reading level at the time, but I didn't need the official word to know I had a huge problem on my hands.

The only way I was going to pull this off was by memorizing my entire part. And that's exactly what I did. I spent countless evenings at home getting help from Maryann with the words. A twelve-year-old sixth grader was helping her eighteen-year-old brother read. I'd sound the words out with her, and then I'd take the script and lock myself in the bathroom and memorize my lines for hours.

The auditions were held at the auditorium. It was Miss Damiano and Mr. Fredericks and a couple other teachers who were involved with the play, and the forty or so other kids who were auditioning or working on the production, filling up the first three or four rows of the auditorium. I was the last one on the roster, so I had the gut-wrenching pleasure of watching all the other kids try out first. I was a complete mess. I felt completely out of place; a "have-not" in a room of "haves." It was absolutely grueling to sit there and watch these well-read, well-spoken college-bound kids perform like masters of the art, and all I had to back me up was the highly regarded performances I had given to my Crest toothpaste and Barbasol shaving cream audience in front of the bathroom mirror. To say I was anxiety-ridden would be an understatement. It was amazing I could even stand up when I heard my name.

"And finally, Joey Pantoliano, you're up."

My heart dropped below the seat of my pants. I walked up the side stairs and crossed over to center stage. Most of the kids who'd auditioned were still hanging out in the auditorium. Miss Damiano leaned over in her chair and said, "Thanks for being patient, Joey. You can go right ahead."

"Okay." Is that my voice? I cleared my throat and jumped

right into it, and I recited my monologue just as I had practiced. I remember like it was yesterday. "Miss Barrett! What makes you think you're so special . . . Are you listening? what I said—what I'm saying—I'm saying you're so special! You're my teacher! So teach me. Help me. Hey teach—which way do I go? I'm tired of going up the down staircase!"

There was some applause from the audience. Miss Damiano smiled and told me I'd done a good job. For a moment there, I was actually feeling good about it. Imagine that. I was getting ready to make my gracious, smooth exit off the stage when I was asked to do one more scene. Not just any scene—I had to read the part of another character, one of the schoolteachers. I started to panic. I hadn't memorized it, I hadn't looked at it, which means there was no way I was going to be able to read it. But what could I say? My whole body was shaking, and I could feel my foot tap uncontrollably on the stage floor. I'm sure it was obvious. As I was directed, I flipped to the page with trembling hands and started.

"It, uh, c-c-come, has c-come to-to m-m-my att-att-ttenshun th-th-at d-d-d-ue to, to, l-l-ax-n-ess on-n y-y-ou-r-r p-p-part, th-th-that-that s-s-o-mm-e s-s-tu-d-d-dents are ch-ch-cheating." I fumbled my way through the whole entire thing. I could hear kids laughing and snickering in the audience and I was mortified. I knew—I absolutely knew—that I blew it. Just like that. My first chance on stage, and I blew it.

I went home and headed straight to my room and locked the door. I sat and thought about how stupid I'd been to actually think that I had what it took. I really sucked. I was every bit a lousy sumanabitch as my mother said I was. I couldn't even read the motherfucking part. I beat myself up for twelve hours straight and barely slept a wink that night.

The next morning I got the part.

We rehearsed for four weeks and performed on Friday and Saturday, December 5 and 6. All of my family came up from Hoboken to see me. It was a huge deal to have them there. I could see Mommy and Florie and Maryann in the third row, Aunt Tilly, Aunt Minnie, Cousin Antoinette, Jimmy and Josie from Brooklyn, Cousin Roseanne and Cousin Peter and the list went on. After the show, everyone in the auditorium stood up and cheered when I came out for my bow. I couldn't believe it.

Everything that Florie had told me over the years and everything I had always wanted to believe was true. But I had always doubted deep in my heart that the fruit from the top branches was within my reach. Suddenly, it all started to make sense. It was the first time I had ever had an ounce of trust in myself and my abilities, even if it was just a tiny little speck. It made all the difference in the world.

It was that night when the fate of the JP Salon somewhere outside of Paramus was forever sealed. That would-be reality was removed from the final cut and was stored in the basement with the rest of the outtakes.

In acting I found something I really cared about. I didn't care much about sports and definitely didn't care much about school. I had never had anyone come up to me before at school and say, "Hey, nice moves on the court," or "Good play on the field, go get 'em, champ," or "Great job on that exam." There had never been anything like that. I had never expected any accolades before, but suddenly I was hearing "Hey, you're real good" and "Nice job on stage. You looked like a real actor." I was getting commended for something I had done. It was the first time I was doing anything I had a real aptitude for and, furthermore, I enjoyed it. It was a genuinely new feeling for me, and I loved it. I had a focus in my life that could actually take me places, even a future outside of the state of New Jersey, outside of John's Pizzeria and the grocery store. And outside of Bergen County Prison. I guess you could say my love for acting made me aware of my own ambition, and that was a very bad word where I came from.

"Who do you think you are, you wanna be an actor? People like us don't become actors. People like us don't go to college. People like us don't get ahead. Don't shake the boat, Joey." That was Mommy's point of view.

How was I supposed to tell her I wanted to go to New York City before the year was over and I wanted to become an actor? That kind of life wasn't part of her set of rules. It wasn't part of her universe. I might as well have been telling her I was gay and coming out of the closet and going to follow Liza Minnelli around on her European tour. And it wasn't only Mommy. It was part of our culture. My aunts and uncles and even my cousins would say the same kind of thing. For most everyone around me, I was trying for more than my fair share in life.

"What, are you crazy?"

"Do you think you're going to go to New York and become a movie star?"

"Who the fuck you think you are anyway?"

"Don't ask for too much, Joey; you're going to be let down. It's better to settle."

This was the prevailing mentality in my world. I was swimming upstream.

Still, it was the first battle I was willing, and eager, to fight. And it was high time I got myself equipped.

I had started going to acting school at HB Studios on Bank Street in the West Village, just around the corner from the site on West Street where Florie had been shipped off to Atlanta Federal Penitentiary back when I was six. Nowadays, Florie was driving me past that same spot three times a week. I never knew exactly what went through his mind passing West Street all those times, but knowing Florie, all that mattered was that he wasn't dropping me off there. Whatever business it was that got him to West Street a dozen years earlier was irrelevant. He was in the business now of making damn sure that wouldn't happen to me. He was doing all he could to ensure that.

Getting me hooked up at HB Studios was one way he was going about it. When I "came out" to Florie and told him I wanted to be an actor, he immediately asked around and within a week took me to meet an actor named Nico Hartos. Nico had a business selling Greek rugs in New York. I got to know the guy a bit and I ran errands for him and his brother Mike. Eventually I auditioned for him. After the scene he told me I had "ability" and he sent me over to HB Studios at 120 Bank Street. I signed up with Herbert Berghof and started studying acting with him. I'd cut my afternoon classes at high school sometimes so I could get there on time, and Florie would be waiting for me outside of Cliffside High to take me to Bank Street.

Mr. Fredericks and Miss Damiano proved to be two of those angels who seem to appear throughout my life. They were just out of college, with dreams and hopes of saving kids like me. All the other teachers seemed to be tenured and, with that, complacent about their role as anything more than a disciplinarian. After seeing the play, Mr. Fredericks decided to take a shot at helping me out. He came up to me and politely told me I had to do my homework if I wanted to graduate.

"I don't know how to do homework," I told him.

He worked with me and he made it a hands-on project. He showed me how it could be fun. He helped me after school. He would boost my confidence. He would read everybody's marks aloud in class after every test. I was usually getting marks in the fifties and sixties. One day he said, "Joe Pantoliano, one hundred percent." All the kids were actually happy for me. He had taught me how to study. He taught me how to do homework and how to memorize, after I'd thought it was beyond me for so long. He kept me after school a number of times, for about a half hour of his time, to reach out and show me how to do what other kids seemed to get so naturally, and his interest was critical to me at a critical time in my life. He paid attention to me when everybody else saw a hopelessly troubled kid going nowhere. He gave me an opportunity and presented me with a challenge I could tackle.

Mr. Fredericks went out to the football field one day to find me during gym class and handed me a book, *Soul on Ice* by Eldridge Cleaver. "You're going to have to learn how to read if you want to be an actor. And I think you should start by reading this," he said to me. "I think you can understand it." *Soul on Ice* is a classic story about a guy who makes something out of nothing. I saw the connection. It was the first book I'd ever read in my life and a really thin one at that. But when I finally put the book down, there was no stopping me.

I started taking speech classes with Alice Hermes and Michael Rado at HB, and since I couldn't afford any of it, they let me work as an apprentice at the school so that I could get the classes for free. Mr. Rado gave me a book on how to improve my vocabulary. I'd learn five words a day and I'd have to weave them into my day-to-day speech. I started taking movement classes as well, and I was picking up more books. I read *The Godfather*, and then I read *The Valachi Papers*. I would read books that interested me, not necessarily the ones that were recommended to me, because I knew it was the only way I was going to get through them. Florie knew Joe Valachi, and that connection was more than enough for a stroke of inspiration to finish Peter Maas's book.

I was doing whatever it took to learn how to become an actor.

And people noticed. Friday night poker games had carried over to Cliff Street, and I was a favorite bit of conversation between Mommy and my Fairview buddies.

"What the fuck is up with Pantoliano? He's talking funny."

It was no longer "Enderson Eveneww"; now it was becoming "Ahnderson Ahvenue" for me. They took every opportunity to pick me apart on it. Mommy was getting a kick out of the whole situation. They were on her side, after all.

And it was only going to get worse when I started bringing up the idea of moving to New York after graduation. She wouldn't hear of it. She'd go insane at the mention of it. Never mind that New York was less than a mile and a half and a twenty-minute bus ride away. She wouldn't have it. She'd "break" me before she'd let me leave. "You faggot!" she'd scream, usually in front of my friends.

Her Italian apron strings were in serious need of cutting, and they might need to be hacked away at some point.

"Everything I've done for you! How could you do this to me?" she'd wail every time I brought the subject up.

"Yeah, yeah, yeah, Ma, you'll get over it" was the only way I knew of trying to shut her up. Little did I know the worst was yet to come. She'd just been dishing out the appetizers, finger food.

There's a calm before every storm. During that time, there were some important matters for me to take care of, aside from my acting aspirations and all the work that entailed. There were minor details I felt compelled to address before I was headed anywhere outside of Cliffside Park. I was eighteen years old, but as far as being a real man, there was still one pretty important thing holding me back from that honor.

It was March 1970, three months before graduation. Our clothes had changed and our hair was growing longer. A patchouli-scented tidal wave of bell-bottom jeans and tie-dyed shirts had washed over us from the party at Woodstock the summer before. That was all good and fine, but free love, my ass—I was probably the only guy in town who wasn't getting laid. Of course, back then they called it balling. "Oh, yeah I balled her." "We're gonna ball like mad tonight." Yeah, everyone was balling everyone. Somehow, I managed to steer clear straight through until I won my second lottery since Nixon's, on a fine May night in 1970.

Even though I was living in Cliffside Park, I was still hanging out at John's Pizzeria in Fairview, the pizza stand where I had had the stunning little fight with Rizzo six months earlier. Fairview and Cliffside Park were close enough to each other that I still was able to walk just about anywhere; not like I had much choice. By then, the Dodge had been repossessed, so we were once again carless. Anyhow, equipped with four wheels or not, I was standing in front of John's, which is what you normally did on a Friday night. Kids would walk by that you knew; you'd be hanging with your friends, usually with more than a couple of guys at a time standing there with you, doing whatever the hell it is you did, which was just about anything that would pull the attention of whatever girls happened to be passing by your way. At one point, though, I remember being alone, and I could see this girl walking north of me on Anderson Avenue, heading south on my side of the street. She was really cute. She had really curly hair, like the old-fashioned Afro-style, which was big and round, moon-type hair. As she walked closer, and she was just passing me, about twelve feet away at the sidewalk, I got up the nerve to say, "How you doing?"

Now, normally, about 99 percent of the time, when you would say "How you doing?" to a strange girl, she would ignore you and keep walking. There would be no indication of free love anywhere at any time. It was the ultimate sucker's lottery; you played, but you never thought you'd actually win. But this girl, she might as well have stood there with a bright shining smile on her face behind a row of floating, numbered white plastic balls and called out my winning numbers. "Hi, how are *you* doing?"

I was trapped and speechless, and I certainly didn't know what the hell had just happened. I had only worked on "How you doing?" so I didn't know what to say or what to do. Automatic pilot took over and I managed to let out an "I'm good." Before I knew it, she had struck up a conversation.

"Do you live around here?" she asked.

And I said, slowly, still in a mild state of shock, "Suuure, yeah."

"Do you to go school here?"

And I said "Yeah."

"What's your name?"

"Joey."

I forget her name.

"Do you wanna get high?"

She probably could have asked if I wanted to strip down naked and run across the George Washington Bridge, and I would've answered her the same. "Oh, yeah, sure."

"Do you got any dope?"

And I said, "Well, I can get it."

So now I realized that if I could get her some grass, then I'd have a very good chance of getting her to fall in love with me, and the rest would be history. I didn't care that I didn't smoke pot. I had never liked it. I had tried it a couple of times, but because of my stepfather's involvement in organized crime, and his "wishes" that I wouldn't do drugs, I was simply too afraid to touch the stuff. I was sure if I ever did, Florie would find out and he would kill me. Really, he would friggin' kill me—as in, make me dead. But this was a whole different game, and the stakes were compounded. There was a girl on the line.

So I ran into John's Pizzeria and found my friend Tommy Warner sitting there, and I said, "Tommy! You have any grass?"

"What the fuck do you want with grass?" Tommy had a way with words, especially with half a pepperoni slice stuffed in his face.

"There's a chick outside and she's really cute and she wants to get high."

"I don't got any," he said as he wiped a healthy layer of grease off his mouth.

"Wait," I said, unrelenting. "Let's go down to Hoboken. My cousin, maybe he's got some."

"I ain't going to fuckin' Hoboken."

"C'mon, Tommy please!" There was no way I was giving in.

He noticed and gave in. "You gotta give me gas money."

That was easy enough. "I have like fifty cents."

"I want a dollar."

"All right, well, I'll give you fifty cents. I owe you fifty cents." This was something I picked up from being reared by a couple of deadbeat gamblers. I knew how to handle my creditors.

We walked over to Tommy's '64 Camaro and piled in the front seat. As she sat in between the two of us, I talked to her and Tommy talked to her, probably at the same time. I don't know what the hell we talked about, but it didn't matter because I was concentrating on the multipart task at hand: charm her on the way to find the pot, find the pot, and become a man. And Tommy could talk to a rubber tire if he had to. But she seemed at ease with this sort of thing, and she was as cool as a chair umpire at a tennis match, and probably looked the part, for the entire fifteen minutes it took to get down to Hoboken.

Once there, we drove slowly around the streets looking for my Cousin Lenny. I had no clue where to find the fucking kid but Hoboken ain't that big a place. Of course, I didn't bother to share that information, or lack thereof, with any of my fellow riders in the Camaro. Lady Luck was wearing her finest red slip that night and she was pointing a finger right at me.

Wait a second, it wasn't Lady Luck, but a shady looking guy with a half-grown beard, and he was pointing a finger right at me from the sidewalk as we were slowing down at an intersection in the middle of Hoboken's projects. I didn't know him, but he seemed to know me. And even better, after rolling down my window, it turned out he knew Cousin Lenny and, to top it off, knew exactly where the kid was hanging out that night. Five minutes later we found Cousin Lenny with a joint in hand. He wanted fifty cents for it. Tommy Garner had to pay for it because I had given him my fifty cents. And Tommy liked to smoke pot anyway, so everybody was happy.

I felt like an asshole for not joining in on the fun, and I was tempted to just grab the joint every time it was passed around and offered to me. But I could hear Florie's warning to me as clear as it had been on the afternoon in the summer of 1969 when he'd sat me down after some of my red-eyed stoned pals had been over the house. "Siddown. I want you to know something. I've been around drugs my entire life, and let me tell you something. Nothing good can ever come out of 'em. Let me try to make it clear for you, Joey. You come into this fucking house and you're fucked up like your pals today, I'm gonna know what you took, and how much you took. And I'm gonna go into the fucking bedroom, I'm gonna come out with the pistol and I'm gonna shoot you in both your fucking kneecaps. And every time you take a step, you'll think of me." What they call today "tough love."

Florie's voice rang in my ears as I accepted the joint on its last trip around, but believe me, I don't care how much you could have paid me then, I wouldn't inhale, really. I was eager to become a man, but I really wanted to have two working legs to enjoy with my manhood.

As we were driving back to Fairview, things started to heat up. This girl started rubbing the inside of my leg and quickly moved to my groin. And I thought, "Holy shit," and kind of snuck a look down. As I did that, I stole a glance over at Tommy's lap because I just assumed she was doing the same thing to him, but she wasn't. And then she whispered in my ear, "You wanna come to my apartment? I have an apartment."

Now, this girl was out of high school, so she was probably nineteen. As I was thinking this, she whispered again, "Come to my place."

I was sure that I was gonna get robbed. This had to be a setup, and there were going to be these guys waiting for me to beat me up and steal my wallet. I was the one that wasn't smoking and I was still paranoid as hell.

So I leaned over to Tommy and whispered to him when she got out of the car, "Wait for me to give you the signal that everything's okay."

She lived on Anderson Avenue and Waller Street, which was about two blocks from where I lived. We went up to a very small one-bedroom apartment and she flipped on her radio as she made a beeline to the bathroom, leaving me alone with Three Dog Night reminding me that "Mama Told Me Not to Come" as the radio hit blasted out of her cheap speakers. I looked under the bed; I looked in the closet—all while she was in the bathroom doing whatever she was doing. And when she got out, I said I had to use the bathroom, and I closed the door behind me and looked behind the bathroom shower curtain. And when I realized that everything was cool, I leaned out the window and signaled to Tommy that everything was okay.

And then, we got into it.

It was everything I'd imagined it to be. I wonder if all guys say that about their first sexual experience. I recognized the feeling of being in bed with this girl and decided right then and there that I believed in reincarnation. It was like I was remembering it and living it all at once, like I'd been there before. To top it all off, she was really cute.

Now, the actual sexual experience probably lasted all of about three or four minutes, and that's by my own subjective clock. And yet, once it was all said and done, she said she really liked me. Not only that, but I hadn't even lifted my head up off the bed when she turned to me and said, "I have a girlfriend who would like you."

And I think to myself, "Boy, you have scored big."

"She's really cute. She would love you. You wanna see a picture?"

I said sure, already confident that I would be awarded North Jersey's rookie-of-the-year award before the night was over. I had struck oil.

She leaned over me toward the bedside table, so that her exposed breasts were hanging nine millimeters from my face, and came back with a picture of a two-year-old little girl.

I flinched. "What, are you kidding?"

And she says, "This is my daughter."

It turned out that this girl had been on her own for a while, since her parents had thrown her out. She was living alone. I don't know where she was getting her money from. I felt bad for her, but somehow she convinced me she was getting by.

Meanwhile, we liked each other enough so we continued a relationship, if you could call it that. It was just sexual. I'd go over there, I'd say hello, I'd fuck her, then I'd leave. And then, finally, about six weeks into my introduction to the sexual revolution, she confronted me on it. Apparently, we never did enough talking. We were all about sex. I said we had nothing to talk about. To that, she said, "Well, I guess we have nothing to fuck about either, then." I disagreed, until I found out later that week that, well, I wasn't the only chip off the block that had landed in her quaint studio. Apparently, she had enough chips off the old block shacking up at that place to build a friggin' pedestrian bridge from Cliffside Park to Newark Airport. She did confess to me, however, that I had been her favorite. I always like to hear that sort of thing. Of course, she told Tommy the same thing two weeks later.

It was probably just as well. I graduated from Cliffside High on June 17, 1970, and I was getting the hell out of New Jersey as soon as I could find a place to live in the city. Meanwhile, that happened quicker than I expected. A friend from acting school who was throwing in the towel and going back to Kansas needed someone to take over the rent at his place on Sullivan Street in Greenwich Village. When I went to check it out, I was surprised by how much the area reminded me of my old neighborhood. Old Italian immigrants ruled the stoops with their American-born grandchildren. There was the cheese shop on the corner. Old ladies were running numbers from their ground floor apartment windows. St. Anthony's Church was on the opposite corner. Mommy would have felt right at home, if she could only have accepted the fact that it was finally time for me to move out and on with my life.

She never took me seriously about moving out of the house after graduation. I guess she always took it for granted that I'd cave in to her wishes and her warnings, just like the old days. Or perhaps she bet on the idea that I'd never have the balls to leave. After a while, I just stopped mentioning it to her. Whatever her true motivation, it was clear that she'd never considered I would actually go through with my plan. That is, until the day I moved out.

"That's right. An apartment in Manhattan."

Mommy looked disturbed as she leaned on the door frame, watching me pick clothes off my bed and pack them in my suitcase. Her face was a mixture of anger, fear, sadness and confusion rolled into a tight-lipped grip on her cigarette.

I thought she was going to bite the filter right off. It was the same expression I'd seen six years earlier on Jackson Street when I'd handed Mommy the phone with the guy from Atlanta Federal Penitentiary on the other end of the line, and the same expression I'd seen countless times in between whenever the wheels of despair began to turn inside the Neapolitan Goddess's head.

Her expression suddenly molded into a devilish grin. "Is that right? 'Cause some guys from NASA just phoned and said they'd love to have you on their next fucking trip to the moon."

There she went with degrading my self-worth again. I ignored her and kept packing.

"Hate to break it to you, honey, but odds are better you being an astronaut on the moon than a fucking actor in New York."

"I didn't ask you. I ain't asking you," I replied.

"Okay, so where you gonna live?"

"Right near Aunt Lizzie's old place, on Sullivan Street."

"Oh, and that's supposed to make me feel better." She paused, as she gathered herself. "Nuh-uh, you ain't livin' anywhere near Aunt Lizzie's old place. You hear? Cliffside ain't anywhere near Aunt Lizzie's old place!"

I was already exhausted. "I don't feel like arguing anymore, Ma."

"You wanna be a big-shot actor, huh? You got the nerve to think you can pull that one over me? You couldn't act your way outta a paper bag!"

My back was turned to her as I labored to zip up the overstuffed suitcase. It jammed once and I started over. It jammed again. "Fuck! Will you leave me alone? I'm old enough to do whatever the fuck I want!" I started zipping again and it jammed again. My head felt hot. I opened up the suitcase to rearrange my clothes. Mommy came over from the doorway and slammed it shut.

"Where the fuck do you think you're going? Either I pay or you don't go! And I ain't fucking paying!"

"I can make my own living. I don't need your fucking money."

SMACK! She slapped me hard across the left side of my face.

"You think so? Who told you that? Huh? Or did you read it in some fucking book!" Her face was turning as red as the left side of mine must have been.

I grabbed the suitcase and she grabbed my wrist to stop me. Her voice suddenly became soft.

"Joey, you can't go. What's everybody gonna think?"

Did I hear her correctly? "What?"

"You know, with you leaving home like this. What's everyone gonna think?"

Oh, this was about *her*? "What!?" I wrestled my hands free from her and went for the suitcase. She grabbed my wrists again.

"You ain't leaving this house unless you're dead or married. And fags can't marry!"

I shook her off and raised my hands in front of my face. This was too fucking much. I started to go off. And as I yelled at the top of my lungs, she started singing that favorite song of hers with the maddest look in her eye, taunting me as I sought some kind of logic or reason from inside of her.

"I'll be ten goddamn minutes away!"

"Who's sorry now?"

"It's only Manhattan for Christ's sake—"

"Who's sorry now?"

"This is something I need to do for myself!"

"Whoooose heeeart is aching for breeeeaaking each vow?"

"For me, Ma! Can't you understand that?"

"Whooo's sad and blue? Whooo's crying too?"

"It doesn't have anything to do with you. It's me, Ma—"

"Just like I cried over you . . ."

"Jesus Christ! Why do you gotta make this so goddamn—" and I stopped myself mid-sentence. Suddenly, I was mesmerized. I stood for a moment and stared Mommy down as she continued in her taunting voice.

Her voice grew louder and her eyes grew bigger as she sang those bittersweet lyrics.

I must have caught whatever Mommy had at that very moment. I'm sure my eyes matched hers in madness as I began to speak in a deep theatrical voice while she kept right on singing. Like mother, like son.

"Your children are not your children."

She didn't seem to care.

"They are the slings and arrows of outrageous wanting."

She just kept singing.

"You are the bows from which your children as living arrows are set forth . . ."

Midway through a lyric Mommy stopped short and stared at me with a puzzled expression. "Slings? Bows? Arrows? Cowboys and Indians? What the fuck are you talking about?"

"They come from you, yet they don't belong to you," I said, still speaking out of my abdomen, not so much my throat, just as I had recently learned in speech class.

"What!?" Mommy was confused.

"I'm quoting Kahlil Gibran . . ."

"Is that the fag you're moving in with?"

I zipped the suitcase closed, grabbed it and made for the door.

"Where the fuck are you going?!" Before I could make it past the threshold of the door frame, she jolted in front of me and slammed the door shut. Standing in front of the door facing me, her scowl dropped to an instant sob as she nearly crumpled to my feet.

"No, Joey! Please . . ." She was staggering like a wounded soldier, grabbing at my sleeve. "Don't go, Joey! Don't leave me! You can't do this to your only mama!"

I was still possessed by my Gibran-inspired counterattack

to "Who's Sorry Now?" My eyes narrowed and fixed on her as the tears poured down her face. And then I told her, in the same tone of voice, "You may house their bodies, but not their souls. For their souls dwell in the house of tomorrow—"

She snapped out of her crying and right back into anger mode as she interrupted me. "Don't talk to me like that, goddamnit!"

I snapped out of Gibran in turn and shook my head. "I'll call you when I get there. Give me a half hour," I told her.

"No!" she snapped back.

"I'll come for dinner tomorrow," I offered.

"Fuck you!" she replied.

With that, I reached behind her to grab ahold of the doorknob she was blocking and I opened the door. I had to push myself out between the door and Mommy, and when I'd successfully managed to get into the hallway, I felt her grab the back of my shirt. With one of her hands on me and with the other bracing herself with a table here and a chair there, I dragged my clinging mother across the living room. She was sobbing the whole way.

"Lemme go, Ma!"

"Ahaaahaaaaaaa!"

"Lemme go!"

"After everything I've done for yoooouuuu! How can you dooooo thiiiis to meeeeee!" She was knocking the chairs over as she grabbed on to them, and I was dragging Mommy, together with our entire living room dining set, over with me on my way to the door. She was beside herself and in rare form, even for Mommy, and I was beside myself, amazed, disgusted and saddened by the absurdity of it all. Right back into Gibran I went as I struggled to get to the door. "Upon the path of infinite, let your bending in the archer's hand be for gladness. They come through you, but not from you . . ."

"Don't talk to me like that, motherfucker!" and with that, she lost her grip on my coat and quickly got to her feet. "You rotten little fuck! How dare you!" Her voice was cold now, separated from her love for me, if she had any left at that moment, by far too many layers of anger and despair. I didn't look back and headed quickly down the stairs. I could hear her yelling from the top of the stairs. "You ain't my fucking son! You hear me? Not my son, motherfucker! Not my son no more!" and that's all I heard as I slammed the downstairs door shut behind me.

When I got to the grocery store, rain had started pouring down hard in the streets. It was an invigorating summer rain; usually the kind you welcome, but not today. I wiped the water off my forehead and slapped a dollar bill on the counter. Florie was making sandwiches for a couple in their early twenties with a toddler who was ogling the junk food in the shop. Mozart was playing from a small transistor radio on the shelf. "Florie, I'm off. Could you hand me some change for the bus?"

Florie went over to the register and I rubbed my face with exhaustion, while trying to cleanse myself from the mess I'd just left back home. He could tell by the look on my face that I hadn't left things all that peachy with Mommy. "You're doing the right thing, Joey. I'll see you on Friday." Just as he said that, I noticed his stare veer off behind me. Whatever his eyes were looking at now, it had frozen him in his tracks. I was afraid to look back. "Turn around, Joey," Florie insisted. I turned around and saw a lone figure staggering up the street in the middle of the rainstorm. It was a truly chilling sight, Mommy in her housedress, barefoot, drenched in the rain, staggering, in between gasping sobs, approaching the grocery store.

"Ooooh, shit." It was the closest thing to the living dead I had ever seen as she pushed her way through the front door.

"Jooooeeeey . . . Noooooooo! You can't . . . do this . . . to meeeee!" she said in between sobs as she scared the living shit out of the little kid in the shop, not to mention the rest of us.

"Mommy, please."

"Joey! You can't!"

"Please, Ma."

"Joey, no!"

"Not here . . ."

"JOEY!"

She grabbed at my sleeve and I pulled away. I pulled away from eighteen years of Mommy's grip on me. I already could feel myself veering off in a better direction. With a certainty that I wasn't yet deserving but felt strongly nonetheless, I knew I was going to win this game in the end. "Who's sorry now, Mommy?"

Her eyes met mine for a split second, and then in an instant she swung her arm toward my face. I ducked and she missed the slap. She must have been sending quite a doozy my way, because the force of her unmet swing sent her tumbling, staggering and crashing into a potato chip stand. Bags of snacks went flying through the air; some of them burst open, and I saw cheese curls spin out in every direction, to the sound of

Mozart's high-note crescendo playing out from the transistor radio and the little toddler's yelps as his mother swooped him off the ground to protect him from the deep-fried projectiles.

I stared down at Mommy on the floor, struggling to catch my breath. I couldn't believe what I had done, or what she had done. She slowly came back to life and started to lift herself back up on her feet as we all stared motionless.

"Ma? Ma? I . . . I didn't mean to . . . ," I said as I reached out to help her, but she violently slapped my hand away. She got up and walked cautiously to the door, as chips and doodles and curls crushed beneath her feet.

For all her skill at drama, she never could have planned this one. It was a kick in the ass for her. "Mommy?"

She paused at the door and turned around. "Get the fuck out of here. You'll miss your bus." And with that, she walked back out into the summer rain.

I boarded New Jersey Transit Bus #156, and by the time the bus rolled out of the Lincoln Tunnel fifteen minutes later, it was partly sunny skies. I felt so much emotion swimming inside my heart, sorrow and horror at first, but then a tremendous sense of release and happiness as I reached the other side of the tunnel.

I had escaped a special breed of nurturing love, the kind that suffocates as it seeks to protect, and the kind that by all means needed escaping at the age of eighteen.

I had escaped a life of the Sixes. A life chock-full of underachievement, a life pigeon-held by my inability to read and my inability to succeed in a place that had already written me off.

I had escaped a prison cell cot that I never got to sleep in.

I had escaped a hair salon in Paramus that never came to be, thank Christ.

I had a lot to escape. But I'm a lucky man, because I escaped it all and kept the best part intact—I had more love and admiration for everything that now resided on the other side of the Hudson River than I ever would have imagined possible while I was there. As I got off the bus at Port Authority and smelled the sweet air of diesel exhaust and week-old urine, it was clear as day. The present had officially become the past.

I had broken free, and I was alive.

Joey Pants, meet the world. World, this is Joey Pants.

Epilogue

Joey, you want coffee?

It's been over thirty years now since I left Mommy resigned and disheveled in her sopping wet housedress. For as much drama as that afternoon dredged up, it was really all in a day's work. I would see her almost every weekend for the next six years until I'd leave for Los Angeles at the age of twenty-five. An overwhelming need for control colored by sudden explosions and inspired lunacy was Mommy's trademark, but so was her ability to let go of her anger, switch gears and instantly forgive—sometimes within seconds of a howling storm of rage. There would be many more performances of this kind, starting as if out of a Donizetti opera and ending with sweet words as if from a flight attendant's mouth as she walks down the aisle with the beverage cart.

I was living at 107 Sullivan Street in lower Manhattan, right next door to Malapo's, the greatest little sandwich shop in New York, studying acting and working as a waiter to pay my bills. In no time, I fell for a girl named Ellen. She was from Virginia and worked as a model. Her mother was a Virginian mint julep type of woman, and her father was a lieutenant-colonel in the Army. Ellen stood for everything I thought I could ever want in a woman, based on everything I had ever seen on the screen. She was beautiful, blue-eyed, five-foot-ten and Barbie-doll gorgeous. I was crazy about her.

I told Mommy about her. My relationship with my mother was back to the status quo, running hot and cold in turn. I had been bringing friends from acting school over to the house for dinners as a diversion so she couldn't break my balls in front of strangers. Explaining that I felt very strongly about her, I asked her over the phone if I could bring Ellen down with me to the shore for the weekend. Ellen would be the first girl I ever brought home.

By that point Mommy and Florie had lost the grocery store. They were playing the numbers to stay ahead of the curve but, as always, they landed flat-broke and far behind that curve instead. They couldn't afford the rent on the store and didn't even have enough quarters to put in the meters for access to the cold cuts. The milk guy stopped delivering and the bread guy stopped delivering, and that was the end of the grocery business for them. Florie had started driving a van for a small children's clothing line where he'd pick up the cuttings in New York and bring them back to Jersey where they'd be sewn together by a group of women, including Mommy. From their meager earnings with the clothing line, they managed to rent a summer bungalow for one week down at Ortley Beach.

To my request, Mommy responded with a condition. "You ain't fucking her in this house." There was a long pause on her end of the line. I waited for the rest, being sure there was plenty more on its way. "You wanna play hide the salami, you do it out of this house. That's your own business. You wanna do it on the beach, under the boardwalk, I don't give a shit. But when she's in this house, she's sleeping in the same bed with your sister and you got the couch."

She didn't really leave much room for interpretation. I knew what the boundaries were and I explained it to Ellen, not in so many words. She was fine with it. I don't think she liked me that much anyway. When we arrived at the shore, Ellen was a hit. Everybody loved her, especially Florie. He was fifty-nine by now, and he was just happy to see any pretty young girl around the house. As for Mommy, I had given her the benefit of the doubt and she hadn't disappointed. She was on her best behavior throughout the weekend.

By Sunday afternoon, I was walking on air. I felt like my dreams had come true, and at twenty years old no less. I already thought of myself as an actor, though most people would define the stage I was in as "struggling actor," I had a beautiful girl straight from cinematic heaven with me and my family had accepted her. And not that it was the make-or-break of my good cheer, but Mommy had just set a fantastic smelling meal of sausage, peppers and onions on the table to eat. We sat down at the table with Mommy and Florie at opposite heads facing each other. I was to Mommy's left and Ellen was to her right. Maryann was to Florie's right, and Joe the insurance man, a pal of Florie's, was to his left.

We were enjoying the wonderful feast and drinking iced tea like any decent family on the shore would. The iced tea glasses had ridges on the inside and while we were eating Maryann was nervously spinning the ice against the ridges of her glass. There had been a minor spat between my mother and sister just before dinner, nothing that was a cause for alarm. Florie, however, was annoyed by the sound she was making with her glass. "Maryann, do you have to do that?"

Maryann snapped, taking the glass and slamming it down on the table as she yelled, "Jesus Christ! Can't I do a fucking thing in this house?"

To me it was business as usual. A meal without an occasional outburst from anyone in the family was like a ballad without lyrics, and I'd expected at least as much. Who likes elevator music anyhow? When I glanced over at Ellen, the look on her face told me the casual use of profanity, especially out of a twelve-year-old's mouth, wasn't a staple of every American home.

Florie picked up on it and he looked at my sister and said, sotto voce, ever so softly, "Maryann, watch your mouth." Those words wouldn't have been spoken had Ellen not been around.

From across the table, Mommy stared at him with steam virtually coming out of her ears. I don't think she'd had a problem creating a comfortable atmosphere for Ellen, but she certainly seemed to have a problem with Florie attempting the same. "She ain't your fucking daughter!" Mommy said to him and paused. "Mind your own business."

It became eerily silent at the table. All you could hear was the sound of silverware scraping against ceramic plates. Joe and I continued to eat as if nothing was going on. I was hoping nothing else would be going on. But Mommy's insult hit Florie hard. He picked up the glass salad bowl in the center of the table and said, "I put the food on this motherfucking table!" as he shook it. He turned around and slammed it down on the floor behind him, breaking the bowl into a thousand pieces, then continued, "Don't you ever talk to me like that!"

Mommy narrowed her eyes and smiled. "Oh, look at Mr. Big Shot! What are you gonna do, Florie, hit me? Fuck you, you *cocksucker*!"

Ellen was looking down at her plate now and began eating again, as if nothing was happening. I was so angry and embarrassed I couldn't hold back from joining in. "You see? You see, you motherfucker. That's why I don't bring anybody in this fucking house. Because of your fucking mouth!" I screamed at Mommy.

I should have known better than to egg her on. She turned slowly away from Florie and toward me and said, "You little cocksucker! Who the fuck do you think you're talking to?" Never one to let an opportunity for drama pass by, she stood up from her chair, took a breast in her hand through her clothes and twisted it like a corkscrew, saying, "I curse the milk that fed you! You shoulda died in my womb! In my womb you shoulda died!"

Maryann was crying and Ellen was staring down at her plate chewing her sausage and peppers like a robot. It was the only thing she could do to avoid the disturbing reality around her. I yelled back at Mommy at the top of my lungs, "That's it, I'm leaving! And I'm never coming back!"

Mommy had her fists above her head now as she screamed. "Get out! You get out, you motherfucker! Don't ever come back! You should drop dead, you dirty stinking dog! If you were on fire, I wouldn't piss on you to put it out!"

The next thing I knew I was outside in front of the little bungalow with Ellen and our packed bags. Ellen was looking straight ahead. She seemed to be praying for a quick delivery elsewhere—anywhere but there. I was waiting for Joe the insurance man to take me to the bus. Florie had already driven off to points unknown.

Joe knew the drill with Mommy. He attempted to persuade me to stay. "Joey, she's your mother. You know how she is."

"Joe, don't start," I answered, still fuming.

He walked over and put his hand on my shoulder. "Go inside and apologize. Say you're sorry."

"*Sorry?* Are you nuts? I didn't do anything! She started it," I said as I jerked away from his touch.

"Joey, she's your mother."

"Joe, I will never, ever set foot in her house again."

As the words left my mouth, Mommy propped open the screen door and stuck her head out. "Joey, you want coffee?"

Without missing a beat, I turned and answered, "Yeah, no sugar. You want any, Ellen?" I asked.

She just shook her head no.

And back in the house I went, leaving Ellen staring after me as she waited outside with Joe.

Needless to say, I never saw Ellen again after that weekend. I heard she ended up marrying her therapist.

That was Mommy in a nutshell. She never stayed mad. She got over it and moved on, until her next performance.

Mommy was the pot stirrer and the instigator, and Daddy, Florie, Maryann and I were her most loyal targets. She loved to light the firecrackers, watch them ripple, explode and light up the sky. When we'd blow our stack her job was done, and everything was okay again. It was a volatile family situation, with chaos always lurking just beneath the surface, but the foundations always remained intact and a strong sense of family unity was always waiting to catch the pieces of the latest explosion and reassemble them without fail, and quickly.

In their autumn years, Mommy and Florie together reinforced each other's tendency to go off at the slightest opportunity like time bombs and they brilliantly maintained an almost Marx Brothers farcical zaniness and absurdity in our family dramas. Even when things were serious or tragic in my family, there always seemed to be an element of comedy woven in as well.

When Mommy's sister, Tilly, passed away on New Year's Eve, 1968, there was a customary first showing of the body for the immediate family at Failla's funeral parlor. Mommy had been very close with her sister, and she was upset because she hadn't been consulted on the arrangements. Aunt Tilly's children had wanted to take care of all the details, which was their right. But even in her grief, Mommy seemed loaded for bear. Mary Ann, Aunt Tilly's daughter, had chosen a beautiful blue dress for her mother to wear. Mommy took one look inside the casket and turned around to glare at Mary Ann, standing right next to her. Cousin Mary Ann must have felt the fumes emanating from Mommy's nostrils and she turned to face her, at which point Mommy said in her grieving, funeral parlor moan, "My sister hated the color blue." Mommy turned around toward Florie and me and moaned in our direction. "I can't believe she put my sister in a fucking blue dress."

"Aunt Mary, don't start," Mary Ann said calmly. "She's my mother, all right?"

Mommy turned to address Mary Ann again. "Blue?" she groaned. "Why blue? I can't believe you, you little sumanabitch. You sumanabitch, Mary Ann, how could you do that?"

The family had begun to gather around the casket as Mommy and Mary Ann argued, Mommy's moans being answered by an increasingly agitated Mary Ann. Cousin Frankie, Mary Ann's older brother; Cousin Phillip; Cousin Cosmo; Patty-boy; me; Florie; my sister were all watching intently. Mary Ann's husband, Dominick, went to stand in between the two women. He faced Mommy and put his hands over her shoulders and asked her to leave his wife alone. Mommy flinched and it appeared to Florie as if Dominick had pushed her. Florie immediately charged at Dominick, but Phillip, Cosmo and Frankie got in the middle of them to calm Florie down. They separated the parties into the far corners of the room until nerves had settled and it was possible to pay respect to Aunt Tilly once again in peace.

As we left the funeral parlor at around five o'clock, it had already gotten dark outside. The air outside was bitter cold and there was a fresh coating of snow on the ground. My sister and I held Mommy as we walked toward Florie's car and we both helped her into the backseat. Florie was standing outside the driver's side door as if waiting for something. "C'mon, get in the car, Flo," Cousin Cosmo said warily.

"Don't worry about me, Cozzie," Florie said as he stared at the door to Failla's, where the rest of the family was still slowly walking out. Then he turned to Cosmo and smiled to reassure him. "I'm not gonna do anything stupid."

Cosmo got into the car and slammed the door shut, making a sound that could have been a shot in the air to start off a race and Florie took it as such. He immediately bolted toward Dominick as he walked with Mary Ann toward his own car. Dominick saw Florie approaching fast and in a split second had let go of his wife to run toward Florie. They were like two bulls charging each other in the ring. Cosmo jumped out of the car and started running and I followed a couple of steps behind. Both of us were trying to intercept them. Cosmo had almost caught up to Florie when he slipped on a patch of ice and hit the ground hard. Florie and Dominick were miraculously distracted by Cosmo's fall and both ran toward him as he lay squirming from the pain in the snow. He had broken his arm in the fall and within ten minutes, the whole family was in the emergency room together telling stories about Aunt Tilly as we waited for Cosmo to get his arm set. Curtain closed.

I was living the life of the out-of-work actor for the first seven years of my career, from the time I started at eighteen. I made a total of seven thousand dollars for those first seven years, an average of about a thousand dollars a year. I was struggling in Manhattan and trying to get an acting job. After I got my SAG card, I started doing extra work to pay off the money I had borrowed from friends to get the card in the first place. I got my first role in a movie while I was living at home. I was an extra in *The Valachi Papers.* Florie and I were both excited. When Florie was in Atlanta with Vito, Valachi had been transferred there. Vito had been trying to have him killed. Even though Florie took care of Vito, made him sandwiches, he still had admiration and respect for Valachi.

On set, I would see Charles Bronson in the flesh—it was a Dino de Laurentiis movie; I'd be surrounded by movie stars. The Sinatra song "The Best Is Yet to Come" was burning in my brain.

That morning at 5 A.M., we woke up and Florie drove me into Manhattan, to the Pierre Hotel, where I was to report for work. At 7:15 I boarded a bus in anticipation of going to my first movie set. I was looking out the window when I realized we were going toward the Lincoln Tunnel. Back on the Jersey side, the route we took was the same I'd been on with Florie just about an hour ago; only now I was heading back to Cliffside Park. I worked on my first movie just three blocks away from my house.

My first scene was a motel scene with an old guy. I was in one cross shot. It was over, and I was on the bus with some of the kids and the old guy. One of the kids noticed that the old actor wasn't moving. The woman beside me realized he wasn't breathing. So I started to resuscitate him, and massaged his heart, while someone called an ambulance.

We wound up in a hospital in West New York, New Jersey. At the same time the wardrobe people showed up, the doctor was coming to give us the bad news. He was shaking his head, indicating that the old man hadn't made it. The woman who'd sat next to me on the bus was bawling in my arms. Without a drop of sympathy, the wardrobe guy then goes, "We're gonna need his costume." It was my first taste of the ruthless side of showbiz. Suddenly, it wasn't all that glamorous. I guessed that it was only uphill from here. The verdict's still out on that.

When I got the role for the character of Maggio in *From Here to Eternity*, it was a huge deal for me and for my family. Frank Sinatra had played Maggio in the original 1953 hit, which had resurrected his career, and here I was beginning mine with the same part. The press was all over this one, asking things like "Can Lightning Strike Twice?" It was my first exposure to the media. I heard even Sinatra himself was keeping an eye on me.

I got a call from Mommy one afternoon and she was whispering on the phone like the old days. She had never completely recovered from the experience of having our phone tapped by the FBI, and anytime her paranoia warranted it, I got a whispered call like this one.

"Joey."

I could barely hear her. "Wha?"

"It's me."

"I know, why you whispering?"

"I don't wanna talk loud. Somebody from *The New York Times* just called me."

"Yeah?"

"They want to interview me, they want to talk to me about you."

I was expecting, with all the press, that they'd be talking to me. But they wanted to talk to my mother, too? This was big. I can't say I wasn't a little excited. "What'd you say?" I asked.

"I told them that you was dead and I haven't seen you in six years and not to call no more." Ah, my first publicist.

Meanwhile, Aunt Rosie wound up being quoted in *The New York Times* because they had called her up after Mommy had hung up on the reporter. Mommy was furious.

And as much as she didn't want me to leave her and chance the mean streets of Manhattan, Mommy began to support me, and was even proud of me, once I started getting roles in Equity showcase plays in some basement here and some cramped theater there on the Lower East Side. I'd go in and audition and get the part and rehearse for three weeks and the plays usually ran for two weeks. My pals who had been derisive of my acting ambitions back in high school changed their tune and became members of my most loyal fan club once they saw that my pipe dreams were materializing across the Hudson. Mommy, Monk and all the Fairview boys would come to see me act. And of course Florie was always there. Florie had been there for me from the start, and he never wavered for a minute in his belief in me.

Everybody pitched in to help me out. When I needed a used bicycle to get around in the city, I called Tonto up and told him. I knew he would "acquire" one for me somehow. So when he and Miller showed up in a pickup truck with four brand-new ten-speed bicycles with the labels still on them, I knew these guys really loved me. It was their way, and it was completely endearing. A gift of swag, Hoboken style, was always a loving gesture.

(Note to reader: Sick, huh? This was all before I sought redemption through professional counseling. Soon to come, Joey Pants's second book: *How I Spent My Ten Years in Group Therapy*, coming next fall from Dutton.)

Mommy pitched in to help in her own way. She got all dolled up on a cold winter afternoon and asked me to take her to Fort Lee. We got in Florie's car and I drove her.

"What are we going there for?" I asked her.

"None of your business . . . and step on it," she said.

She told me where to park. She crushed out her cigarette and climbed from the car. "Shut the engine off. Money don't grow on fucking trees," she yelled back to me as headed up a long walkway of stairs toward an upscale suburban home. She rang the doorbell. A blue-haired woman answered and looked at my mother, staring at her for a second before she gave her a big hug. They went inside.

Forty-five minutes later, I was still sitting in the car freezing my ass off. I could barely make out Mommy saying goodbye at the door through the car window, which was frozen and frosted from my breath. She was hugging and smiling with the blue-haired woman. The woman looked across the street and waved at me. My mother got into the car and said, "Start the fucking car. It's freezing in here."

I started the engine, scraped the window, pulled off the curb and drove away. "Fuck him. We don't need him," Mommy said.

"Who?"

"Who what?"

"Fuck who?" I said. "Who don't we need?"

"Frank."

"Frank who?"

"Sinatra."

"Who was that?" I said.

"His mother."

I slammed on the brakes. "I didn't know you knew her," I said.

"I've known her for thirty-five years."

"No kidding." I paused. "When's the last time you saw her?"

Mommy paused. "Ah, thirty years ago at least."

I can only imagine what it took for my mother to swallow her pride and seek Mrs. Sinatra's help that way. But she did it, quietly and with tremendous grace. She had come to understand how determined I was to become an actor. And she would do anything to help her boy.

My family became my most loyal supporters. The first time I ever worked in summer stock was as an apprentice at the Carriage House Theater in Little Compton, Rhode Island. I was getting ten dollars a week and I was appearing in *Lovers and Other Strangers*. I looked down and saw some familiar faces in the audience. Florie, Monk, Mommy and Maryann had driven all the way to Rhode Island, and they spent the night in the same barn that the whole company slept in. Monk actually got a heat stroke the day they were up there, and we were afraid he was going to have another heart attack. But they were there for me through thick and thin.

For the next seven years, whenever I did plays in little theaters in New York City, my three parents would be there. They put their tumultuous history aside to support me. Side by side they'd sit, Daddy, Mommy and Florie, and their eyes all gleamed equally with pride.

Years later, I was working on an episode of *NYPD Blue*, and an actor I was working with mentioned he'd seen me in "that play *Orphans* years ago." I had starred in the world premiere of the play in Los Angeles.

I was surprised.

He smiled at the memory and said, "I've gotta tell you something that was very touching to me. The night I saw it, your father was sitting next to me." He meant Florie. "During the curtain call, you came out to take your bow, and he was so proud he kept hitting me and saying, 'That's my boy. That's my boy up there!' "

On Sundays and holidays, the three of them were always together. Mommy would cook, and after dinner Daddy would wash the dishes and then go home. Daddy certainly didn't visit for lack of activities and loved ones. He came because they were his family and any bad blood between them boiled away with each passing year. He had been living with his girlfriend Betty since he returned from Florida. But for a long time, he didn't bring Betty along because of Mommy's hostility toward her. Even during their separation, he catered to Mommy.

My parents had never actually gotten divorced. In fact, they were never even legally separated. There was no need for formalities. Everyone knew where everyone else stood. In the end, the three of them were old friends if nothing else. They were old friends bound by a common past and a common love that ran deeper than anyone on the outside looking in would have imagined. They had each done their part to raise two children in their own quirky ways, and their dedication to us never faltered.

However cantankerous, dramatic and loud we might be—as a family we were one.

In 1982 I had just returned from Rome, where I had a small part in a movie called *Monsignor*. The plan was to spend a weekend so I could go to my cousin Rosanne Guidese's wedding in New Jersey. Morgan, my wife at the time, and I were to stay with Mommy and Daddy in the senior citizens' apartment with our baby Marco.

The wedding was great. I hadn't seen my cousins in a long time. They were all there, just like old times, minus some of the folks who had died. Uncle Popeye was gone at this point, so we spent some time reminiscing about his off-key concerts. We were having a blast. Daddy had just finished doing his false teeth bit, and it was the last slow dance of the evening. My mom asked me to dance with her. We were dancing, and my cousin Peter Guidese came over and wanted to cut in. And Mommy tenderly goes, "Peter, let me dance with my boy." We had a nice time that night.

The next morning, not unexpectedly, Mommy's mood pendulum had swung back to its more unpleasant side. Mommy was sitting at the coffee table doing a slow burn, drinking a cup of coffee, smoking her morning cigarette and calling Daddy and me "bridiaggon bastards." Morgan was nursing my son

Marco and covering his ears at the same time because Mommy's voice was frightening him. Mommy was pissed off that Daddy, myself and all the men were carrying on the night before. We had just been drinking and having a good time at the wedding.

I defended our evening. "C'mon, we didn't drink that much. It was about fun."

It might have been Dopey Gus himself talking to her. She was forever nervous about the mixture of men and alcohol since she'd lived in her father's house. She said that Daddy and I were an embarrassment to the human race.

"Will you stop? We were just having a good time."

"You call making asses of yourselves a good time? You're all no good sumanabitches, every last one of you." She dragged out her words for emphasis.

I was feeling light-headed from the night before and decided now was as good a time as any to get deep with Mommy and do a little amateur analyzing. "Ma, what's your problem?" I could see her eyes widen and mouth tighten, preparing for a vile response. Okay, maybe that wasn't the right approach, I thought. So I tried again, attempting to make some headway. "Look, Mommy, let me ask you something. Why do you hate men so much?"

She took a deep breath and replied, "Let me tell you something . . ." With a cigarette in her hand, she took a last big puff. By that time my mom had cataracts, so she had these big thick glasses like Coke bottles that made her look like a fly. She was quite a sight. As she was putting out the cigarette in the ashtray, she said, "Let me tell you something. The best man in the world ain't good enough for the worst who-wa."

And that, I can proudly pronounce, is her epitaph. That was the way she went through her life. No matter how good a man was or how hard a man tried, in the end men were always a piece of shit.

And Morgan said, with no malice, just in a matter-of-fact manner, "That's it. I'm going home now." She got up and went into the bedroom to pack.

I had been planning to go back with Morgan and Marco that evening, but I had done an audition on Friday for the movie *Eddie and the Cruisers*, and it had gone well, so I had to stay until that Tuesday. I couldn't leave, but I didn't want to stay at my mother's because I was still pissed off at her. She had a way of doing that. I was angry with her because what she'd said encapsulated her lifetime view of men. Throughout our relationship, it had become a wall and barrier of misunderstanding that I had never been able to break through. And it gave me a feeling of futility and helplessness about communicating with her. It had distorted so many aspects of her life. So to keep my distance, and the possibility of other tiffs at bay, I went to stay with my buddy Michael Kell at his apartment.

By this point, Mommy had had several small strokes. She had one in 1979 and one in 1980, and she was also a diabetic. Then she had an additional stroke and her artery was corroded and blocked, so they did a bypass, repairing the artery with a vein from her leg. But in doing that operation, they somehow damaged her vocal cords. So the last several years of her life, Mommy sounded like Louis Armstrong. And between her voice and her new glasses, when she talked to the baby she'd make him cry. Marco would just see this fly woman and freak out.

Mommy loved that baby and it would break her heart when he cried.

At this point in my mother's life, even though she was sick, as a rule of thumb I didn't believe anything she said. She was always exaggerating things. It was hard for me to believe that she was really sick.

My reluctance to deal with my mother's complaints about her health was more complicated than a wariness of her illnesses or her characteristic lies. I do think I had trouble dealing with her mortality, and the idea I might be without her someday. She was such a pillar of strength and love, despite her moods and dramatics. I could never imagine her not in my life.

When I left her that day, I was more angry with her behavior than receptive to her warnings that she wasn't feeling so well. I thought nothing of it when I went into the city that Sunday night and crashed on Michael's couch.

I called her on Monday, but there was no answer.

Early Tuesday morning the phone rang. Michael answered it. It was Florie at the hospital. My mother had had a heart attack. I got on the phone. "You'd better get out here right away," Florie said.

I hung up, told Michael and got in the shower to go to Jersey. As I showered, I fumbled with the thought she was really sick. I began to blame her condition on her need for attention. When I came out of the shower, Michael was sitting on the bed. As I stood there and began getting dressed, he said quietly, "Listen, man. She's gone."

I was completely caught off guard. "What? What are you talking about?"

He said, "Florie just called back. He said . . . your mom . . . she's dead. . . ." Of all the reactions I could have, I started laughing.

Throughout my life, all of the fights that I had with her were instantly resolved. Even if we didn't discuss the details, we just resolved them by talking to each other again. This time I never had that chance. I never got to call her. The last thing that I heard my mother say to me was that the best man is not good enough for the worst who-wa.

As far as I know, she died mad at me.

After making arrangements for Mommy's funeral at Failla's, I told Jack, the funeral director, "I want a half hour with my mother. I don't want anybody to walk in." It was the first time I was able to talk to my mother when she couldn't answer back; she had to listen. I always joke that it took her death for me to get her attention. But in a way it's true; I could make my peace with her now.

I kneeled at her casket, the same one I had kneeled on as a child next to her, and said, "Why did it have to be this way? What was it about you that made it so difficult? You didn't have to live a life this way. It could have been different."

By the time I had sifted through my thoughts, I had spent myself. In my time with her that day, I had a complete metamorphosis; I was laughing, I was crying and I was yelling. It was sad, it was comical and it was cathartic. At that moment in my life, I realized that she had done the best she could; whatever she was and whatever she had done. It was not her fault and the hurtful things she did were not deliberate. I had reached an understanding with her.

At the wake the night before the funeral, I had to decide who would be in the family car. I insisted that Florie be in the first car along with Daddy, Maryann, Aunt Dannah and Aunt Rosie. I was in the front seat with the driver.

We buried her in a beautiful turquoise dress. It was her favorite color.

A year or two after Mommy died, Florie said, "You know, as much as she made me crazy, I miss her." He loved her; Daddy loved her; we all loved her.

I always thought that my mother was the glue between these two men, and that their relationship existed because of Mommy. When she died, in the back of my mind I thought, "Well, that's the end of Florie and Daddy. There's no reason for Monk and Florie to see each other anymore." But that wasn't the case. In the end they were good friends. Mommy and us kids weren't their only common loves; they loved each other too.

Although the Monk flourished in his golden years, Florie never recovered from being cut loose from his ancient wiseguy ties. He had worked in the dirty business for most of his adult life, and money had always been a problem after he'd left it behind. He couldn't make a consistent amount of money like a working-class Joe. My cousin Patty-boy loves to tell the story about Florie and Mommy in their later years. Florie would always be sitting and reading behind the store window in the corner of the store while shaking his head, saying he wished he were back in prison so he wouldn't have to deal with my mother.

At one point I'd gotten a job as a maître d' at O'Neal's Balloon in Manhattan, but I wanted to learn how to be a waiter, and after several months, there was a spot that opened up and my boss said, "You gotta get somebody to replace you." So I brought Florie in. He was a lunch guy and a night guy, and after a while he became the manager. But he had to retire when he couldn't breathe because of his emphysema. By the end of his life, at seventy-seven years old, he was picking up dirty laundry from the apartments of rich, upwardly mobile professionals who lived in the Horizon House. That was his last job. It was a far cry from the guy that came off the airplane from Atlanta in 1963.

For all the help Florie gave me, I guess all of us—Monk, Mommy, Maryann and I—saved Florie too in some respects. He finally had a family. He might have died in prison otherwise.

A few years after my mom died, Florie called me and said, "I got bad news."

I said, "What?"

And he said, "Marsha's dead."

And I said, "Marsha. Who's Marsha?"

"Remember?" he goes. "My wife."

I said, "You married?"

And he said, "Yeah."

I asked, "You've always been married?"

He goes, "Yeah."

I said, "How long you been married?"

"I don't know. Thirty-two years?"

"When was the last time you saw her?"

"Ah shit. Twenty years?"

Florie was a guy that I thought I knew intimately. He lived with my mother for twenty years, and I never knew he was married. It was just part of the denial, the secrecy and the irony was that my family would say anything to each other and scream at the top of their lungs. Yet when I thought that everything was out in the open, I found out that Florie was married to somebody else for thirty years.

Marsha had lived on the Lower East Side of Manhattan. She had always lived and worked there. In the end, she left Florie her entire life's possessions.

In the late years, Florie's health sank with his emphysema. My father took care of him. He couldn't walk two feet. He gave Monk his car so that Daddy could get around to help him out. Florie was going in and out of the hospital a lot in those last years of his life. He had no Blue Cross and no medical. He couldn't afford it. He was always in and out of the hospital, but they liked him. There were no computers then, so I guess it took them longer to find out that he was broke.

By this time Florie was alone. Mommy was gone, and all of his old cronies were either dead or in jail. I was living in California. Florie was still in the senior citizen's building that Mommy lived in when she died. Ultimately Daddy turned out to be Florie's keeper. Daddy would go over to his apartment and clean for him. He bathed him, shopped for him, got his medications for him and took him to the doctor.

In contrast to Florie, the Monk was social. He loved to dance and party and go out. He always played bingo at his senior citizens building. Florie was more introverted. Florie didn't feel comfortable socializing, or taking advantage of the senior functions and activities in his building. In Florie's mind, he was still a big-shot tough guy and these things were beneath him. But Monk would play bingo, and through that social avenue, he would find out who the new widows were and call on them offering comfort and the company of a charming date. He was a sly guy. In the end, he had traded getting dead men's clothes for getting dead men's wives.

One day in 1987 Daddy called me and he was crying.

"What's the matter, Daddy?"

He could barely talk. "Florie's dead. He died in my arms, Joey. He couldn't breathe. He suffocated in my arms. The last thing he said to me was, 'Monk, I'm dying. I'll see you later, pal.' "

Four months to the day, I got a call from my father, who said that his arm had swelled up and he didn't know what to do. I told him, "Go to the doctor."

Three hours later I got a call from his doctor saying, "Mr. Pantoliano, I don't mean to alarm you, but your father has all the symptoms of inoperable lung cancer." It had spread everywhere and cut into the blood vessels to the arms.

When Monk died, two hundred people came to his funeral, including three mayors. Only twelve people came to Florie's. They were two different men who gave me all they had. I know I benefited from their strange differences in so many ways.

Many years later, when I saw *GoodFellas* and saw the graphic ways in which wiseguys supposedly operate, for some reason it crystallized in my mind and though I understood and admired that code of honor many real wiseguys actually live by, I thought, "Oh my god, was that what Florie was doing? This was the life that he had chosen? However hard this reality was to process this was, after all, a man that I loved. The film made me physically ill. I felt helpless. I couldn't confront him because he was gone. I couldn't say, "Hey, Florie, did you really do that kind of stuff?"

Just as I had not been able to say I was sorry to my mother two days before she died, haunting, unanswered questions arose with Florie. I will really never know. Or perhaps I don't want to know.

And with all my love for him, for what he had given me, I now understood that his criminal life had been a really terrifying one. I could begin to understand why his nights were consumed by nightmares.

In the end, I am left with the tragic fact that the one person in my life who made me feel I could be something did some very terrible things. Florie would, by some standards, be considered a horrible person, who may have tried to rectify his deeds through helping encourage my confidence and success with his unconditional love. He was the sweetest wiseguy I ever knew.

I guess in many ways I have never really left the fire escapes, the rooftops and the clotheslines of Hoboken. It was, after all, my Italian-American Eden. There were so many angels there for me. I have had a truly blessed life thanks to my childhood home. I loved funerals as much as I loved weddings. There was always a big party afterward; a celebration of one's beginning or one's end. Laughter and love were always the key elements to our community.

I still keep an apartment there with keepsakes from my childhood and all that is precious to me, including my Marx Brothers and Abbott and Costello posters. I never left; like

Francis Albert, who came back anonymously in the pitch black of the night at four in the morning to show his friends where he began, I will always be from Hoboken.

And—sorry, Daddy, about this—how can an actor from Hoboken write a book without paying tribute to the haunting presence of Sinatra, who touched the lives of countless millions across the globe who never heard of Hoboken?

When Frank Sinatra died, I was in Sydney, Australia, doing *The Matrix*. It wasn't until that point in my life that I realized the magnitude of the impact this man had on the world. Even in Sydney they were paying tribute to him. It was all over the newspapers, CNN and the rest of the media. Sinatra was big, bigger than I could ever imagine. He cut across boundaries of prejudice, ethnicity, age, nationality, language and geography with his singular and irreplaceable talent, his boundless skills and great heart, and a voice so fresh and distinctive, so passionate and romantic and wise it would stop you cold in your tracks. My good friend Chazz once had the pleasure of running into Sinatra himself; Frank offered these inspiring words about me: "That poor son of a bitch ain't ever gonna be the most famous guy from Hoboken."

My mother often said to me, "When I'm dead, you're going to bite here," she pointed with her right index finger to her opposite elbow, "for all the times you miss me."

How right she was.

She could make you feel worthless, and she could make you feel like royalty. Perhaps she didn't realize how hurtful she could be when she put you down with her vicious tongue, because I have the feeling she was most honest when she made you feel loved. It was through fear, paranoia and bitter resentment that she knew how to express herself best. Her childhood taught her that, as it taught her to be a cynic to the idea of owning dreams and aspirations beyond what was readily available to you. She didn't want her children to rock the boat because she had no faith in the rose-colored view of the world. Her early cynicism about my chances for success as an actor contrasted to her excitement to seeing me on stage told me that her fears were conquerable, they were only a thin but resilient layer that dressed her emotions.

Mommy never allowed my father to be a father, she never allowed me to be a brother to Maryann; in some sense she wanted us all to herself. In many ways she tore us apart, and in others she held us together. Antoinette visited Mommy almost every day when Mommy became ill and the two of them would reminisce about the old Hoboken and the chapter in the history of that square-mile city that had already begun to close. They'd gossip about incarcerated cousins and new wives and husbands and children who were just like their parents. They'd remember the old establishments, the old bakeries and cheese shops and social clubs that had turned into Irish bars and Mexican restaurants. Several days before she passed away, they would reminisce about the old Hoboken and the chapter in the history of that square-mile city that had already begun to close; they'd gossip about incarcerated cousins and new wives and husbands and children who were just like their parents. They'd remember the old establishments, the old bakeries and cheese shops and social clubs that had turned into Irish bars and Mexican restaurants.

When I began writing this book, I thought I knew all it was possible to know about the mysteries of my astounding mother: how she came to be what she was and what forces had shaped her. But thanks to a long conversation with Antoinette May in 2002 in connection with creating this book, I discovered things that were revelatory and that explained a great deal to me about her. Above all, they contained an answer to the last question I ever asked my mother: Why did she hate men so much?

I think it would best to have my Cousin Antoinette speak in her own words as she did to me that day. They were words she could not have spoken to me when I was younger; they were words direct from the heart:

"Yeah, Mary was wild. Did you ever hear the expression, '*mina kativa*'? It means a 'little wild person.' That's what your mother was. She was a good woman down beneath.

"Your mother took so much; your grandmother Mamie suffered so much. And Mary was always sticking up for her and protecting her.

"After your wedding, I used to go to your mother's every day. And your mother sat there and said to me, 'Antoinette, I'm so sorry for what I did to Monk in my life.' And you know what it meant for her to admit that. She only died shortly after, and she said she was sorry . . . she did the wrong thing by living with Florie."

Antoinette paused and said, "She was really rough. But she

loved you, Joey. She gave you life, and she was so happy to have you. Don't curse her. Remember her name."

MOMMY: What are you, writing a book?
JOEY: Yeah, Mommy.
MOMMY: Well then, kiss my ass and make it a love story.

Well, this is my love story.

ABOUT THE AUTHORS

Born in Hoboken, New Jersey, Joe Pantoliano landed his first professional role in 1972 when he played Billy Bibbit in the national touring company of *One Flew Over the Cuckoo's Nest.* He worked in regional theater and has appeared in over forty Off-Broadway productions, including *Vision of Kerouac* at the Lion Theater and *The Death Star* at the Theater of St. Clements.

In 1976, he made his move to Hollywood and appeared in the ABC series *McNamara's Band*, and *Free Country* starring Rob Reiner. He was next cast in the coveted role of Maggio in the NBC miniseries *From Here to Eternity.*

He returned to the stage in Los Angeles, winning a Dramalogue Award and a Drama Critic's Circle Award for Best Actor in *Orphans.* His second Dramalogue Award as Best Actor was received for *Italian American Reconciliation*, written by John Patrick Shanley.

Joe was nominated for a CableACE Award for an episode of the horror series *Tales from the Crypt*, directed by Richard

Donner. His other television credits include roles on *NYPD Blue*, *L.A. Law* and *Civil Wars*. He also starred in HBO's *El Diablo*, the NBC series *The Fanelli Boys*, and the critically acclaimed CBS drama series *EZ Streets*, for which he was nominated for a Viewers for Quality Television Award.

On the big screen, Joe has appeared in over forty films, including *Risky Business*, *Running Scared*, *La Bamba*, Steven Spielberg's *Empire of the Sun*, *Midnight Run*, *The Fugitive*, *Bad Boys*, *Bound* opposite Academy Award–nominee Jennifer Tilly, and Warner Bros.' *U.S. Marshals* with Tommy Lee Jones and Wesley Snipes.

Joe also starred in the Avi Nesher–directed drama *Taxman*, costarring Elizabeth Berkley, which Joe also associate produced. The suspenseful drama received highly acclaimed critical notice.

Joe teamed with the Wachowski brothers to costar opposite Keanu Reeves and Laurence Fishburne in Warner Bros.' smash hit *The Matrix*.

Joe can now be seen starring in HBO's hit drama *The Sopranos*. He portrays gangster Ralph Cifaretto and is currently in production on the fourth season. Joe also starred opposite Carrie-Anne Moss and Guy Pearce in the critically acclaimed independent hit *Memento* for director Christopher Nolan.

Joe Pantoliano resides in New York with his wife, Nancy Sheppard, and their three children.

David Evanier has published articles in *The New York Times Magazine*, *New York* magazine, *The New Republic*, *The Village Voice*, *The Nation*, *The Forward*, *New American Writing*, *Dissent* and many other publications. His most recent book,

Making the Wiseguys Weep: The Jimmy Roselli Story, was a *New York Times* Notable Book of the Year. *Making the Wiseguys Weep* was also a finalist in the Ralph J. Gleason Music Book Awards. David has been a winner of the Aga Khan Fiction Prize. His story "Mother" received the Mcginnis-Ritchie Award for Fiction. His previous books include *The Swinging Headhunter*, *The One-Star Jew* and *Red Love*. David lives with his wife in Brooklyn, New York.